STRENGTHS-
LEADERSHIP
HANDBOOK

Pernille Hippe Brun,
David Cooperrider
& Mikkel Ejsing

Illustrated by Jens Hage
Foreword by Lyell Clarke

Crown Custom Publishing, Inc.
1210 Teakwood Lane
Brunswick, Ohio 44212
(330) 273-4900
www.crowncustompublishing.com

Ordering Information

Individual sales: This book can be ordered directly from Crown Custom Publishing, Inc., at the address above.

Quantity sales: Special discounts are available on quantity purchases by corporations, associations, and others. For details, contact Crown Custom Publishing, Inc., at the address above.

Orders for college textbook/course adoption use:

Please contact Crown Custom Publishing, Inc., at (330) 273-4900.

Orders by U.S. wholesalers:

Please contact Crown Custom Publishing:
Tel: (330) 273-4900 | Fax (330) 225-9932
E-mail: carl@crowncustompublishing.com
Web: www.crowncustompublishing.com

ISBN 978-1-933403-22-9
Printed in the United States of America

Library of Congress Cataloging-in-Publication Data
First Edition 10 9 8 7 6 5 4 3 2 1

Publisher: Carl Wirick
Copyediting: Marianne Miller
Design: Tia Andrako

ABOUT THE BOOK

If you want to succeed as a strengths-based leader, you need to invest in the process with presence and authenticity and understand the philosophy behind the concrete tools offered by this paradigm. Part One of the book introduces you to the history and research behind the paradigm, definitions of the approach, and the underlying philosophy of strengths-based leadership. Part One concludes with two chapters describing how you can identify and bring your own strengths into play and how you can identify and deal with your weaknesses.

In Part Two, you are introduced to concrete strengths-based ways of dealing with typical management challenges such as conducting strengths-based conversations, giving feedback, dealing with stress, enhancing teamwork, and leading a change process. This part of the book is more tool-oriented, but it is fundamental that you understand the philosophy behind the paradigm before using these tools in your daily leadership practice. Therefore, we encourage you to read the book in chronological order.

Throughout the book, we have attempted to make concepts specific and accessible using quotes, cases, models, and reflection boxes and providing concrete exercises. We strongly encourage you to try these exercises as soon as you can. It is one thing to read about a subject and another to put it into practice. True learning takes place and the real adventure begins when you take yourself out of your comfort zone, dare to fail, and experiment.

LITERATURE

The end of the book provides a list of literature you can turn to for inspiration if you want to further explore the topic of the strengths-based paradigm. This literature also served as background literature for the book, especially in regards to research and an explanation of the overall paradigm.

INTRODUCTION BY THE AUTHORS

We live in a wonderful world that is full of beauty, charm and adventure. There is no end to the adventures that we can have if only we seek them with our eyes open.

— Jawaharlal Nehru

We have come to love the word *adventure*. It invites two seemingly opposite experiences: sensational excitement and disorienting risk. The excitement is easy to embrace and understand, for we thrill to the adventurous moment, including the novelty of unexplored pathways, expansive vistas, and a sense of the possible. Explorers love adventure. However, there is another side of authentic adventure. It can lead to a wake-up call of new awareness. And even when the shock is positive, it still can disrupt and challenge one's assumptions of the status quo. Positive dislodgement of certainty can alter lives, sometimes forever and in just an instant. An adventure always involves risk.

The same is true of big ideas, which is what this applied book is all about. What this book does is to bring three revolutions into one unified whole, yet in an applied and experiential way. Marcus Buckingham was one of the first within the strengths-based paradigm to notice that someday three threads could come together seamlessly to provide everyone with a coherent set of strengths-based mind-sets and useful positive tools that could unite and span the domains of family life, business and management, and individual psychology. What was it that he noticed?

According to Buckingham, three movements were beginning to interweave. First, there was "The strengths revolution in management" that was articulated early on in Peter Drucker's 1966 management theory on *The Effective Executive*. Second, Buckingham traced the call in the field of organization development and changed management for an *Appreciative Inquiry into Organizational Life* (introduced by Cooperrider and Srivastva, 1987). This book called for a reconstruction of the 20th century's predominant problem-centric focus in almost every applied field from medicine to management to a life-centric focus on "what gives life?" when living systems are at their generative best, excelling, flourishing, and actualizing (where change = *creating* the elevated and better future, not just getting rid of something or *solving* the past). Third, as Buckingham described it, there was an invitation to the entire field of psychology for a reversal. Instead of a science preoccupied by what's wrong with the human being, there would be a vast refocusing into studies of the good life, the meaningful life, and the engaged life (that is, the christening of the field of positive psychology). What was emerging across all three, he argued, was a richer and more complex whole of mutually reinforcing ideas and solutions.

And what was the core idea? It was that leadership might be all about strengths.

When we fuse the word *positive* from the field of positive psychology with the word *strengths* from the domain of strengths-based management, it may be no exaggeration to say that the premises, the tools, and the across-the-board opportunities of the positive-strengths revolution might well be the most far-reaching development in the human sciences of the past half century.

One sees it happening everywhere now, and one can sense something of a rebirth, of whole disciplines breaking out anew. Alfred North Whitehead, the brilliant philosopher of his day, spoke in unforgettable terms about what he called *The Adventure of Ideas*. He was referring to thrilling times when new fields are born, eras are defined, and profound shifts in foundational beliefs are unleashed, all through the power of ideas.

In our view, the strengths revolution is one of those adventures. Why? Because it re-constructs how you actively see the world. And if you change the way you see your life, you change your life. If you change the way you see the world, you change the world. The strengths revolution in change challenges one bias after another.

The first bias is the negativity bias. It's the brain's tendency to be more alert to and to give more weight to negative information. Why, for example, would a parent focus on an F when seeing his or her child's report card of A, A, B, and F? Why doesn't the parent spend more time studying the success dynamic in both A's? Or why, for example, are the headlines in newspapers more focused on bad news, not great news—events that provide a vision of what could be and stories of solutions, success, and strengths we can build on?

The second bias is "the deficit-based change." This theory says that to improve things, to actively manage change, you first need to define the core of the problem and then diagnose the root causes of that problem. What happens in terms of cognitive bias is what Nobel Laureate Daniel Kahneman calls "anchoring," or the predilection for relying too heavily on one piece of information (in this case, the initial framing of a problem *as a problem*). Think of a team that's labeled "low morale." Is this the best way to increase a team's morale: to conduct, in medical model fashion, a diagnostic *low* morale survey? That's what organizations often do, and it's a routine bias. Yet why *not* get that same team to ask rigorous and "more beautiful" questions of times of near perfect performance or study the most inspired, effective team they've ever seen—one that might give vivid insight into what all of the team members want in their next stage of team development.

A third bias is the "neutral bias." Imagine that a colleague says, "Roberta, we need a meeting; *I need to give you feedback*." What's Roberta's first thought? Even though the word *feedback* is neutral, she probably thinks, "Oh no. What did I do? What's wrong now?"

The fourth bias is the underestimation bias. You underestimate "the universe of strengths" people have at their disposal. You do this all the time. An important *counter* example of this bias is the science of biomimicry. It's an invitation to emulate life's strengths [for example, studying how the wings of a butterfly (with strengths honed over eons of evolution) might exponentially increase the productive power of a solar panel]. When organizations start using biomimicry, a whole universe of strengths and resources opens wide. With 30 million species on Earth today, there are millions upon millions of strengths stories, and some of those have survived 3.85 billion years of testing and rigorous selection. What a resource base! Once biomimicry is introduced, it becomes a way of knowing "more than human" strengths transforming entire industries. It was precisely this *strengths stretching* discipline that led CEO Dee Hock to grow the revenues at VISA International over 10,000 percent during his leadership.

One more cognitive predilection is mentioned here—the generality bias. Ask someone what his or her signature strengths are, and you are likely to hear broad, not very useful, generalization such as "I'm good with people." But is that true under all circumstances? When, more precisely, is that actually happening? Could it be that you are good with people when you are teaching or are serving as an expert? Could it be that you are good with people when you have a passionate purpose (and what kind of passionate purpose) to win in business or to help people heal or to lead a social movement? These are huge differences, and each leads in a different career direction.

In our own work with leaders, parents, change agents, and others, we've been intrigued with how very small changes in perception and how challenging the preceding five biases can make seismic changes.

For example, Mayor Frank Jackson reframed Cleveland's focus on "the quiet crises"—a newspaper series tracking economic decline, ecological degradation, and loss of population as the old industrial economy fell apart. How did he reframe it? He called the whole city together—leaders from business, civil society, government, and universities—for a decade-long series of "whole-system-in-the room" Appreciative Inquiry Summits and studies into the region's strengths. The topic was as follows: How might we create "An Economic Engine to Empower A Green City on a Blue Lake." It's since been featured widely as a model of urban development renaissance. People were asked what their vision was, and the overarching response was "Cleveland will surprise, amaze, and inspire the world with its transformation to a bright green city on a blue lake."

Where once there was doubt and depression, there is now a palpable community of confidence and collective activation. There are urban farms. The rivers are filled with fish. Green economy jobs are multiplying. Offshore wind energy systems are going up. Regional brain gain is near the top in the nation as young people flock to the city where housing rentals are at 98 percent occupancy. And every citizen in Cleveland now can get 100 percent of his or her energy from clean, renewable sources—in fact, residents must opt out of this amazing program.

But here's the point. The brain's negative bias, the deficit-based change bias, the anchoring bias, the neutral bias, the underestimation bias, and the generalizing bias were all holding the city back, a city that was endlessly caught in its narrative deterioration. But stopping massive deterioration (or ending it or slowing it down) does not easily, if ever, equate into a renaissance. In fact, all studies of industrial-age deterioration would not give anybody in the city new knowledge or a clear image of what a vibrant *green city on a blue lake* could be—and what strengths patterns or bundles would create it. If people don't search for positive deviations, they won't know their causes.

Excellence is not the opposite of failure. Consequently, most inquiry continues to focus on studying unhappy customers to create happy ones, studying sickness to learn about health, removing the problems of bureaucracy to learn about enterprise innovation, and ending depression to get to *where*? Any study of how to end depression will not teach much about the pathways and disciplines to overall personal flourishing. And guess what happens to Mayor Jackson's industrial decay if the establishment of a green city on a blue lake eclipses the decay. That's right. A problem gets solved, certainly not by solving it directly on its own terms, but by *creating* something new.

That's why small changes in perception can be seismic. You live in the world your questions create. When you study the best and aim higher with your vision, you become what you study. When you study the best possible city, you learn about all of the indicators, root causes of success, pathways, and possibilities. When you study the worst possible city, you see none of those things. That's why the father of management theory, Drucker, disliked the lack of innovation in bureaucracies. Bureaucratic officials were, in his view, too often focusing on tiny deflective problems and thereby squandering precious time and *return on attention*. Bureaucracies often are experts at, in Drucker's words, "feeding the problems and starving the opportunities."

Your strengths are your multiplier. Your strengths magnify you. They represent *you* at your best. Seeing them—in your teams, your institutions, your world, and yourselves—requires the gift of new eyes. This book contains research studies that document the many personal, collective, and business benefits. There are citations to many other great works that can expand your strengths library. There are frameworks such as appreciative inquiry models that give solid logic. And what may be most important, the book is full of concrete applications.

Almost every chapter contains *things you can do* to invite the strengths way of life into your world. These applications are there to open the doorways of the mind. They broaden and build your resources in ways that will make you better leaders, collaborative colleagues, and parents or coaches. They help undo past patterns, especially the many cognitive biases mentioned. They build resilience and hope. And they help you soar into a developmental adventure.

The American author Helen Keller said, "Life is either a daring adventure or nothing." She was deaf and blind, but she saw strengths everywhere, beautiful ones inside and outside, and so many things others simply could not see. And Jawaharlal Nehru, whose quote appeared at the beginning of this introduction, lived and led in times where beauty, charm, and adventure might have been hard to see or find. But by pointing at the ability as human beings to find them—if they only look for it—he started a whole new era, not only as the first Prime Minister of India, but also for a continent and a world, who desperately needed to find again this ability to see what was best, possible, and next.

Give yourself this gift. Learn to see what's best, what's possible, and what's next. Bring your questions and curiosity to the journey. Take on the risks. Experiment in tiny ways and get bolder. And then, as in any adventure, you might find surprises with lasting impact.

We have seen that using the strengths-based leadership paradigm promotes a greater sense of security and trust within the organization because weaknesses are addressed rather than "swept under the rug." We have experienced how organizations are energized when every person in the organization is allowed to bring his or her strengths into play. And we have seen how this energy creates results and happiness and how the organization flourishes, ultimately achieving better and more sustainable work flows, ways of collaborating (inside and outside the organization), and products. This is a positive spiral, where things are interlinked. We do not see efficiency at the cost of well-being or innovation. We see well-being generating efficiency and better products. And we see that achieving results and doing something great in the world promotes well-being. In other words, we see more humane organizations moving into the surrounding community in a positive way.

And we believe this is what the world needs. We live in a time where too many people burn out, where efficiency is put above thoughtfulness, mindfulness, and sustainability for the individual and society and the environment. We believe that a new paradigm for leadership is needed and that the strengths-based revolution offers a valid approach, helping leaders and organizations excel but not at the cost of the employees or the environment.

We think the world needs a new form of leadership where people collaborate rather than compete—where they seek to understand before they judge—and where every leader looks at every employee, colleague, other leader, collaborator, board member, and competitor as another human being who has the same needs and interest: living and leading in a safe and peaceful world. With the problems the world faces today regarding climate change, war, poverty, injustice, and inequality, we believe a more innovative, humble, kind, collaborative, engaging, and sustainable mind-set is needed to solve these problems and the strengths-based leadership style promotes this.

We wish you a happy adventure exploring and trying out the strengths-based leadership paradigm.

— Pernille Hippe Brun, San Francisco; David Cooperrider, Cleveland; Mikkel Ejsing, Copenhagen
Spring 2016

CONTENTS

FOREWORD

My name is Lyell Clarke. In 2007, I was the farthest thing from being an appreciative and strengths-based leader. I was the president of Clarke Mosquito Control, a 60-year-old family-owned and family-operated company in the field of mosquito control and aquatic habitat management. I had spent most of my work life in my family's business and had been in the role of president and CEO since my father transitioned to the position of chairman in 1996. In 2007, I would have characterized myself as a fairly conventional and conservative business manager and would have characterized our company as a tired, old pesticide manufacturing, service, and distribution company. That said, we enjoyed significant market share, were respected within our industry, and were considered a leader in our field. We weren't in crisis. But we were about to make a change that would have a profound effect on our business, our employees, and our industry. The question you might want to ask is: "Why change?"

This is a story of how I and my company implemented the strengths-based paradigm. It wasn't done overnight. In fact, it has taken us seven years, and we are not done. So by telling my story in detail, you can get an insight into the fact that however "easy" the tools and ideas found in this book might seem, it takes courage, time, and effort to implement them. But it is worth it!

Each leader has his or her reasons for wanting to make a change. As I reflect back on my reasons, there were five major factors. It started with my attendance at a three-day self-awareness retreat. At the end of the retreat, the walls were covered with a myriad of inspirational sayings and quotes. The facilitator encouraged us to consider these as souvenirs of the experience. My souvenir, which I still keep in my briefcase, simply said: "If you don't do something different, you're going to wind up where you're headed." I realized that we were facing a fork in the road.

I also was becoming aware of a different business model—a sustainable value business model. A great deal has been written on this subject by Chris Laszlo and leaders such as Ray Anderson from Interface Carpet and Yvon Chouinard from Patagonia—pioneers in the sustainable value business model. This growing awareness of business that could *do well by doing good* was the second factor in our change journey.

The third factor was happening inside my company. After having adopted a deliberate product development strategy a few years prior, our efforts were beginning to show significant promise. We had new products in the pipeline that had the potential to revolutionize our industry. We were facing a decision. Were we going to handle those new products in the same way we had handled all of our conventional products, or were we willing to do something significantly different?

The fourth and most personal factor was the adoption of my son Joseph in 2008. Joseph was just 24 months old and had spent the majority of his life in a crowded Russian orphanage. Conditions in the orphanage were spare. And like many children there, Joe was undernourished and sickly. We brought him home where he had access to good health care, a healthy and balanced diet, and an abundance of love and attention. Within just a few weeks, his weight was coming into line with standard growth charts and his curious mind and bright and charming personality was beginning to shine through. With Joe, I learned in a very personal way that I could make a real difference in the world.

And finally, perhaps the most important factor was something that came from deep within my soul. I found myself contending with a nagging feeling about the legacy I would be handing to the next generation of potential family owners. Would I be leaving a legacy of a tired, old pesticide service and distribution company? Or would I be leaving a legacy that the next generation would be proud to be part of, one that would align with the millennial and postmillennial generations' desire to work for or create a company consistent with their values and that would appeal to their lifestyle? As I contemplated this, I began to realize that within me was a pent-up desire to create a company with greater purpose.

At that year's annual planning retreat, I took a first step in what would be my own journey to become a wholly human, authentic, and strengths-based leader: I allowed myself to be vulnerable as I explained to our management team that I wanted us to make a change. I didn't know exactly what that change would be or where it would take us; I just knew it was time for us to do things differently.

Our journey started with an exercise in discovery and dreaming, exercises you will find in this book. You will discover what already works for you and what you might imagine or dream of becoming in the best version of yourself as an individual and as a company.

In our working groups that day, we were asked to create a picture of the current company identity. We were invited to cut pictures from magazines of images that represented our current reality. The images that the teams presented were very telling. We were Chevy Silverado trucks. We were Rambo. We were a big black bear. We were solid, reliable, and tough.

And then we were invited to draw a picture of us as the best version of ourselves. After a moment of hesitation and cautious uncertainty, the team began to collect pictures of nature. We were birds. We were green. We were Kermit the Frog. And in one amazing and profoundly emotional moment, one of groups announced that we were salmon swimming upstream, willing to sacrifice ourselves to protect future generations.

In that moment, I realized that the struggle I was having was also a struggle deep within our employees. This visioning exercise revealed that our employees also were hungering for something different. They didn't want to work for a mosquito control company. They wanted to work for a company that saved lives and focused on public health. They wanted to work for a company with meaning and with greater purpose. And so we set out on a journey to become that company. It wasn't easy. We faced many challenges as we worked to discard our old, tired ways and to ignite a fire and goodness in our people. Three pivotal moments propelled us forward.

The **first pivotal moment** took place in October 2008. Coming out of that transformational planning/visioning retreat, we decided to invite all of our employees into the conversation with a first ever all-employee meeting. This gathering of 150 employees was where I again allowed myself to show real vulnerability. I explained to our employees that I felt this desire and responsibility to lead the company in a different direction. As I shared with them what I had learned about the sustainable value business model, I openly admitted to my company that I didn't know how we were going to get there. I told them I needed their help and asked them for their ideas on how we might become a more sustainable company. In that one day, our employees came up with 800 ideas—some very simple and some very audacious ideas that helped us begin to chart a road map for our journey.

Two years later we had completed a brand change—from the icon of the "upside down, dead mosquito" that represented us as a "trusted partner in mosquito control" to "the shield" serving to "make communities more livable, safe, and comfortable." We articulated our values. The first, *Caring for the Planet*, was aspirational. The others—*Caring for People; Being Passionate About What We Do;* and *Doing the Right Thing, Even When It's Hard*—were an articulation of the values and strengths we already had within us. We were transforming our brand and focusing our strengths toward a more aspirational future. And with the creation of our first sustainability committees, we had begun to make progress in reducing unnecessary waste, improving efficiencies, and becoming a (slightly) more sustainable company.

But we hadn't yet embedded these new concepts into our DNA. We had activated a small group of passionate employees, many of them the millennials who represented the next generation of leadership. In time, we began to realize that there was a significant organizational gap between my vision and the vision and passion of the employees who had joined these early committees. Our efforts were too often seen as extracurricular or as something that would pass. Employees received mixed messages. They were torn between getting involved and getting "back to work."

If we were to achieve our vision of making sustainability one of the primary lenses through which we made every business decision, we needed to elevate our efforts to effect a holistic organizational change. This realization led to our **second pivotal moment**. With information and ideas gathered from other companies that we looked to as role models, we established "Project Greater Purpose." Project Greater Purpose created a formal organizational structure around our sustainability efforts and created processes to help us maintain progress in, and pay attention to, key business, environmental, and social priorities. Our Sustainability Advisory Board, made up of top management and leaders in key focus areas, provides oversight, guidance, and direction to five committees: Health and Wellness, Social Responsibility, Awareness and Education, Good Earth, and Sustainable Business.

Through these five committees, we take action on a wide array of activities and initiatives designed to increase our awareness of sustainability issues and topics, reduce our environmental impact, engage with the community, and elevate the health and wellness of our workforce. We invite our employees to vote with their feet and to become involved wherever their passion points them. Today, close to 80 percent of our employees are actively engaged in one or more of the 70+ programs and initiatives that are being pursued under the Project Greater Purpose structure. We no longer view sustainability as an extracurricular endeavor. Today there is an expectation that our employees will get involved, and this involvement is integrated into job descriptions and performance management and reward systems.

The momentum of Project Greater Purpose led us to and prepared us for our **third pivotal moment**. Our first Appreciative Inquiry Summit. Dubbed Clarke+, we imagined a summit that would "accelerate a sustainable Clarke," a summit that would engage all of our stakeholders and inspire us to become radically innovative as we sought to secure our shared global future. The way we conducted the summit was aligned with what is discussed in Chapter 12 of this book. Basically, we followed the steps in David Cooperrider's 5D model and were inspired by the thoughts behind strengths-based change processes.

In February 2012, we invited all of our employees and 60 outside stakeholders to spend 2 1/2 days discovering our collective strengths, dreaming, and designing programs and initiatives that would help us create that shared future. This event was the catalyst we needed to accelerate our transformation. During those days, our employees and outside stakeholders came up with ten areas of opportunity, including ZERO Waste, EXTRAORDINARY Health and Happiness, Radical Partnerships, and alliances that would challenge us to be a Bold Catalyst for External Change. We aspired to accelerate the development of our Next Generation of products and to adopt Transformational Energy solutions. We envisioned expanding our aquatic management efforts to a broader Water Resource Management platform. We imagined broadening our Clarke Cares philanthropy efforts and Elevating our Customer Experience. We also created an aspiration of a Clarke Campus of the Future—a facility that would be a brick-and-mortar manifestation of our mission, vision, and values and that would create a bridge between science and nature and business and the community.

At the end of our summit, I asked our head of Human Resources and Sustainable Development: "What's the next step?" Her response was reminiscent of my appeal to the team back in 2008 as she said to me, "Honestly Lyell, I don't know. But I do know we will figure it out."

So we started again to map out a plan to propel the momentum and energy of our summit into actionable plans and initiatives. Over the next nine months, we again leveraged the strengths of our passionate employees to review and prioritize not just one prototype, but three to five on which they wanted to take action. Some initiatives were immediately actionable (such as the adoption of a Paid Time Off policy to replace our traditional Vacation and Paid Sick leave programs). Most programs, however, were more complex and needed further consideration. In a series of half-day sessions, Opportunity Area leaders refined their recommendations, prepared their "business" case, and created action plans for immediate midterm and long-term initiatives. At the end of the summer, we were positioned to integrate our initiatives seamlessly into the next year's operating budget and into our existing Strategic Planning and Project Greater Purpose management structures.

Prompted by a desire for greater purpose and propelled by the collective capabilities of our system, we've made amazing progress. Twenty-five percent of our revenues are generated by products and services that focus on green chemistry. We've reduced our carbon emissions by 25 percent, resulting in millions of dollars of operational savings. We've cut our operational waste by 64 percent and are recycling or repurposing 81 percent of the remaining waste. We've adopted a flexible work policy to engage a more relaxed and nimble workforce. Forty-eight percent of the energy we use comes from renewable sources, and with the installation of a 100 kW solar array at our new Clarke Campus (of the future) facility, we're generating 20 percent of its energy needs through onsite renewable energy.

We recently won the President's Green Chemistry Award, a national award for our work in creating softer greener chemistry for the public health market and twice have been an honored recipient of the Illinois Governor's Sustainability Award.

Our business is healthy and profitable. We're engaging with our customers in new and different ways. We're working with dynamic partners, and innovation is coming from every corner of the organization. In addition, we're attracting and engaging a workforce of talented and passionate people who are encouraged to imagine a bold future.

These are proof points for a journey that has been both profound and simple. Putting myself out there—articulating a personal struggle and desire while admitting that I didn't have the answers—may have been the most difficult moment in my career. And yet it was also the moment where my work became easier and more meaningful. That instant of vulnerability was the spark that lit the imagination and capabilities of our organization. And that spark continues to ignite and propel us forward as we prepare to bring our system back together for a second Appreciative Inquiry Summit. This time we're challenging ourselves to go deeper, to be braver, and to think bolder in our work to create a prosperous and flourishing company and a prosperous and flourishing world.

Through appreciative inquiry and an endeavor to lead in a manner that leverages the strengths of our organization, I have become a strengths-based leader and have fostered an organization that is rich in appreciative and strengths-based leadership. It started out with a personal aspiration, but to transform a whole company, one must commit fully to the strengths-based philosophy and adopt many of the concrete tools offered in this book. You can learn more about Clarke and our journey to become a Company with Greater Purpose by looking at our website and Sustainability Reports at www.clarke.com.

I hope you will be inspired by our story—my story—and by this book. My name is Lyell Clarke, and I have the greatest job in the world!

PART ONE

STRENGTHS-BASED LEADERSHIP IN A NUTSHELL

STRENGTHS-BASED LEADERSHIP ORIGINS AND DEFINITION

This book begins by taking a closer look at the origins of strengths-based leadership as a management discipline and at the definition of strengths-based leadership. It also provides an introduction to some of the basic research that underpins this discipline.

CONTENTS

THE ORIGINS OF THE STRENGTHS-BASED LEADERSHIP APPROACH

How can we tell when a particular approach—a particular "movement" or paradigm—is born? The answer is rarely at the moment it is born. When did we see the first book, the first statement, the first management training course within the strengths-based approach? Who initiated the approach? Who were the front-runners? Who were the first to foster the ideas and the thoughts behind the paradigm? We'll try to address these questions now, with the knowledge that some of the people we refer to may not have characterized themselves as the front-runners of a strength-oriented approach. Nevertheless, in a contemporary perspective, we see them as having played an important role in shaping our thinking about strengths-based leadership and having helped initiate research on the effects of strengths-based leadership.

Peter Drucker and the task of leadership

The first management book that paid real attention to strengths was the late Peter Drucker's book from 1966, *The Effective Executive* (1966). Drucker (1909–2005) is characterized as the leading founder of modern management. Before his death, he authored close to 50 books on management and leadership, and he has left his imprint in the hearts and minds of many business executives. He continues to do so after his death through his books; the many interviews he gave; and his to-the-point quotes about leadership and organizational change, which are often cited. His thoughts, ideas, and perceptions about management and leadership are still considered groundbreaking. Drucker was a front-runner and an advocate of decentralization, empowerment, and delegation (just to mention a few management issues about which he had an opinion), and he saw the leader's prime task as creating the right conditions for the employees to perform and excel and bring their strengths into play. In *The Effective Executive*, Drucker makes the first mention of studies that show that to succeed, efficient leaders build on their own strengths and the strengths of their employees, their colleagues, their superiors, their customers, the organization, and the larger environment.

In one of the last interviews Drucker gave, he made the following statement when asked about the prime task of leadership (Cooperrider et al., 2005):

The task of leadership is to create an alignment of strengths making our weaknesses insignificant.

In all simplicity, this statement reflects the essence of strengths-based leadership.

Our task is to align our own and our staff's strengths in such a way that our weaknesses are no longer an obstacle to performance, efficiency, innovation, well-being, and growth to the benefit of the world.

David Cooperrider and Appreciative Inquiry

In the 1980s, the strength-oriented approach began to gain ground with one of this book's coauthors, David Cooperrider. He developed an organizational framework—Appreciative Inquiry (AI)—designed to identify and amplify the things that work in society, in an organization, in a person, or on a team. With its structured and simple method for developing communities, organizations, teams, and individuals, AI has proved its capacity for generating impressive results for organizations and solving complex social and environmental problems around the world. On a large scale in relation to organizational development in restructuring projects, change projects, and vision and strategy implementation projects, the change process has proven its worth, as it also has done on a smaller scale in improving dialogues, enhancing communication, and increasing understanding internally in the organization and in relation to the organizations' partners and customers (Cooperrider et al., 2005, 2008). The basic message in AI is the same as the conclusion that Drucker reached:

It is more effective and healthy to focus on strengths and on what works than to focus on weaknesses and what does not work in order for the company to succeed on a broader scale.

This point has been widely confirmed by subsequent research, case studies, and organizations' experience in using the method (see, for example, Lazlo et al., 2014; Watkins et al., 2001; Anderson et al., 2008). Organizations that focus on strengths and "what works well" thrive and grow—and survive—as the two case studies in Chapter 12 show. Those case studies are descriptions of projects that we as consultants have been involved in delivering. For other case studies, look at the web page of AI Commons. It is full of case stories from both public and private companies that have benefited from using the AI method in developing and transforming their organizations during the last 20 years.

Since the "invention" of AI in the eighties and nineties, the approach has been developed and expanded and it created a movement involving thousands of leaders and organizations from all over the world. For more information, refer to the website for Case Western University—the Fowler Center. The AI process continues to inspire organizations to rethink how they are structured and how they lead—and how they may be of benefit to the world. With the "Business as an Agent of World Benefit" (BAWB) movement, the approach has been taken to the next level, letting the strengths-based paradigm lead the way for organizations striving to be sustainable. The BAWB movement's "Global Forum" in 2015 had the headline "Flourish and Prosper," and more than 600 executives discussed how to lead, manage, and organize in a manner promoting sustainability, flourishing, and good results.

Martin Seligman, positive psychology and positive organizational scholarship (POS)

In the nineties, the AI movement was supplemented by a more psychologically oriented movement headed by Martin Seligman (1998, 2003). Seligman was elected president of the American Psychological Association (APA) in 1998. Candidates holding this position must pick a theme or topic that will receive particular attention during their presidency. At that time, Seligman chose a rather unknown branch within psychology, today known as *positive psychology*. This is the part of psychology that studies and addresses what makes people thrive and overcome troubling times—what brings out the best in people and makes them happy, resilient, and filled with hope and optimism. This is opposite the part of psychology that studies and focuses on what makes people ill, unhappy, and filled with negative feelings such as anger and hostility. In his president's address in August 1999, following his one year as president, Seligman said the following:

> *Entering a new millennium, we face a historical choice. Standing alone on the pinnacle of economic and political leadership, the United States can continue to increase its material wealth while ignoring the human needs of our people and of the people on the rest of the planet. Such a course is likely to lead to increasing selfishness, alienation between the more and the less fortunate, and eventually to chaos and despair.*
>
> *At this juncture, psychology can play an enormously important role. We can articulate a vision of the good life that is empirically sound and, at the same time, understandable and attractive. We can show the world what actions lead to well-being, to positive individuals, to flourishing communities, and to a just society.*
>
> *Ideally, psychology should be able to help document what kind of families result in the healthiest children, what work environments support the greatest satisfaction among workers, and what policies result in the strongest civic commitment.*

This was seen as a liberating development that allowed American psychologists to study what is right with people and their surroundings rather than what is wrong. In Europe, positive psychology soon brought about the same attention it had in the United States. Today there are innumerable books on positive psychology describing the profound underlying research conducted in the field for the last 15 years. Seligman kick-started a series of research studies that has thus far proved, in essence, that:

> *The leaders who are capable of triggering positive emotions such as hope, optimism and resilience among their staff achieve superior results than the leaders that trigger anger, fear and hostility. The leaders who think (or learn to think more) positively and who generally look for the things that work (what is right in and for the organization, the situation and the employees) achieve superior results.*

One result of the outcomes that followed from Seligman's proclamation of the emphasis on positive psychology during his presidency of the APA was a movement that took the approach to support studies looking into "positive deviances" within organizations. This movement, called the "Positive Organizational Scholarship" (POS) movement (Cameron et al., 2003), supports the exploration of organizations that excel in their field, achieving extraordinary results and thriving and performing above their (expected) level—sometimes against all odds. The emphasis is on identifying the positive things that happen in these organizations and the conditions that make the foundations for their success.

The basic statement behind the POS movement is as follows:

> *If we want to identify what creates success and extraordinary performance, we would be wise to examine the cases in which it already occurs.*

This sentence holds an important point and wisdom within the strengths-based paradigm: That which generates success, well-being, and progress in an organization is not simply the opposite of or the absence of negative factors. Positive factors and negative factors are not characterized by opposite conditions and consequences; their root causes are fundamentally different. Thus, we do not necessarily learn about success by studying failure. Focusing on positive factors is a special area that deserves greater attention in companies and in research, simply because we cannot conclude what it takes to succeed (as an individual or an organization) by stating "just do the opposite of what it takes to be a failure." You can read some of the case studies conducted in this movement and their different findings on what it takes to succeed at http://positiveorgs.bus.umich.edu. You also may be inspired by Malcolm Gladwell's book *Outliers: The Story of Success* (2008). It describes different factors for human success. Likewise, the book *Good to Great: Why Some Companies Make the Leap . . . and Others Don't* (2001) by Jim Collins describes different factors for long-lasting organizational success, as does his follow-up book *Great by Choice: Uncertainty, Chaos, and Luck—Why Some Thrive Despite Them All* (2011).

Since the start of Seligman's Positive Psychology movement and Kim Cameron's Positive Organizational Scholarship movement, other organizations interested in studying positive deviances and the benefits of using a strengths-based approach to development of organizations was born. One of them was The British Center for Applied Positive Psychology (CAPP). In a summary from 2012, the Center came with the following evaluation:

BENEFITS FOR LEADERS AND COMPANIES OF BUILDING ON STRENGTHS

- Putting untapped talent to use throughout the organization
- Recruitment and retention of the employees that the organization needs
- Improved individual performance
- Achievement of engagement
- Development of flexibility
- Improved teamwork
- A positive emphasis on differences
- Greater openness to change
- Better handling of dismissals
- Enhanced job satisfaction for employees and achievement of individual goals.

Marcus Buckingham and the research of the Gallup organization on strengths-based leadership

The most recent addition to the strengths-based approach comes from England, where for the past 15 years, Buckingham has revolutionized the perceptions of performance, efficiency, and achievement of results through strengths-based leadership (Buckingham, 2005, 2007, 2008, 2011; Buckingham & Clifton, 2002). At Gallup, he and his colleagues have carried out quantitative and qualitative studies (via thousands of interviews with employees, teams, and leaders) of what generates efficiency, high performance, and results in organizations. In summary, here is what they found:

> *The highest levels of performance and accomplishments co-occurring with the highest levels of well-being, employee satisfaction and commitment are found where leaders take an interest in and support the employees' ability to bring their strengths into play.*

In 2003, a Gallup survey concluded that leaders with a strengths-based approach to management were twice as likely to achieve success and positive results as leaders who did not focus on the strengths in their organization (Clifton & Harter, 2003). This led to a series of follow-up surveys to identify whether leaders focused on the strengths of their employees, whether the employees believed they were able to bring their strengths into play, and what the relationship was between this possibility/focus and the results the organization achieved.

The results were unambiguous. In 2005, Gallup published a study demonstrating that workers' engagement was highly dependent on whether management focused on their strengths. In fact, in the cases where the leaders focused on the employees' strengths, 99 percent of the employees felt engaged in their jobs. Conversely, the number fell to 60 percent when the leader largely ignored the employees and to 82 percent when the leader focused on weaknesses, showing that attention matters even if the attention focuses on the weaknesses. Ignorance is the biggest problem of leadership. But focusing on strengths generates more engagement, and a direct link was found between engagement and productivity (Buckingham, 2007).

This sparked additional research. Gallup then carried out a survey of 36 companies in multiple countries. The survey included interviews with 198,000 employees, all of whom were asked 12 questions. These questions were chosen because they had been found to correlate with productivity and engagement. They have since become known as Gallup's Q12 engagement survey, which is used to measure good management. You can learn more about the survey and other results from Gallup's research on strengths and engagement at www.gallup.com.

The statement that was found to be most closely correlated to productivity was statement 3, which is:

At work, I have the opportunity to do what I do best every day.

Again, this shows how important it is to be able to use one's strengths at work every day. This is significant because of the correlation between being able to do what one does best and being productive. It also is important because using one's strengths is correlated to being happier and to achieving satisfaction in one's work (Gallup, 2013).

A meta-analysis comparison study of engagement surveys from 2013 used data from more than 22 million respondents, 2.5 million business units or workgroups, and 1,079 organizations. The following box provides the results of the study (Harter et al., 2012).

TEAMS AND ORGANIZATIONS WITH HIGH Q12 SCORES HAVE POSITIVE CORRELATIONS WITH THE FOLLOWING

- Customer metrics (referred to as customer loyalty)
- Profitability
- Productivity
- Lower turnover
- Fewer safety incidents
- Less absenteeism
- Less shrinkage
- Higher patient safety incidents
- Higher quality
- Fewer defects

The people who replied "Strongly agree" to statement 3 on the Q12 were found to be members of high-performance teams with very low staff turnover, a high degree of well-being, and a high degree of customer satisfaction (Harter et al., 2002, 2012). The discouraging aspect of the same study, though, was that only 17 percent of the people surveyed strongly agreed that they were able to do what they did best every day. That is less than one-fifth! What a waste of resources and energy. Imagine if that number could be raised to 30 percent? What would that do for companies' performance, well-being, and ability to do something great in the world?

In summary, the strengths-based approach has proven to be a valid tool for promoting effective and healthy organizations. Let's now turn to a definition of strengths, weaknesses, and strengths-based leadership before we dig into the underlying philosophy behind the strengths-based paradigm in Chapter 2.

DEFINITIONS: STRENGTHS AND WEAKNESSES; STRENGTHS-BASED LEADERSHIP—WHAT ARE WE TALKING ABOUT?

Definition of a strength

What is a strength? First reflect on the following:

REFLECTION

What is your perception of a strength?

Where do you think your strengths lie?

In your opinion, what is the difference between a strength and an ability or a competence?

Where does talent fit into this?

Below is a review of what the literature says about this.

Talent *is innate*. It is a particular ability or gift that someone has, a special capacity that makes some things easier for that person. It is the recurring patterns of thoughts, actions, and behaviors that are characteristic of a person and that occur persistently and consistently and naturally. Talent cannot be changed. We have been given a certain amount of talent in certain areas. Research has found a striking similarity between the personality features and talents we display at 3 years of age and the ones we display at 26 or 66 (Buckingham, 2007). Thus, our talents and personal preferences are difficult to alter. What we can alter, however, are our *competencies* and our *knowledge level*.

Knowledge level is what we develop by studying a field. It is the internal, cognitively structured intelligence we achieve in a given area.

Competencies are the same as ***skills***. It is what we are capable of doing as a result of training and practice and the knowledge we have acquired by studying. However, it does not reflect whether it was easy or hard to acquire this competence, and in itself, it does not reflect whether the competencies acquired (for example, typing, doing handstands, working with Excel spreadsheets, or talking with a customer) lie within our area of strengths. As we will see, a true strength has to do with "ease," whether something feels easy and natural for us to learn and practice. Thus, competencies are what we can and must be able to do to hold a certain job or carry out a task. Management competencies can be described as the basics required to do our job as leaders in the context in which we work as leaders.

When we talk of ***strengths***, the word tells us that the concept is related to energy, power, and muscles. We can use the word *strength* in connection with activities in which we put an effort: "It takes real strength to lift that block of concrete. She is very strong." It also gives us a hint that strengths are something we can build. We are born with the muscle—the talent. We can acquire knowledge and competencies, but strength only develops once we use our muscle/talent in combination with the knowledge and competencies we have developed in the field in which we bring our strengths into play. This counts not only for individuals, but also for organizations (Cooperrider, 2008; Mohr et al., 2008).

Tom Rath describes a simple formula for defining and developing our strengths (2007).

TOM RATH'S STRENGTH EQUATION

Talent (an innate and natural way of thinking, feeling or acting)

× investment (the time you spend training, developing your skills and adding to your knowledge within the field)

= strength

To optimize a strength, we need to have a particular talent and to make a considerable investment in developing that talent. If we have great talent but fail to invest time in it, that talent will fail to become a strength. If we lack innate talent, we can work hard and become good at something, but it will never become a strength.

The equation can serve as a tool for assessing where we should devote our time and energy when we want to develop our leadership. If we don't have a talent for resolving conflicts, that will never be one of our strengths. If we have a talent for developing and executing a strategy or crunching numbers, with the right investment, that can become a real strength (Linley, 2008).

CASE

In 1955, a research study was carried out in Nebraska to determine the teaching styles of various literacy teachers and the related learning outcomes for the students. The study produced an unexpected result. It found that there was little correlation between teaching style and literacy outcomes. Provided the teachers had practiced their particular teaching approach with commitment and knowledge, there was no difference in the students' progress. However, the unexpected outcome of the study was that the struggling readers only improved very slightly. They did progress a little—from minus 10 to minus 4. By contrast, the students who already had a good reading speed and few errors improved considerably. They went from plus 10 to plus 40 (Glock, 1955).

What this study shows is that it is only possible to achieve a mediocre performance in areas in which you have no talent, but you may achieve the extraordinary in areas in which you are already strong.

Collins takes this to the organizational level when talking about organizational performance in his books *Good to Great: Why Some Companies Make the Leap . . . and Others Don't* (2001) and *Great By Choice: Uncertainty, Chaos, and Luck—Why Some Thrive Despite Them All* (2011). The organizations making the leap from good to great build on their unique strengths—the things they can be and are extraordinarily good at combined with their passion and good eye for whether they can earn money from this talent.

Thus, using Rath's definition:

> *A strength is an innate talent that we have invested time and energy in developing and which we—if we use it in the right manner and at the right time—may use to create high performance for individuals and organizations.*

Buckingham goes one step further than Rath in his definition of a strength. According to Buckingham, having invested time and energy in our talent is not enough for us to call it a strength. We also must be *successful* in using our talent and find ourselves *energized* from using it. According to Buckingham, success requires that we combine our talent with our acquired skills and knowledge, and like Collins, he states that the timing—that we use it at the right time and in the right context—also counts. Thus, we achieve success when we acquire knowledge about and training in what it takes to apply our talent at the right time and *in the right context*. However, in addition to this, we should also feel energized by using our strength. That is the hallmark of a strength in Buckingham's definition. We'll return to this point later.

Buckingham summarizes this in a model with four interconnected parameters that, taken together, indicate a strength. He calls it the SIGN model (Buckingham, 2007).

THE SIGN MODEL

Success: Your strengths lie within areas /activities at which you are successful (in other people's assessment).

Instinct: You perform the given activity where your strength unfolds naturally and with ease—you have a natural talent.

Growth: You cannot wait to learn new things and techniques in relation to the field—you want to develop and improve.

Need: You feel a need and an urge to engage in activities where you use your strengths. You are energized when you use your strengths. Therefore, only you can determine whether something is a strength in your own case.

So to determine whether something is a strength, we need to notice whether applying our talent energizes us. Whether we look forward to applying our talent and whether the activities in which we use our talents seem easy or hard are important. This also counts for teams and organizations as a whole (Fredrickson & Losoda, 2005; Cameron, 2006).

Whether we are successful in an activity is not merely up to us to judge. Whether we are successful depends on our own assessment as well as on other people's assessment. If our goal is to become a really good listener as a leader and our employees and/or customers give us a 3 in our next 360-degree review, have we been successful? We have clearly succeeded in improving if our previous rating was 2.5, but that doesn't necessarily mean that "listening" is one of our strengths. At least others' assessment is that we aren't particularly good at it. So it wouldn't be enough to call it a strength of ours. And if the organization claims that it has the best product in a given area or is the best at responding to customers quickly but the customers don't agree and numbers show it isn't true, this isn't an organizational strength even though the organization may claim it is.

Talent alone is not enough. Hard work alone is not enough. Whether a talent unfolds to become a strength for us or the organization depends on whether we are successful in the situations in which we use our talent, whether we have grown in the area in which we seek to develop, and whether we have an instinctive urge to seek out new knowledge and grow within the field (Buckingham, 2007; Rath, 2007).

According to Buckingham, to define the strength even more specifically, we need to notice *in what situations* a strength occurs. He points out that we often tend to be too general when we define our strengths, which ultimately means that they are watered down. For example, we might say that empathy is one of our strengths. Indeed, the test described later in this book (the StrengthsFinder test), which can be used to chart strengths, describes strengths in this general format.

However, Buckingham encourages us to thoroughly examine the following:

- When
- In what situations
- With whom …

… the strength of empathy is expressed. By taking an even more radical stance, he further adds that individual strengths are played out in specific activities in which people use their skills and knowledge, not in the generalized domain. As an example, he mentions that a person may have a *talent* for assertiveness (speaking his or her mind without being hurtful), a *skill* of checking a guest into a hotel, and a *knowledge* of local restaurants. All of that adds up to the strength of "taking charge of each guest's experience."

In Buckingham's definition, a strength is something we *do*. And it is something we can *continue to do consistently*. We don't do it just once, but are able to repeat it and thus achieve "consistent near perfect performance in an activity" (Buckingham, 2007, 2011).

In summary, a strength is defined as follows:

A strength consists of equal parts talent and investment and can be expressed repeatedly in situations where one feels strong and energized, is successful, and wants to contribute.

Definition of a weakness

Inspired by Buckingham (Buckingham & Clifton, 2002), we apply the term *weakness* to refer to anything that *hinders you in excellent performance, both as an individual and as an organization.*

A weakness is defined by hindering you in your ability to be successful.

Often the term *growth area* is used to refer to the weak points of people or organizations. But in fact, it is not helpful to speak of strengths and growth areas. With this terminology, we give ourselves and others the impression that the weak points are the only ones that we should try to improve and that are open to improvement. *In the strengths-based approach, both strengths and weaknesses are seen as growth areas*. Moreover, the strengths are seen as primary growth areas, whereas weaknesses need to be dealt with, a point that will be explored in subsequent sections and was briefly touched on in the case earlier in this chapter.

Just as a strength is expressed in situations in which we or the organization feel strong, weaknesses are expressed in situations where we feel weak or drained. Thus, indicators of weaknesses are the opposite of strength indicators and can be defined as follows:

A weakness is expressed in situations where a person feels drained of energy. It is characterized by hindering a person or an organization in the ability to be successful and by a lack of instinct/ease/talent or the desire to be in these situations or to learn more about the situations where the person is forced to draw on his or her weak side.

Definition of strengths-based leadership

In 2008, different practitioners and researchers and theorists within the paradigm of AI asked themselves this question: What is meant by a strengths-based organization? (Mohr et al., 2008). A special edition of the *AI Practitioner* sheds some light on this question and discusses, looks at examples of, and begins to identify parameters of strengths-based organizations, which may help us define strengths-based leadership as well. Therefore, let's take a look at what they found:

The image we are beginning to discern is that strengths-based organizations:

- Systematically identify and leverage both individual and organizational strengths in their strategic pursuit of superior and sustainable mission performance—be it in the public, corporate or not-for-profit sectors
- Are consciously designed with a focus on strengths that is evident both in what they do (service delivery/product creation) as well as how they build, sustain, adapt and innovate (strategic planning, continuous improvement, process reengineering, technology implementation, restructuring)
- Affirm, nurture and sustain life at the individual member level and in their interactions with customers and stakeholders
- Articulate a vision of workplaces fueled by generative conversation, evolving vision, emergent, more democratic structures, and cultures rich in meaning and relationship

DEFINITION: "Strengths-based organizations are organizations, including groups, families and communities, explicitly designed and managed for the elevation of strengths, the combination and magnification of strengths, and ultimately, the amplified refraction of our highest human strengths outward into the world." (Mohr et al., 2008)

Inspired by this and by Buckingham's and Rath's definitions of strengths and weaknesses, our definition of strengths-based leadership can be summarized as follows:

The main goal of strengths-based leadership is to identify, build on, and amplify the strengths in all the people of the organization and the organization as a whole—at the same time as weaknesses are dealt with in a constructive way—making everybody pull in the same direction for the organization to succeed in an area of common good.

The last part of the definition is important. The chapter hasn't included much discussion about "the common good." But the strengths-based approach is valid only if the case we work for as an individual or an organization is for the common good of the world. The strengths-based approach is a way to create something of importance in the world—such as a great, new, innovative, and sustainable product or a process that lessens people's suffering in a given area or reduces inequality. A necessary revolution is needed, as Peter Senge states in his 2010 book *The Necessary Revolution* (Senge et al., 2010; Lazlo et al., 2014).

In the rest of this book, the preceding definitions will guide us in our journey of becoming better at leading from the strengths-based perspective. They form the underlying conceptual framework. But as with any conceptual framework, it is only when we begin to use it in practice that it makes sense. Thus, if at this point the definitions seem somewhat broad and general, that will be alleviated once we understand the philosophy behind the paradigm and begin to work with the concrete leadership tools presented in the second part of the book.

2

THE PHILOSOPHY BEHIND STRENGTHS-BASED LEADERSHIP: THE IDEAL PIT

It is essential and important that we understand and know the philosophy behind the paradigm of strengths-based leadership if we want to practice the concrete strengths-based methods, processes, and tools described in the second part of the book.

Our success in using the tools and the benefits we gain from them depend on our understanding of the philosophy. The intention behind using the tools is also paramount. If we want to use them only to create more efficiency, we misuse the tools. It is important that we be humble, open, and curious as leaders and that we view the tools as a way to create not only efficiency, but also healthy and human organizations working for a common good. So let's take a closer look at the underlying philosophy behind the strengths-based leadership paradigm.

In a nutshell, the approach rests on the following philosophy—the ideal pit—where *pit* may refer to "the seed inside the fruit/the core of an implosion weapon" or as *pit* in botany, where it refers to the part of the plant cell walls that allows the exchange of fluids [Wikipedia].

The ideal pit is the ideal way of implementing the strengths-based paradigm, allowing for the desired effects of the paradigm to take place.

THE IDEAL PIT—OVERVIEW

I lluminate/shed light on what you want more of
D evelop the strengths; compensate for the weaknesses
E xperiment, learn, modify
A ccept what is and should be authentic
L ook for good intentions, reasons, and explanations

P ositivity matters
I nvolvement is key
T iming and presence are paramount

CONTENTS

Before continuing, we'll take a moment to reflect on the leadership philosophy/the ideal pit outlined above.

REFLECTION

When you look at the philosophy that underlies strengths-based leadership, what are your first thoughts?

Do you, for example, agree that positivity is key? Do you already practice this?

What about involvement?

And do you believe that development happens best when the main focus is on strengths and that weaknesses need to be compensated for, not developed?

Are you already practicing a leadership philosophy that resembles the one outlined above, or is this something you consciously would have to remind yourself of when practicing leadership?

Would you like to base your work on this philosophy? Why or why not?

In what situation would something be natural for you, and in what situation would you struggle?

Now, let's review each of the eight statements that make up the strengths-based leadership philosophy.

1. Illuminate/shed light on what you want more of

If we're looking for signs of inefficiency and low performance, we're likely to find some. Naturally, these factors exist in all organizations, but the opposite also is true if we look for it. And we find what we look for—and what we find we get more of (Bushe, 2000). Before we proceed, let's test this assumption with a small exercise that gives us an opportunity to examine and notice what happens to problems when we look for their causes and what happens when we look for solutions to the problems.

EXERCISE

Think of a challenging issue you are facing as a leader. Write it down.

____

____

(continued on next page)

EXERCISE (CONTINUED)

Now answer the questions below. To enhance the effect, you may want to have someone else interview you.

Problem-Focus Questions

1. What is the cause of the problem?
2. Who especially contributes to the problem?
3. Why are you and others unable to do much about the problem?
4. What makes it worse?
5. What is the most difficult aspect of the problem?
6. What are the obstacles to a solution?
7. What solutions do you see?
8. What must you do?

Now that you've answered the questions, what are your thoughts about the issues? What feelings are you filled with right now?

____

____

Next, answer the questions below based on a challenging issue you face as a leader.

Solution-Focus Questions

1. What do you hope for or want to see happen?
2. Who makes the problem smaller; that is, who might help solve it?
3. In similar situations, what has made the problem smaller?
4. What is already working well even if it is just a little thing?
5. When is the problem smaller/not present?
6. Who has done something useful, clever, or smart aimed at solving the problem?
7. What solutions do you see?
8. What is a first step in solving the problem?

Now that you have answered the questions, what are your thoughts about the issues? What feelings are you filled with right now?

____

____

(continued on next page)

EXERCISE (CONTINUED)

Reflection

What is the difference between the thoughts and feelings you wrote down after answering the two types of questions?

What impact do you think the difference in your thoughts and feelings might have on the way you handle the issue?

Which type of question gave you the greatest sense of personal responsibility?

Which type of question gave you more energy and the most ideas for solving the problem?

What thoughts did you have as a result of the two types of questions?

Our guess is that both types of questions produced ideas for solving the problem but that the solution-focus questions produced more ideas and more energy. In our experience, the feelings that leaders write in response to the problem-focus questions are more positive than their responses to the solution-focus questions, and what grows in their mind with the two approaches is not the same!

When we shed light on something, it grows. An intense awareness of problems makes the problems grow larger. On the contrary, an awareness of possible solutions pushes the problems into the background (Cooperrider & Srivasta, 1999; Whitney et al., 2008). It's not the same as stating that the problem doesn't exist or fooling ourself. It's a matter of choice and awareness—what do we want to see grow? And by focusing on this, what give us the most energy and the possibility for change?

Let's deliberately use this insight. The following model illustrates how, in the same problematic situation, we can choose to focus on weaknesses and the causes of problems or on solutions, strengths, and those things that have worked in the past or those things that work despite the problems. Going forward, we can choose to keep talking about the problems, or we can begin to talk about the solutions. The question is where we choose to direct our focus and spend most of our time and energy.

In the strengths-based leadership approach, we're encouraged to make a deliberate effort to turn our focus *away from* the problem *toward* what works or what might make things work in the future—the solutions and strengths. The assumption behind the model is that if we want to address our challenges, we'll find the best answers and the best energy on the strength axis.

At first glance, it may seem like a good idea to look for the cause of a problem to solve it. And that approach works well when we're dealing with physical systems (for example, engines, cars, and computers). But that approach doesn't work well when we're dealing with people/social systems. When we dig into what went wrong and what weaknesses each of us, a team, or an organization has, at some point, we start pointing fingers. It is someone's "fault" (our own or somebody else's) that we're not more successful and that there are weaknesses. Then feelings of guilt or blame arise, and those feelings are not the best basis for addressing and solving the problem. On the contrary, we find our best energy to do something about a problem when feelings of hope, self-esteem, confidence, and optimism are present (Fredrickson, 2000, 2009). These are the feelings that emerge when we shed light on already existing strengths—the things that work or could make things work in the future and on all the great things people may have already done to solve the problem.

When we're on the problem axis, we learn a great deal about problems. What we shed light on here (the problems) becomes clearer to us, and in the worst case, they actually grow. The skeleton in the closet suddenly grows because we shed light on it. All the other great things that may exist in a situation, a person, an organization, a system, or a community go unnoticed because the skeleton is the only thing we shed light on, as illustrated below.

What you shed light on grows.

Problem talk takes us down the problem axis toward the undesired future; it helps us learn about problems, not solutions. In the strengths-based paradigm, we solve problems in two ways: (1) by identifying the problem (so we do in fact talk about the problem) and (2) by looking for examples of things that we or others have done in previous similar situations that helped solve the problem and/or by looking for existing strengths in the individuals, the team, or the organization that we can use to solve the problem.

Sometimes this way of dealing with problems can produce solutions that are so quick, efficient, and sustainable that people become skeptical, convinced that something must have been overlooked or "left out" (Watkins et al., 2001). However, by working with the problems on the strength axis, we introduce a positive and optimistic spirit that accelerates and speeds up the process toward finding and implementing solutions.

Of course, it may be necessary to move down the problem axis to vent frustrations and discuss experiences that should be avoided in the future (Goleman et al., 2013). The question is how long we stay on this axis. As leaders, our responsibility is to be aware of the effects of remaining on the problem axis for too long. We must keep an eye on whether staying there will add anything to the analysis or whether it will drain us or the system/organization and not take us any closer to a solution. As mentioned, it creates a difference in mood whether we're on the problem or the solution/strengths axis.

Part Two of this book explores different ways that leaders can help themselves, their employees, their teams, and the organization make a deliberate choice of going down the solutions axis after a problem has been identified and is understood. What we illuminate grows in our minds, what grows in our minds shapes what we can imagine for the future, and what we imagine may become our best ideas for solutions. So a strengths-based leader should illuminate other people's great ideas, contributions, achievements, and strengths (Whitney et al., 2008). How often do leaders do that?

2. **D**evelop the strengths; compensate for the weaknesses

Most of us are taught that to develop, we must focus on fixing our shortcomings. However, we don't develop nearly as much as when we focus on developing our areas of strength. Our greatest development potentials lie within the areas in which we are already strong. Many of us still believe that our greatest development potentials lie in the areas in which we are weak. With this book, we hope to challenge that perception.

In fact, research has found that we can benefit more from focusing on bringing our own, others', and the organization's strengths into play (and using these strengths to overcome the weaknesses) than we can by focusing on "improving" where we are weak (Hammond et al., 1998; Anderson et al., 2008). It's about time we realize that no one is perfect on his or her own, but that *together* we can achieve perfection.

Unfortunately we don't have the tendency to develop or aren't likely to focus on developing our areas of strength. This may have to do with what we learned in school and were told about how to solve a problem "properly."

Most of us are raised to think that to develop, we need to fix our shortcomings/weaknesses (Buckingham, 2006). We are told that to become a complete person, we need to address the areas in which we're weak—where the "holes" are. We're encouraged to take courses to "catch up" and to practice until we master the areas in which we're lagging. This begins in childhood, as parents and preschool teachers and other well-intentioned adults take note of children's "overall" development, checking whether they are learning to walk, speak, read, write, master a foreign language, do math, write stories, write long-hand, or master social skills. There is great emphasis on checking whether children are developing well all around. If they are found to be lagging in certain areas, a special effort is made to bring the child up to speed. Maybe a speech therapist is involved, or perhaps the parents spend more time reading with their children if the children are struggling readers. And maybe the well-intended grown-ups around the child forget to notice, mention, and amplify the fact that the child might have excellent social skills.

REFLECTION

When you were growing up, where were you told to place your main focus—developing the areas in which you already did well or the areas in which you did poorly?

As a child, when you brought your grades home and you had both good and bad grades, which areas did your parents encourage you to spend time on developing?

If you have children, what do you focus on with regard to their grades and any feedback you get from school regarding them? Or if you had children, what would you focus on to support their growth and development?

As a leader, when you look at your staff, what do you think your staff should work on primarily in their development—their strengths or their weaknesses?

And what about you? Where is your focus in relation to your own growth and development as a leader? Should you spend most of your time developing the areas in which you are weak or the areas in which you are strong?

With regard to solving problems, what have you learned to do? What should you focus on?

When children receive their grades in school, most homes tend to focus on the low grades and ways to make them better: "Why are you not doing well in this area? Don't forget to read. Do you need help?" Of course, it is important for the child to catch up in the area in which he or she is struggling, at least to the extent that will impact the overall performance of the child in the long run. One very low grade can reduce the average score and perhaps eventually prevent the child from being accepted into the education program of his or her dreams.

But research-based evidence shows that investing special effort in areas of strength also leads to improvements in the areas in which performance is lower. This has been documented, for example, in studies of language training, where immigrant children who were given training in their first language subsequently did better in other subjects (Thomas & Collier, 1997, 2003). One hypothesis that explains this is that the child gains a higher self-esteem when he or she is supported in an area that feels natural to develop in and that the child then uses this feeling of higher self-esteem to develop areas in which he or she struggles and is weak.

With training, we can get up to par in areas that are not our primary areas of strength, where we do less well. However, we'll never excel and we'll have to devote a great deal of energy just to keep up. Rather than making us struggle, the strengths-based approach encourages us to discover what we find to be easy and what we like to do and then to use our strengths to compensate for our weaknesses. It recommends that adults begin to notice in what areas their children are strong and to help their children improve in those areas. For example, parents may ask, "Why are you getting such good grades in that subject?" and "What is it about this subject that energizes you—why do you think it's fun?"

The strengths-based approach also recommends that as a leader, we begin to look for the employees' strengths and areas of contribution rather than focus on their faults and shortcomings. As mentioned earlier, this shift in focus helps build self-esteem, but it also proves to be a far better use of the employees' resources. It's not the employees who are the most important resource of the organization; it's their strengths.

No one can excel at everything, but everybody has one or more areas in which they can make important contributions.

The following case provides an overview of a classic learning study from 1982 that compared the learning potential of focusing on strengths versus focusing on weaknesses when aiming for improvement and positive development in a given area—in this case bowling (Kirschenbaum et al., 1982).

CASE

How can we best improve bowling skills?

In 1982, a learning study was carried out at the University of Wisconsin-Madison. Two bowling teams attempted to improve their performance over a period of a few weeks. Both teams received instructions from a coach who focused on a few select parameters. One team was instructed to keep a record of its bowlers' experiences of succeeding and of the characteristics of these situations. The other team was instructed to notice what happened when the bowlers failed.

Both teams improved, but the team that was asked to notice when they succeeded improved 100 percent more than the other team!

The researchers concluded: When we want to learn something that is novel or difficult, we achieve greater positive improvement by focusing on the times we do things right rather than on what went wrong.

Also, with regard to organizations, a focus on what works well makes the most positive, quickest, and most desired development, as many of the case studies in this paradigm show.

The last topic that will be mentioned in this paragraph is the history of how we are taught to solve problems. As stated above, we have a tendency to dig into the causes behind a problem when we're trying to solve it but that this often leads to feelings of hopelessness, blame, and guilt—and rarely to solutions and an open-minded, innovative mind-set. The usual problem-solving ability we were taught in school is to (1) identify the problem, (2) look for the root causes of the problem, (3) look at the consequences of the problem, and (4) come up with ideas and solutions to the problem.

However, based on research, problems—at least within social systems such as organizations, teams, and groups of individuals—are better solved by going down the solution axis. Development also speeds up if we choose this focus rather than a "problem focus."

3. Experiment, learn, modify

When developing, it is important that we have a clear picture of where we want to be as individuals, a team, or an organization. Our role as leaders is to help ourselves, our employees, our teams, the organization, and society move in a desired direction. Everyone's points of view need to be brought into play with regard to the desired direction/future and the best and fastest way to get there (more about this later). But a main point in the strengths-based paradigm is that it is important to be willing to *experiment* when developing and going in the direction of the organizations, vision (Rothwell et al., 2005; Barrett, 2012).

The present changes constantly, which is why it is so crucial to be able to experiment, improvise, and act quickly based on the facts at hand. When developing, we might benefit from making a plan on how to get to a desired future. However, it is important that we look at this plan as a draft and don't expect to stick to it no matter what comes up (for example, new information, obstacles, or help). The key for us, as strengths-based leaders, is being willing and open to look at and learn from the present moment—and to dare to experiment in the here and now. Then we don't become slaves to a plan, which may be outdated before the ink on the paper is dry.

It takes courage to practice strengths-based leadership. We should try things without having had lengthy training in leadership and without knowing how our experiment is going to work or be received. But we need to dive in, test the various methods, experiment, evaluate, change direction, and feel our way through. We shouldn't think that we can plan or train for everything. Instead, we are encouraged to envision the goal and then take the first steps. Remember John Lennon's brilliant observation:

Life is what happens to you while you're busy making other plans.

That is also true of management and of growth and development for the organization and the employees. Life, including organizational life, can't wait for us to reach the point in the strategy plan when something new is supposed to happen.

When we experiment, we learn and are able to change direction and modify our plan if it is better to do something other than what we planned. Eric Ries, a start-up entrepreneur from Silicon Valley, created a revolution using his approach, called "the lean start-up." The philosophy behind this paradigm is what we talk about in this basic part of the strengths-based philosophy: to experiment, learn, and modify. Ries talks about being able to pivot if the direction we're taking leads us astray. As he says, "What does it matter if you stick to your plan, being on time and on budget, if you are driving off a cliff?" (2011)

We may have a great idea about something and a clear vision of what implementing the idea will lead to, but we need to test it out before we know whether what we wish for will happen. For instance, when conducting product research, we might ask our customers whether they want this particular product. If they answer yes, we might start developing it. Months later, when the product is finished and we release it, those same customers may not buy the product. They may have changed their mind, their financial situation may have changed, or someone else may have offered the same product or a better product. The point is that we can't count on what people say they will do—only what they do in the moment. As strengths-based leaders, we must be willing to release part of a product—a prototype—before it's ready. That's the only way we'll be able to test how the product is working in real life, to learn from that, and then to modify it.

The same is true for strengths-based initiatives. We can begin experimenting by asking strengths-based questions at meetings, for instance, instead of waiting until we've drafted a turn-around plan using the strengths-based process model. There is no excuse for not getting started immediately. We should try, see what happens, learn, and then modify. We can find concrete ideas on how to "go with the flow" and learn to experiment and apply this philosophy by reading Frank Barrett's book *Yes to the Mess*. In his book, Barrett describes his "surprising Leadership Lessons from Jazz" and the way jazz musicians stick to a few golden rules and then listen to and learn from each other in the moment to create a wonderful and present piece of music.

4. **A**ccept what is and be authentic

We are who we are with our innate talents. The same is true of our employees. That is the starting point. We need to start accepting—and perhaps acknowledging—what is. Then we can start changing things for the better. The following quote is from the famous Danish philosopher Søren Kierkegaard (1849, 1980 trans.).

> *If you really want to help somebody, first of all you must find him where he is and start there…*

In other words, we need to accept and acknowledge what is and isn't working well for ourselves, our employees, and our organizations to be able to see and understand the starting point in its fullness (Goffee & Jones, 2006; Goleman et al., 2013). Then we can start developing. And when we're developing, we should stay authentic. We shouldn't try to change ourselves, others, or the organization away from the "core"—away from what is and feels most natural to deliver. That is where the talent is; once we've acknowledged that fact, we can start investing our time and energy and develop from there.

In that respect, we should strive to discover our inner motivation, our inner "drivers," and try to bring everything into play that come naturally to us and the organization. What is our employees' and our organization's authentic, most natural "core"? We all have things that are more "us," that feel more natural to us, and that we do with ease. Each of us can do things with ease that others struggle with, and these are the areas, the activities, the strengths that we should attempt to build on.

Unfortunately, our upbringing and other people's expectations of us may have pushed our personal desires and the things that felt natural to us into the background (Buckingham, 2008). Some people may have always done what was expected of them, without checking whether it felt "right" or "natural." Maybe it's hard for us to simply feel what comes naturally to us. Therefore, the first step we should take in practicing strengths-based leadership is to discover who we are, what we find easy and hard, what energizes us, and what drains us. Then we should use these experiences to discover our own strengths and to encourage other people around us to do likewise. We'll learn how to do this in Chapters 3 and 4. With regard to the organization as a whole, we must start asking ourselves the same questions: "What can we become the best at for the world? Where do our main strengths lie? In what areas does the organization contribute with ease, and where do we struggle?"

We may as well breathe a sigh of relief and begin to accept ourselves, others, and our organization "as we are/it is." We don't have to change in a direction that feels unnatural or difficult. The good thing is that when we put the best of ourselves into play and others do the same, we create a whole. We don't have to handle everything ourselves. We don't have to excel at everything. We can begin to specialize, to find niches, and begin to turn down those areas in which we have less to contribute. This counts for individuals as well as teams and organizations.

This, of course, requires that others can cover the areas in which we are weak—if these areas need to be covered.

Some might see this as selfish. Can we really do that? Can we simply use the "excuse" that this isn't an area of strength for us so we don't want to do it? Yes, we can.

In the long run, results will improve if people, teams, and organizations stop doing what they aren't good at and begin to excel in the areas they've have mastered and about which they feel passionate.

Of course, there will be a transition period when we begin to take a strengths-based approach. This will be a period of change when people continue to do things that they may view as a "chore" and that they're not passionate about and when organizations continue to do things that aren't within their core but right now earn them a living (as is the case for many newspapers). But over time, these areas of weaknesses and drainers should be minimized. It may not be possible to eliminate a particular task entirely, but too many of us spend too much time doing things that we're not very good at. In today's organizations, too few people have sufficient opportunities to bring their strengths into play on a daily basis. Recall from Chapter 1 that only 17 percent of the labor force has the opportunity to do what they do best on an average workday (Harter et al., 2012).

This means that more than 80 percent of employees perform at a mediocre level. This is one of the things that strengths-based leadership aims to change—that is, to create the conditions for most of us to be able to bring our strengths into play most of the time and to contribute using our best capabilities every day. By doing this, we improve the well-being of individuals as well as the performance of every one of us and the organization as a whole and move in a direction where reaching the goal of common good becomes not a chore, but a play (Lazlo et al., 2014).

5. Look for good intentions, reasons, and explanations

This point is an extension of the illumination principle and the idea of accepting who we are and who our team or organization is. With the realization of who we are (and where we have the most to offer) comes the possibility of contributing our best—the possibility and the desire. Research suggests that the two go together (Keyes & Haidt, 2002; Lazlo et al., 2014). From early childhood, everybody instinctively tries to contribute, to help by emptying the dishwasher, comforting others, or picking things up (toys or a cup that fell off the table). Any parent or anyone who has spent time with children has observed these instinctive attributes. Upon reflection, this is quite natural. Humankind didn't survive as a species by taking and demanding without contributing. We survived thanks to our instinctive creativity and our urge to contribute and make meaning. Therefore, we should always expect and think that others have a good reason to do as they do and that their intentions are not bad but rather are based on an instinctive wish to be of good use. Of course, those instincts might have been inhibited or damaged in some people, who now no longer find meaning in doing good. Fortunately, that involves a small number of people (Weisbord & Janoff, 1995; Kofman, 2006; Keltner, 2009).

When conflicts arise, they are not usually the result of negative intentions, but of varying perceptions of what the situation calls for. It is with this mind-set that the strengths-based leader encounters the world, the employees, and any problems. Meeting other people with trust, openness, and (most importantly) curiosity is key for the strengths-based leader. Keeping an open mind to the idea that people have a good reason for doing what they do and to the idea that everybody has a contribution to make is important, as is curiosity to see what good ideas the employee has to offer. In fact, when you do that, happiness may follow, as what happens in happily married couples, which is illustrated in the following case (Gottman, 1995).

And as we will learn next, when we look for the best in other people (as happily married couples do), it enhances not only the level of happiness, but also the other person's ability to *be* his or her best.

Looking for and believing that everybody has something valid to offer has natural consequences for our leadership practices. As a strengths-based leader, we don't mind "taking chances" by facilitating empowerment and delegating responsibility because we believe that with the right time, learning, and training, the employee will be able to handle a given task or situation in his or her area of expertise. And as a strengths-based leader, we don't see it as a fatal error when employees make mistakes. We view it as necessary for them to make mistakes and to learn from them. Mistakes are part of growth and development and of product development (Kelley, 2001). Consequently, we don't blame employees for making mistakes. Of course, the employees are expected to learn from their mistakes, but they are expected to learn more from their successes.

CASE

Happy long-term relationships

Studies of the factors that characterize happy long-term relationships reveal that happy couples look for examples of their partner's good intentions and strengths to a much higher degree than unhappy couples do. And that's not all—the partners even exaggerate each other's strengths.

One hypothesis that explains why the partners do this is that it confirms to them that they picked the right partner when they decided to commit to marriage or a long-term relationship.

Whatever the explanation, it remains an indisputable fact that when partners look for good intentions and for their partner's strengths, the satisfaction with the relationship increases (Murray et al., 2000).

In the strengths-based perspective, errors are not characterized as mistakes, but as attempts to do the right thing. It's expected that the employees are willing—in fact, want to contribute with the best they have to offer. With this perspective, something called the "Pygmalion effect" or the "Rosenthal effect" happens, resulting in superior performance, as demonstrated by an experiment in the American school system in the 1950s (Rosenthal & Jacobson, 1968).

CASE

The Rosenthal study

The study set out to investigate what effect teachers' expectations of students' skills and knowledge had on the students' performance. In the study, new classroom teachers were told which students were high performers and which students were low performers. In fact, there was no connection between what a test showed about the students' performance at the time and what the teachers were told, but a connection soon developed.

After just three months, the students about which the teachers had high expectations did far better than the group of students about which the teachers had low expectations. In fact, the difference was so pronounced that the study was aborted for ethical reasons.

What happened? A review of video clips from the lessons revealed that when asking questions, the teachers were more likely to pick the students who were expected to know the right answer, ignoring the others, who also may have raised their hands to give an answer. The study also found that the teachers assisted the supposedly smarter students when they did get the answer wrong; conversely, the teachers didn't help the students whom they considered to be low performers.

(continued on next page)

CASE (CONTINUED)

One might wonder why. An explanation might be that teachers, like everybody else, like to affirm their original perception of a student. It is a human inclination to look for indications that support our perception of the world and the people around us as we perceive them (Langer, 1990; Schiller, 2002).

When a "good" student does get it wrong, the teacher tends to think that it had to be a mistake. Otherwise, the teacher would have to adjust his or her perception of the child. Thus, the teacher wants the "good" students to be right, and when they fail, it must be a mistake. Hence, the teacher will make comments such as "What you meant was ..., wasn't it?" to which the "good" student answers, "Yes, that's exactly what I meant." Whereas if a "bad" student gives a wrong answer, the teacher provides no help because existing basic assumption have been confirmed.

When the experiment was aborted, the researchers told the teachers how their expectations had produced different behavior patterns in the students. When the teachers learned what had happened, they were shocked, but then something interesting occurred. Once the teachers became aware of the importance of not treating the students differently and of having positive expectations of all the students, the teachers were able to change the pattern, helping every student to excel.

What does this study tell us? If we expect our employees to take responsibility and if we expect them to be willing and able to do their best, there is a much better chance that they can and will. And once we begin to notice how our perceptions of others affect their behavior, we can make a deliberate effort to have positive thoughts and expectations of everybody.

We know that expecting the best of other people is more easily said than done, especially when we're dealing with someone who has disappointed us in the past, has proved undeserving of our trust, or has taken advantage of us. In those cases, we may not be able to develop positive expectations, but we may be able to find something to respect in the person and maybe an explanation, an underlying cause, for the person's "bad" or "wrong" behavior. When we look for the good reason, the motivation behind a certain behavior, or something we can respect in the person, something is bound to change in our relationship with that person—and research has shown that it will (Grimes, 2005; Keltner, 2009; Goleman et al., 2013). Try it!

EXERCISE

Think of someone you find it hard to have positive expectations of, have difficulty showing appreciation of, or have difficulty communicating with.

Write down good things you can say about this person and/or reasons for you to respect him or her.

List at least five things, preferably more.

Begin by considering positive things that others say about the person and things you see as a quality in the person. For example, you might say that the person is persistent, creative, goal-oriented, serious, and good at reasoning. Include anything you see that is positive about the person.

1. ______________________________
2. ______________________________
3. ______________________________
4. ______________________________
5. ______________________________
6. ______________________________

The next time you are with this person, recall all the good things you can say or respect about him or her and begin to gather evidence of the person's value, importance, and positive contributions on an everyday basis. Then begin to notice what this does to your relationship—that is, your communication and the person's performance.

6. **P**ositivity matters

When we are in a state of alert—when we are busy getting tasks and chores done, protecting ourselves, responding to outside threats, and developing a sufficient armor to shield us from the harm that may occur on any given day—we have a narrowed action repertoire (Fredrickson, 2000; Fredrickson & Losada, 2005; Boyatzis & McKee, 2005). When we are under a great deal of pressure and fail to take time to pause and consider an appropriate response in a given situation, our body automatically chooses a fight or flight response or a freeze response. This limited action arises because we are capable of just these three fairly rigid responses when we're under stress. When we feel threatened, our instinctive and initial inclination is to fight (give a snappy answer, act aggressively, pound the table, yell), flee (leave work early, back down in a discussion, work more at home), or freeze (become invisible behind our desk, sit still, stare into space). In modern society, most threats are complex social patterns. They're not a matter of life or death as they were in primeval times, but are more likely to involve thoughts such as "Am I going to get fired?" or "Do the others like me? or "What if our competitor gets to market first?" or "Why don't my employees show enthusiasm about my latest idea for improvement?"

Those kinds of thoughts lead to negative emotions, and negative emotions limit our action repertoire. Positive emotions, on the other hand, expand it. Research has found that people become more creative, better problem solvers, and more flexible when they are in a positive mood characterized by hope, happiness, and humor (Fredrickson, 2009). A number of studies have looked into people's ability to handle pressure-filled challenges and problems when their emotions had been affected positively or negatively prior to the challenge. The studies all found that people deal with a challenge or problem (such as diagnosing a patient, doing mental calculations, or pointing to the company's most important current strategic effort) faster and with greater precision and accuracy when they are in a positive emotional state (Goleman et al., 2013; Goleman, 2013).

To illustrate this point, look at the picture below. Who is better at solving the problem—the people on the left or the people on the right?

A good mood has a considerable impact on our efficiency and ability to think out of the box—not only when we work on our own, but also when we work with others. The close link connecting positive mood, efficiency, cooperation, innovation, and performance has been documented in several studies (Seligman, 2012; Goleman et al., 2013; Fredrickson, 2009). We might wonder whether the good mood is due to the general good performance, but research suggests that a deliberate effort to promote positive feelings such as optimism, hope, trust, joy, confidence, engagement, and high spirit can turn negative results positive. Therefore, it's a crucial point in the strengths-based approach that as leaders, we should seek to maximize positive feelings in ourselves and our organization, particularly when we're under pressure.

It's important to point out, though, that we're not supposed to sweep things "under the rug," forget about or ignore problems, or act overly optimistic. Basically, we should strive to be in sync with our employees and organization in the sense that we recognize problems and acknowledge their negative effect on the organization. But we also should make a deliberate effort to cultivate and enhance positivity whenever that feels right.

Resonance means being on the same page as our employees and on the same wavelength as the general mood in the organization and being able to empathize with other people's thoughts and feelings. When we achieve resonance, we can amplify the feelings in a positive or negative direction, depending on our skills as a leader—and how good we are at instilling energy, hope, optimism, and self-esteem in our staff and others around us (Boyatzis & McKee, 2005).

Leaders who operate on autopilot, who are out of touch with their own mood, or who cannot tell how they affect their surroundings with their energy set all sorts of things in motion without any control. And that is not particularly constructive or efficient—especially when the leaders are inclined toward negative emotions. Research has found that leaders who spread their negative mood contribute significantly to undermining the organization's performance. A leader's bad mood, mood swings, and negative aggressive outbursts affect the employees more than may have been realized previously (Pescosolido, 2000; Fredrickson, 2009).

Leaders who are in resonance with the staff and who are able to guide the organization toward hope, optimism, joy, and engagement achieve higher levels of well-being, engagement, and performance.

This means that if we want to practice effective leadership, we must take responsibility for the energy we give out and create around us. Some may think that "energy" is a strange, intangible concept that is hard to specify. But we should take a moment for reflection.

REFLECTION

What is the mood in the room you are sitting in right now?

What is the energy in your workplace right now? Is it high or low, shrill or subdued? How do you gauge that?

What sort of energy exists between your superior and yourself as a leader and among the employees? On what do you base this assessment?

What will or can you do if you sense negative energy?

The more we reflect on the type of energy level in the workplace and the effect we and others can have on it, the clearer it will be to us what this "energy thing" is. We can also begin to experiment with affecting the energy ourselves.

EXERCISE

Try taking initiatives that affect the energy in a positive direction in your workplace. Set out by simply noticing how it affects the energy if you, for instance, are clearly present a whole day—not just physically, but mentally too.

What happens when you take the time to listen?

What happens when you are truly present in the moment during an entire meeting?

What happens when you make an active effort to generate a positive atmosphere?

What happens when you take responsibility for putting others in a good mood and giving them confidence or hope in relation to a task?

An important point is that resonance is essential, as we previously discussed. That is a precondition for attempting to generate hope, optimism, and joy. If we try to generate a good mood in a situation in which there is every reason for pessimism, doubt, and uncertainty, we're not in resonance. For example, if the company is facing a severe situation because of a diminishing demand for the company's product or service or if an increase in demand is leading to everyone pulling double shifts, resulting in higher stress levels, there is no point in denying these facts. In that case, resonance is about empathizing and expressing that we understand the situation that everyone is facing.

Next, as leaders, we can take steps to keep people from becoming discouraged. We might express our conviction that the organization as a whole, including its employees, has what it takes to succeed or that we intend to take measures to change the situation for the better. The key point is to see the situation as it is, for better and worse, and to address the facts as they are (Collins, 2001; Boyatzis et al., 2013).

CASE

The Stockdale Paradox

During the Vietnam War, James Stockdale (an officer in the U.S. Navy) was captured by the Vietnamese. Like his fellow prisoners of war, he was subjected to systematic psychological and physical torture and faced the constant threat of being killed at any moment. He saw several of his fellow captives succumb to the ordeal. After the end of the war, he was asked in an interview what characterized the men who didn't make it out alive, and Stockdale's somewhat unexpected reply was:

Oh, that's easy, the optimists. The optimists didn't make it. (Collins, 2001, p. 85)

Why? Did we not just mention the crucial importance of hope, optimism, and faith? Yes, but what Stockdale was referring to was blind optimism, optimism that fails to face up to the facts. The optimists who told themselves "We're going to be out by Christmas" succumbed and lost the will to live when Christmas arrived. The survivors, on the other hand, were more pragmatic and maintained a more realistic outlook, combined with an ability to focus on the bright points and good things that did occur despite the traumatic nature of their everyday existence. They told themselves and the other prisoners of war things such as "We might not be out of here at Christmas, but we still have food to eat."

This mind-set can be summarized as follows:

Face the brutal facts, but never ever doubt that you will prevail!

This is an important point for a leader to remember. Remember to face the facts, but also remember to instill hope and faith that you or the organization as a whole will prevail (Collins, 2001).

7. Involvement is key

As strengths-based leaders, we don't consider ourselves as having all the answers or as being the wisest and most decisive people in the room. Instead, we're curious to hear others' ideas and input and want to involve them when making decisions. We try to be in resonance with our employees, customers, colleagues, leader(s), stakeholders, and society. Our most important task is to maintain the broad overview, making wise decisions based on a given situation and a broad spectrum of information and making sure the decisions are followed up by concrete actions that lead to the execution of a strategy that helps the organization reach its goal of creating something of value for the common good. The key is to align the employees' strengths in a way that gets everybody pulling in the same direction. It is, in other words, not just about bringing everyone's strengths into play, but bringing them into play in a coordinated manner (as shown on the cover of this book) and pulling the organization in a desired direction (Barrett et al., 2000; Bryan, 2007; Anderson et al., 2008).

One way to do this is by (1) *being as open as possible about the current state of the business*—about what does and doesn't go well, (2) *communicating a clear vision for the company*—what we want to achieve and help alleviate in the world, and (3) *involving everybody in making the correct strategic decisions of "how to reach that vision."*

When we're open (or as open as we can be) about current company information, communicate this information well, and then listen to and involve people in sharing their best ideas on "what to do to succeed," we make sure people understand and support the decisions being made in the company. If we just tell people what to do, we can't take for granted that they will understand why we made a decision or support us in implementing a strategic action plan. Therefore (and because employees, stakeholders, and others often come up with good ideas), involvement is key.

When Jack Welch retired as CEO of General Electric in 2001 (after successfully holding that position for 20 years), he was asked what he thought it would take for the company to continue to succeed. He said that the company would have to create "a culture that breeds an endless search for ideas that stand or fall on their merits, rather than the rank of their originator, a culture that brings every mind into the game" (Rothwell et al., 2005). The management and leadership challenge that Jack Welch indicated was this:

how to bring every mind into the game

This management challenge has not diminished over the years, but we believe that strengths-based leadership offers a good approach to meeting this challenge. It all begins with trusting that as leaders, we can benefit from listening to the employees' ideas and involving them in the daily decision making. We benefit when we empower people to do their job without asking us for permission on every detail. But we have no choice than to do this because the rate of change is so rapid. People don't have time to wait for their leader to understand, check, and approve everything (Goffee & Jones, 2006). Also, it is unmotivating for the employee when leaders don't involve them, and the strengths-based leader wants to create a culture in which energy, flow, efficiency, and, yes, happiness dominates. Involvement is key in creating this culture. More about this topic is provided in the closing remarks of the chapter.

8. Timing and presence are paramount

When we want to apply a strengths-based approach to leadership, we begin by training ourselves to see the work, other people, problems, and dilemmas in the perspective outlined above. We look at the world, its problems, the solutions, ourselves, and other people through a certain lens—the strengths-based lens.

For us to excel as strengths-based leaders, however, timing is crucial: how, how much, and when, for instance, we bring ourselves into play and in relation to whom. How much we get involved, when we bring in more positivity, and what we illuminate are key. Timing and presence in the moment are paramount to everything else. The key to this is awareness—and all awareness training begins when we notice where our awareness and our attention are. We need this insight to check whether we're focusing on strengths or weaknesses (our own or others'), whether we're focusing on what we're doing or aren't "present," whether we're working in the right direction or going off on an unconstructive tangent, and whether we're emotionally in resonance with others or have gone astray. We need these insights to get our timing right for the initiatives we take and to ask questions in the right way and at the right time.

How do we ensure timing and presence in the moment? This is a basic leadership skill and a prerequisite for our ability to sense what the right timing and the right actions might be here and now. It's a skill that some master and some don't, but it is a skill that can and should be taught (Gardner, 2006; Goleman, 2013; Carroll, 2007; Dolman & Bond, 2011; Bregman, 2012).

The ability to be present in the moment is not something that is the focus of much systematic leadership training in the Western world, though (Goleman, 2013). Therefore, we will outline some ideas for how we as leaders can work on becoming more present and attuned to ourselves, others, and the situations we face on a daily basis as leaders.

First, we are dealing with a mind-set that is often referred to as mindfulness in modern terminology. Mindfulness (focused attention) is a relatively new term in the Western world. It describes a state in which we're particularly attentive to what our consciousness is focused on and what it compels us to do (Kabat-Zinn, 2005; Goleman, 2013; Gelles, 2015). This attentiveness enables us to make deliberate and appropriate choices and take deliberate and appropriate actions that benefit us as well as others (including the planet as a whole). These actions are the result of insightful reflection and are often creative, different, and more profitable than the things we do on autopilot simply because "that's what we normally do" or because we don't think, consider, or notice that things could be done differently (Boyatzis & McKee, 2005; Langer, 1990; Scharmer, 2009; Senge et al., 2005; Gelles, 2015).

The man in the drawing is not mindful. Or is he? Take a moment to reflect on this.

Mindfulness can be defined as follows:

Being intentionally and disciplined aware in the moment— with an open and kind attitude

The training of a heightened state of mindfulness for leaders and literature on the topic has exploded in recent years. A large number of books have been published on the topic, and we believe it's because mindfulness training has proven useful for the leader who wants to create resonance and make wise decisions and see more permanent results (Gelles, 2015).

Jon Kabat-Zinn of the University of Massachusetts was responsible for introducing the approach to the Western word. In the early 1980s, he introduced the concept as part of a course he taught called Mindfulness-Based Stress Reduction. It was offered to people suffering from pain and stress. The approach soon had a significant impact on the participants' ability to manage and live with chronic pain and the after effects of long-term stress (Kabat-Zinn, 1991).

Since then, various people have described mindfulness training as having a positive effect on leadership as well as organizational development (Goleman, 2013; Tan, 2012; George, 2010; Gelles, 2015). The training is based on a millennia-old Buddhist tradition of practicing a special way of being in the world with a deliberate open, unprejudiced, curiously explorative, trusting, kind, and patient mind in relation to the world as it appears right now (the part of the real world one is aware of). Thus, the training encompasses the capacity to focus and "rein in" one's awareness as well as certain basic attitudes and approaches to life, oneself, and other people, also when under pressure.

We can practice being present in the moment/mindful in many ways. Here we will mention four ways to become more mindful as a leader. We can find more exercises and read more about mindfulness in an organizational context in books by, for example, Richard Boyatzis, Daniel Goleman, Chade-Meng Tan, Michael Dickman, Michael Carroll, and David Gelles. (For inspiration, look at the Literature section at the end of this book.)

EXERCISE

Exercises to become a more mindful leader

1. In your daily life, pause as often as possible and turn your full attention to what you are doing at the moment. Notice what emotions, thoughts, and bodily sensations are at play and notice what is going on around you. Based on this information, you can make deliberate, appropriate choices. This is "mindful living"/awareness

(continued on next page)

EXERCISE (CONTINUED)

training. You anchor yourself in the present moment (for example, via your senses) and experience yourself, other people, and the situation in which you find yourself at that moment. You may begin to notice little things that used to slip right by you (for instance, that one colleague gives you energy, whereas someone else is draining you; that it's nice to walk in the rain; that you're snapping up customers and assignments in contexts you never used to consider; that the walk to and from meetings helps you recharge; or that there are many inspiring things to look at along the way). Although this way of being in the world is new, it may make you feel more alive, fully present and in touch with yourself and the people around you. It may feel awkward and time consuming at first, but soon you will learn how it pays off in the long run because you don't make as many mistakes or miss important information or moments as you used to.

2. Sit down and practice being present in the moment, training yourself to focus and to take an open, curious, accepting, trusting, patient, unprejudiced, kind, and nonstriving stance toward yourself, the world, and other people. If you find that your mind wanders or that you become distracted, register the distraction that "hijacked" your attention and bring your attention back to where you want it to be—again and again. By deliberately training your ability to refocus your attention, you exercise your "attention muscle." By deliberately noticing what distracts you, you learn more about yourself and your environment. These distractions may hold important information. The main point is that you notice that you have been distracted and that you train yourself to return to the present moment repeatedly, training yourself to "harness" your attention.

3. Train your sense of presence by noticing what it takes for you to be present in the moment. A common experience for most people is that with adequate sensory stimulation, they have no problem staying focused. It is when they get bored or are understimulated or stressed that they lose their focus. So ask yourself this question: "What could keep me sufficiently stimulated?" It might be to bring one of your strengths, such as asking questions/being curious, into play. It might be to lead a conversation in a more strategic direction. Pay attention and when you lose your focus, deliberately do something to bring it back.

4. A concrete way for you to learn to be more present in the moment is to do something other than what you normally do or to challenge yourself to look for something new in a situation. When you do, you hone your senses. It's during your automated everyday routines that you become absent. It's in the dull, predictable everyday situations, where you think you know what is going to happen (but never do), that your mind leads you astray and you stop focusing on the present moment. Instead, you focus on something that is going to happen later or something that happened yesterday. And that means you're absent, not present, and inattentive to the moment. To counterpose this, change your habits, challenge yourself to change the way you're seated at meetings (why not stand up?), change the way you ask questions, or change how much you speak compared with how much you listen.

Summing up

To lead from a strengths-based perspective, we need to establish a culture and structure in which everybody can bring his or her strengths into play, can make decisions quickly and independently, is innovative and creative, can help one another, and can think and act for the benefit of the whole system. In this culture, positivity flourishes; people are present and connected; people accept things and others as they are; and people experiment, learn, and modify and look for good intentions, reasons, and explanations in others and in the system—most of the time.

Leaders should reflect for a moment: Do the structures and culture of my organization hinder or foster that? Does my leadership style or the general leadership style in the company enhance or diminish these things? If the conditions are not in accord with the ideal pit, what can I and others do about it?

Even if conditions are not optimal in the organizational culture or structure, as leaders who want to establish a strengths-based culture, we can experiment with delegating, empowering, asking more questions, being curious, thinking in terms of establishing more positivity, and conveying meaning (Morh et al., 2008). We've seen examples of individual leaders who worked as strengths-based leaders in organizational environments not at all suited for promoting the paradigm, and little by little, their example conveyed the benefits of changing the organizational structures and leadership culture of their company.

Conversely, we've also seen leaders who had a great culture and structure in which to act as strengths-based leaders, but who personally failed to delegate, listen, introduce positivity, help employees work across borders, look for good intentions, and be innovative. They didn't have the courage, humbleness, and/or trust it takes to delegate, to face employees who were wiser than they, or to display curiosity and interest in others' ideas.

So it all starts with us as leaders. It's not about us, but it starts with us and the way we look at leadership and development, ourselves, others, and the world in general.

To take the next step in leading from the strengths-based paradigm, we must begin to identify our strengths and weaknesses and begin to bring our strengths into play and manage our weaknesses. We must be honest with ourselves about who we are and what energizes and what drains us.

3

IDENTIFY AND BRING STRENGTHS INTO PLAY

Every time we spend an hour dealing with our weaknesses, we should spend at least three hours focusing on our strengths and what brings us forward. In those who lead from a strengths-based perspective, that is the distribution of time we see between strengths and weaknesses. Those leaders manage to bring their own and their employees' strengths into play. We also see this distribution in some of the top athletes of the world.

In the book *Training a Tiger*, Tiger Woods's father, Earl Woods, describes the process that he and his son applied to golf, which ultimately created a great golfer (1998). This is the tale of a talent that is nursed into a formidable strength. Throughout his career, Tiger Woods's growth and development as a golfer has been driven by enjoyment, energy, and the desire to learn—and training, training, training.

CONTENTS

CASE

Creating a top athlete

At an early stage in his career, the already legendary golf player Tiger Woods was well on his way to becoming number one in the world rankings. He was already the best at hitting long, straight shots onto the green. But he only came in 62nd in terms of escaping the sand bunker. He needed to improve to develop and become an even better golfer.

To the astonishment of many fellow competitive golfers and experts, Tiger Woods chose to develop his game by working intensely on his long shots, something he already excelled at. Of course, he also practiced his weak bunker shots so that he would not be completely lost when he hit the ball into the sand. But the better he was at the long, straight shots, the more precisely he would strike the green. This reduced his need to rely on his weak bunker recovery shots. By training his strength, he made his weakness less important in his overall success as a golfer.

Our growth and development and our particular strengths as leaders also should be driven by energy and enjoyment—and a great deal of training. As leaders, we have the opportunity to develop our strengths on a training track that involves many dedicated and competent people. Even the less dedicated and less competent people around us give us an opportunity to practice our skills. This chapter examines how we can discover our strengths and bring them into play more often so that the best qualities of our leadership make up the majority of our leadership practice. Later, we can turn our strength perspective to the outside world and begin to work with our employees' and colleagues' strengths. But let's begin with ourselves. Trying the exercises and the methods described in this and the subsequent chapters will enhance the leader's self-awareness and enable the leader to begin developing his or her strength. Doing that will help not only the leader, but also his or her entire team, as a recent published survey from Gallup points at (2013).

> *It is not surprising to see gains on engagement scores and other outcomes when every employee on the team receives an opportunity to develop his or her strengths. However, Gallup still found substantial increases in teams' business outcomes when only the manager underwent strengths-based development. How is it that the entire team benefits when only one person—the manager—receives the strengths intervention? Gallup has found that a manager's approach to strengths has a profound effect on employees' engagement and performance because he or she plays an important, direct role in maximizing employees' chances to use their strengths every day.*

So being a strengths-based leader starts with undergoing strengths-based development. Let's get started.

IDENTIFYING STRENGTHS

We can choose one of two approaches to identify our strengths. One requires that we spend an extended period of time (at least two weeks) writing down the situations that we find energizing. The other approach is test-based. Both methods will be presented below before discussion on how we can bring our strengths into play in our daily management practices.

Strengths journal

To chart our strengths by means of a strengths journal, we must complete three stages (Buckingham, 2006):

1. Capture our strengths.
2. Clarify our strengths.
3. Confirm our strengths.

1. Capture our strengths

As we saw in the definition of a strength in Chapter 1, one of the most essential features of a strength is the energy related to those activities in which our strengths are brought into play. The strength drives us and comes into play in situations where we are truly motivated. Thus, to explore our strengths, we must first check our energy and motivation barometer in different situations.

Imagine a scale from 0 to 10, where 0 indicates that we're completely drained of energy and engagement. We don't feel any joy when engaging in this activity/situation. At the other end of the scale, 10 indicates that we're bursting with energy, joy, and engagement. We're highly motivated, and our contribution in the situation is completely driven by our desire to engage. We can hardly wait to be in a similar situation again, and we look forward to getting started with the activities connected with the situation.

The idea is that we now begin to track our energy barometer and note which situations fill us with energy. We should write this down in a journal, which also will contain notes about our weak sides. (We'll tackle those in the next chapter.) The journal may be a notebook or a computer or telephone. We can take notes during the day, or we can take 15 minutes every evening to update our journal. The exercise is most useful when we take notes several times a day. Otherwise, we tend to forget what our energy level was, when we felt drained during a meeting, and when we were bursting with energy. The notes need to be that detailed for the exercise to be useful.

We must explore which tasks and types of challenges give us energy. When we write it down, we can use the notes as a guide that tells us where we can make the greatest contributions.

Our inner energy barometer is our most important guide for telling us where our strengths are, where we are our best, and where we have the most to offer.

At first, we shouldn't interpret our notes or think about why our energy barometer looks the way it does. We also shouldn't think about whether we are successful in the activities that we find energizing. That comes later. We should simply note which activities fill us with energy. One leader who went through the process of jotting down strengths and weaknesses for a two-week period commented on the exercise this way:

> *It was really interesting, inspiring and a learning experience. First, we kept a journal about what gave us energy, and what drained us of energy over a two-week period. At the end of each day, we had to write down in very specific terms what sort of situations had made us feel energized. And which had made us feel tired and drained. There were several good things about that. First, there was the really simple point: simply sitting down and thinking about one's day, reflecting on what had happened. And it was inspiring to see how much learning this holds, if one takes the time to do it. I, for instance, learned more about my own response patterns and about what I like to do. And when it is that I really feel that I unfold my best potential. In this sense, using my strengths automatically became more prominent without any effort on my part, because I began to aim for the situations where I could bring them into play, once I discovered how it boosted my energy. So over this two-week period, eventually I didn't have many situations left that left me feeling drained. Also, I used the situations where I felt strong to resolve energy-sapping situations instead of avoiding them.*
>
> —Jane Johansen Pade, Head of Section at the Danish Ministry of Culture

EXERCISE

Strengths journal—capture your strengths

The first two weeks: Keep a journal of your energy barometer. On a scale of 0 to 10, note what your energy level was in a situation when you felt strong, motivated, and engaged. Were you all the way at the top at 10 or closer to 5? (If you drop below 5, you're are probably not dealing with a strength, but with a weakness.)

Next to the numbers, you might write down statements such as these:

- I was filled with energy when…
- I just loved…
- I found myself completely absorbed by…
- I was really engaged and excited when…

Write down what you were doing, what the task involved, who was present, and which part of the situation or activity most lit your inner fire.

The more specific and precise you are, the easier it will be to detect the patterns in the journal.

To notice how we feel in various situations, we must pay special attention to ourselves. Although that might seem a little self-absorbed, we must spend time looking at ourselves and feeling what works and what feels good for us. We've seen many examples—as in Jane Johansen Pade's story—in which the very act of focusing on our strengths will have a positive effect on our activities.

2. Clarify our strengths

When we've spent two weeks taking notes, we're ready for the next step in the process.

EXERCISE

Patterns in your strengths journal—clarify your strengths

After two weeks: Sit down and read through your journal entries. Try to detect a trend with regard to the situations and tasks that give you energy. Look for patterns and connections. You might discover that you get energized by standing up and making a presentation to a large group of people or by planning large-scale projects. Be specific and then articulate three strength statements that describe the situations in which you feel strong.

I feel strong when: ____________________

I feel strong when: ____________________

I feel strong when: ____________________

The statements might sound something like these:

- I feel strong when I make a presentation.
- I feel strong when I have a one-on-one dialogue with an employee.
- I feel strong when I visit clients and make presentations on behalf of the company.

When you've written down your three strength statements, ask yourself the following questions:

1. Who is involved in the situations in which I feel strong?

This is important. Is it when you're with people you know well or just the opposite? Is it when many people are involved or few? Young or old? Educated or less educated? Well read, unskilled, successful, novices? What sort of people are involved in the situations in which you feel strong? Write it down.

2. What is the specific nature of the activity?

For example, do you feel strong when you teach? Do you feel strong in a dialogue? If so, which dialogues make you feel strongest? Be specific.

(continued on next page)

EXERCISE (CONTINUED)

At this point, your strength statements are probably clearer. Now they might look something like this:

- I feel strong when I make a presentation on the topic of X to a large group of people (more than 50), where it is clear that I know more about the topic than they do.
- I feel strong when I have a one-on-one dialogue with employees who are stuck and need specific motivation and advice to move on.
- I feel strong when I present the company's product X to clients whom I've not met before.

What stands out when you look at the situations in which your strengths are brought into play? Are they familiar? Are there any surprises? What does that tell you about yourself as a leader?

3. Confirm our strengths

The last part of the process of identifying strengths via journaling aims to help us make sure that what we've identified is in fact a strength. That's the purpose of this last exercise.

EXERCISE

Confirm your strengths

Once you've written down your three strength statements and clarified them, you should test them to see whether they express your strengths.

Ask yourself questions within the SIGN model framework.

1. **S**uccess. Am I successful in this form of activity? Do others agree? Have I won any awards with the strength?
2. **I**nstinct. Do I feel like doing the activity (almost) every day? Do I volunteer for this type of activity when the opportunity arises?
3. **G**rowth. Do I want to learn more about how I can improve my competence within this activity? Is it easy for me to learn?
4. **N**eeds. Do I need to do the activity? Does it give me great satisfaction to do it? Do I look forward to doing it? Do I feel punished if I can't do it?

If you answered yes to the questions above, you probably discovered your strengths, exemplified with things you do in real-life situations.

When we complete the journal, the real work begins: unfolding our strengths even more in our everyday business. We'll get back to how we can do this once we've reviewed the other approach we can use to identify our strengths: a strengths test.

Strengths test

Another way to identify our strengths is to use a test. A test can be a good addition to the strengths journal, but it shouldn't stand alone, as it risks becoming too generalized. We should identify when specifically (in which situations, with whom, and in doing what) the strength unfolds. As mentioned earlier, strengths are related to specific situations, whereas talent is always with us. A test, however, can provide a different set of concepts and ideas about our strengths than we would have achieved by working with just the strengths journal. The general concepts of strengths that the tests offer are based on research-based studies of strengths categories and may give us an overview of some of our general strengths or talents.

Two tests in particular help in identifying strengths, and a third one involves mapping the strengths on a team. Below is a brief introduction to each of them.

VIA Signature Strength Test

This test is available at www.authentichappiness.sas.upenn.edu.

The free test was developed by Martin Seligman and Christopher Peterson.

The website provides a wide range of free tests that measure various aspects related to positive psychology (for example, Happiness, Meaning, and Gratitude). It takes about 45 minutes to complete this online test. VIA Signature Strength Test identifies 5 main strengths out of 24 universal strengths, which include, among others, curiosity, fairness, forgiveness, and appreciation of beauty. Upon completing the test, the test taker receives a report that summarizes his or her test score. The report doesn't contain any recommendations, only the test results. If the test taker wants to better understand the results and learn how to develop his or her strengths, he or she can purchase the book *Authentic Happiness* (Seligman, 2003).

StrengthsFinder 2.0

This test is available at www.strenghtsfinder.com.

The test was developed by Tom Rath, who elaborated on the original StrengthsFinder test, which was developed by Donald O. Clifton. To take the test, a person needs a personal code, which is found in the book *StrengthsFinder 2.0* (Rath, 2007). In addition to explanations related to the test, the book provides background for the perceptions people apply to the world when they set out to develop themselves as leaders on the basis of their strengths.

Completing the online test takes about 30 minutes, but the test taker must buy the book first. The test is in English. StrengthsFinder 2.0 identifies 5 main talents within 34 general areas. As mentioned previously, Tom Rath has developed a model where a strength is treated as the combination of talent and effort. The test identifies a person's talent; then it is up to that individual to develop his or her strengths—hence, the title StrengthsFinder. Upon completing the questions, the test taker receives a thorough report that explains his or her score for each of the five talent areas. The person receives a personal description of what characterizes him or her and his or her specific talents—what makes the person stand out from the crowd. And as an outline of a plan of action, the report suggests ten ideas for specific action the individual can take in relation to each of the five talents.

The VIA Signature Strength Test applies to life in general, whereas the StrengthsFinder offers a more direct indication of talents and strengths that can easily be transferred to challenges in a person's work life and personal development as a leader. The StrengthsFinder test is very precise in relation to the recommendations it offers.

StandOut

Buckingham developed a test especially designed for leaders who are applying the strengths paradigm with their employees. This test is called StandOut (Buckingham, 2011). To simplify, he suggests that teams take this test because it gives each individual just one signature strength, compared with StrengthsFinder, which gives five. Buckingham has divided these strengths into nine roles.

THE DOWNSIDE OF STRENGTHS— THE STRENGTHS-PITFALL MODEL

An interesting detail in StrengthsFinder is that in describing a person's talents, it also offers examples of what might be difficult for that person based on his or her five specific strengths. That encourages an important reflection on how an individual's strengths can turn against him or her, producing undesirable behaviors if they're overused or not used in the right context. This reflection adds an important level of nuance to understanding strengths. If a person overuses them, he or she might not be allowed to bring them into play in other situations because people may develop "allergies" to that person using them at all. So it is important that a person learn to "harness" his or her strengths. The following model helps a person understand the downside of—and thereby harness—his or her strengths. The model, originally called the talent-pitfall model, was developed by Daniel Ofman in 2004. In this book, the name was changed to the strength-pitfall model to align with the previous definitions of talents and strengths. The model describes the challenges, "allergies," and pitfalls that accompany any strength.

THE STRENGTHS-PITFALL MODEL

STRENGTH: What a person instinctively finds easy— a natural way to think, feel, and act, which the person has put energy into developing.

PITFALL: If a person overuses a strength, the strength becomes a pitfall and a weakness.

CHALLENGE: This is what a person should be doing but finds challenging because it requires the person to harness himself or herself/not overuse the strength.

ALLERGY: People whose strengths are opposite those of someone else might turn off that person and vice versa. This often pertains to people who are very different from each other.

A strengths-pitfall model might look like this:

STRENGTH: Getting many ideas and sharing them with others.

PITFALL: I get so many ideas that other people become overwhelmed, and none of the ideas are implemented.

CHALLENGE: To harness myself and make sure my ideas are implemented or disregarded before I involve others in my next idea.

ALLERGY: People who never have new ideas and who never think outside the box. These people may be just the ones who can help me implement my ideas, however. So even if I find them annoying, I can benefit from listening to them and collaborating with them.

In the next exercise, we try working with one of our strengths based on this model. We should discuss the model and some of our strengths with someone we trust and whose feedback we would appreciate.

EXERCISE/REFLECTION

Dealing with the downside of a strength

Strength: ____________________

Pitfall: When and how have I exaggerated this strength so that it turned into a drawback? So that it annoyed or hurt other people or prevented me from achieving my goals? What might this strength prevent me from achieving?

____

____

Challenge: What should I do to avoid overdoing my strength and thus end up in a pitfall?

____

____

Allergy: Why am I annoyed with other people when they use a strength that is opposite mine? How do I respond when I am in a situation with a person like this? How might these same people help me overcome my pitfall?

____

____

We can use the model with all the strengths and talents we identify during our strengths process.

The strengths-pitfall model adds nuance to the image of our strengths and increases our awareness of the importance of being present in the moment, being authentic, and noticing what goes on in every situation. When we know both the upside and downside of our strengths, we can improve our timing and our sense of the situation (George et al., 2007; Goffee & Jones, 2006).

Now that some of the most important paths to identifying personal strengths have been introduced, the next step is to make sure we bring the strengths into play even more than we might today. How we do that will be covered in more detail in the next section.

BRINGING STRENGTHS INTO PLAY: STRENGTHS TRAINING WITH THE CASE MODEL

This section introduces a model that can help bring our strengths into play at work to a larger extent than they might be implemented today.

There are four exciting and challenging paths for us to take to make this happen. All four methods require time, effort, and persistence. If we want to become stronger in a given area—get in better shape—we need to invest time in building this strength—just like we would if we wanted to be physically stronger. It's like training a muscle. If we quit exercising, our strength/shape slowly fades away. Developing our strengths is a process that requires continuous attention and training. If the training and the attention stop, our strength dwindles. Recall Tom Rath's equation:

Talent × Investment = Strength

We may choose to focus on the four paths to building our strengths and putting them into play to a higher degree one at a time or at the same time. Based on inspiration from Buckingham and others' experience, the following model was developed for strengths training. It's called it the CASE model.

CASE MODEL

Challenge yourself and the conditions.
Acquire new skills and techniques and increase your knowledge.
Share with others what you love doing and want to do more of.
Explore the things that already work well.

Let's examine each of these points.

1. Challenge yourself and your conditions

When you challenge yourself, you try to bring your strengths into play in situations where they have not yet been tested. In other words, you expand your action repertoire. You expand the area in which you can use the particular strength; you experiment and you take risks. Following are some of the questions you can ask yourself and others to discover new ways of using your strengths on an everyday basis.

CHALLENGE YOUR STRENGTHS

Pick one of your strengths and answer the following questions:

In what situations might it be advantageous to use this strength more?

What might be preventing me from doing so already?

What changes can I make to my planning and priorities to bring this strength into play more often?

What tasks, projects, or areas of responsibility do I want to take on where I might have a chance to bring the strength more into play?

What tasks, projects, or areas of responsibility should I turn down or pass on to others?

What challenges do I face in other contexts in which this strength might be helpful?

To whom could I talk about making some of these adjustments?

How will these adjustments affect others?

What will it require of me to accomplish this change? (Do I have any strengths I could use to achieve that?)

2. Acquire new skills and techniques and increase your knowledge

You should consider reading a book about those things you are passionate and in areas in which you have a strength. Take a course in something you are already good at, go to a conference, exchange ideas with others who are strong in this area or at this particular skill. Find a role model who is highly competent in the area in which you have a strength and learn from this person. There are many ways to learn. A condition for you to learn anything, however, is to open your mind and heart to your own and other people's thoughts and ideas. Let go of what you think you know and be curious. View all situations as learning opportunities.

ACQUIRE LEARNING

Pick one of your strengths and answer the following questions:

What do I need to learn to build my strength and get even stronger in this area?

To whom can I turn for inspiration?

What books, courses, conferences, and blogs might I benefit from?

Who can give me feedback on my use of the strength?

3. Share with others what you love doing and want to do more of

So far, your strength process may have been highly personal and private. Now it's time open up to the people you work with and others around you. Tell your own leader what you love doing. That will enable him or her to give you more of the tasks and responsibilities you enjoy. In connection with this talk, you also might tell your leader more about the things that drain you so that those tasks and areas of responsibility can be given to others who enjoy doing them. You can't count on your leader or others to discover your strengths for you. People are not mind readers, and even though something is obvious to you (for instance, providing details for a budget), others may not know that this activity drains you or know to what extent it drains you. You are responsible for shedding light on those things you want to spend more time on.

In relation to your employees, it might also be helpful to open up and talk about what is important to you as a leader. Be courageous and tell them where you see your strengths—and maybe your weaknesses. That will help them understand why you handle some situations better than others. And by the way, telling employees and others around you about your weaknesses is important if you want to be perceived as authentic (Goffee & Jones, 2006). If you're not used to having such an open dialogue about highly personal issues, ease into it gradually. You also can combine this self-revealing talk with a dialogue about the employees' strengths and weaknesses to turn this into a process that you are working on together. (You can find additional inspiration for this process in Chapter 9.)

SHARE

Pick one of your strengths and answer the following questions:

How will I talk with my leader, my employees, and other relevant people about my strengths and my hopes of expanding them—that is, bringing them into play more often?

Where and with whom might I offer to bring this strength into play more often?

What can I share about my areas of strength that other people could benefit from?

Explore the things that already work well

You already have a notebook full of situations in which you were full of energy and probably brought various strengths into play. You may have discovered a wide range of situations that work well for you and energize you. That process of discovery continues with this approach. Here you need to explore and search for the situations where the strength on which you're focused is already in play. You may be in for a surprise when you begin to examine your leadership practice from this new perspective. Set your modesty aside and honor yourself in the areas in which you have strengths and already bring them into play. Identify the situations in which your strengths have helped you be a great leader. This approach should leave you full of confidence and keen to do more of what already works well.

EXPLORE

Pick one of your strengths and answer the following questions:

When is the strength typically in play?

What results have you achieved because of this strength?

Have you seen other people take notice when the strength was in play?

What did they say about it?

When have you been proud and energized as a result of your performance in connection with this strength?

How does bringing the strength into play benefit the employees and the organization?

How do you benefit from using it?

CLOSING REMARKS

We've worked on identifying our strengths and bringing them into play even more than we do today. Next, we must focus on maintaining what we've learned and develop a habit of reminding ourselves to use our strengths. Remember that our strengths weaken if we don't use them.

EXERCISE

Establish new strengths-based habits

Every day: Set out to bring at least one strength into play.

Every weed: Think about the coming week and find a way to include more activities in which your strengths come into play.

Every quarter: Look back at the past three months and tell at least one other person (possibly your supervisor) when and in which area you have successfully applied one of your strengths. Describe the outcome.

Every year: Reflect on how the past year has brought you closer to a job situation in which you bring your strengths into play most of the time. Also consider what it will take to increase that. If your situation is such that you aren't bringing your strengths into play to a higher degree than a year ago, what will you do about it?

The next step in our personal strength journey concerns our weaknesses. They are, of course, the other side of our personality, and we have to pay just enough attention to them to make sure they don't prevent us from succeeding. Then we'll also appear as more complete and authentic individuals with self-awareness and the ability to deal with our weaknesses; we won't ignore them or let them hinder us in reaching our goals (Goffee & Jones, 2006; Boyatzis et al., 2013).

4

IDENTIFYING AND DEALING WITH WEAKNESSES

CONTENTS

All of us have sides of our personality with which we're less happy or about which we're embarrassed, and all of us have traits that make us do less well or do poorly in certain situations. In our position as leaders, we need to learn how to deal with our weaknesses to keep them from preventing us or the people around us from thriving and being successful.

Maybe we need to find someone else in the organization who handles particular tasks or situations better than we do and who then can help us or take over the tasks we don't excel at. In some cases, we may need to engage in situations that we find draining. And in other cases, we might find out that we don't need to engage in those situations at all. In this chapter, we discuss how to best handle weaknesses based on those different approaches.

We need to learn to embrace our weaknesses as a natural part of ourselves and our role as leaders. If we fight them or try to convince ourselves that they're irrelevant, they'll only be exacerbated or we might bring them into play in the wrong situations. When dealing with our weaknesses, generally, the goal isn't to change ourselves, but to make small changes in our behavior that make a difference to us and the people around us. In a non-strengths-based approach, it might be seen as cheating to evade our weaknesses in this manner. With that perspective, we may stay in the dark hole, struggling with our weak sides and fighting our demons. But in the strengths-based approach, it's okay to sidestep the pothole or to take a different road entirely. If it works, it works. We aren't blind, after all; it isn't like we're trying to kid ourselves; we acknowledge our weaknesses. We're aware of them, and we're dealing with them when necessary—and that's when they're preventing us from being successful or from reaching our goals.

Regarding whether our weaknesses are preventing us from being successful at work or in life in general, the hull of a ship provides a helpful metaphor. If there is a hole in the hull below the waterline (if our weaknesses prevents us from doing our job properly or from bringing our strengths into play), there is a risk of shipwreck. We must fix this hole sooner rather than later—deal with the weaknesses and do something about them until they don't hinder us in reaching our goals anymore. However, if the hole is above the waterline, we don't need to spend much time on it—we can just patch it up so that it doesn't get bigger. All we need to do is make sure the hole isn't at risk of expanding and eventually spreading below the waterline or undermining other aspects of our performance.

As with our strengths, the first step in dealing with our weaknesses is to identify them.

IDENTIFYING WEAKNESSES

The way we deal with our weaknesses is similar to the way we worked with identifying our strengths. For two weeks, we note when, where, and for how long we feel drained and unmotivated. This will capture our weaknesses. Then we can clarify them, and finally we can confirm them—just like we did with the strengths (Buckingham, 2007).

1. Capture our weaknesses

Using the same approach as we did when we tried to identify our strengths (and possibly at that same time), over a two-week period, we can write down those situations that leave us drained of energy. We aren't supposed to do anything to extract ourselves from these situations; we can just jot down our energy level and the task we're doing in that specific situation. When doing this, it may well happen that we change our behavior and invite more strengths-based activities into our lives and start to avoid some of the situations we may find draining. But we shouldn't consciously work on this yet.

CAPTURE YOUR WEAKNESSES

First two weeks (simultaneously with the strengths): Keep a journal of your energy barometer. On a scale from 0 to 10, note how drained of energy you were in a given situation. You may write down statements such as these:

"I felt drained of energy when…"

"I really did not like…"

"Things did not go so well when I…"

"I hated having to…"

Write down what you do, what the task is about, who is present, and what part of the meeting or the activity was particularly draining for you. The more precise and specific you are, the easier it is to identify patterns in later entries.

2. Clarify our weaknesses

After two weeks, concurrently with our strength notes, we continue with the next steps.

CLARIFYING YOUR WEAKNESSES

After two weeks: Scan the journal entries. Try to discover a trend with regard to the situations and tasks that drain you and make you feel weak. Look for patterns and connections. You might discover that you feel drained whenever you type numbers into a spreadsheet or when you take part in large group meetings or when you start a debate. Try to be specific and then articulate three weakness statements that describe what situations leave you feeling drained.

I feel drained when ______________________________

I feel drained when ______________________________

I feel drained when ______________________________

After you've written down your three weakness statements, ask yourself the following questions to clarify your weakness statements:

- Who is involved in the situations in which I feel drained? That's important, just as it was with regard to the strengths.
- Specifically, what is the activity about? For example, do all meetings or only certain meetings drain you? Do you feel drained from initiating all kinds of projects or only projects that last more than two months? Be specific.

(continued on next page)

CLARIFYING YOUR WEAKNESSES (CONTINUED)

At this point, your weakness statements are probably much clearer. Now they may read something like these:

- I feel drained when I must start a debate with people I already know well and am fairly sure what their opinions are on the subject.
- I feel drained when I participate in meetings in the cafeteria on Monday mornings with a large group of people I don't know from the company. It's okay if the meeting involves people from outside the company I don't know.
- I feel drained when I must type numbers into a spreadsheet that the assistant already knows and can do better than I can.

What stands out when you look at the situations that drain you? Are they familiar to you? Are there any surprises? What does this tell you about yourself as a leader?

3. Confirm our weaknesses

The final part of the process of identifying our weaknesses using journal entries is making sure that what we've identified as weaknesses are in fact weaknesses. That's the purpose of this last exercise.

CONFIRM THE WEAKNESS

After you have written down your three weakness statements and qualified them, you need to test them to see whether they reflect actual weaknesses.

Again, use the SIGN model:

Success. Is there a lack of success? I've always struggled with these situations; they're difficult for me; and I rarely succeed, something others confirm to me.

Instinct. I don't feel like doing this activity. In fact, I avoid it.

Growth. I have no desire to learn more about this area, but if I must, I find it hard to concentrate.

Needs. I have no need to engage in this activity. I'm happy when activities of this nature are canceled or finished.

Do you recognize these points? If so, you've probably identified your weaknesses.

After we've identified our main weaknesses, we can begin to deal with them.

DEALING WITH OUR WEAKNESSES

The first step in dealing with our weaknesses is to accept them. We shouldn't fight them or spend time blaming ourselves about things we aren't good at. And most importantly, we shouldn't blame others because they're involved in bringing us into situations in which our weaknesses become an issue. Instead, we must assume responsibility for moving our management approach toward our strengths.

The second step in dealing with our weaknesses is to assess how essential the weaknesses are. Using the metaphor about the ship's hull, we should assess whether the individual weakness is above or below the waterline. We may consider asking for someone else's assessment. Our employees, our leaders, or our spouse may have some interesting points of view that we hadn't considered in terms of our strengths and weaknesses. If a particular weakness is above the waterline and isn't crucial to our work as a leader, we should forget about it and move on to the next one. If the weakness lies below the waterline, we should begin to deal with it, which is the next step.

Dealing with our weaknesses in the framework of the CARE model

We can essentially choose four different approaches to dealing with our weaknesses. As leaders, we should CARE enough to avoid spending too much time on actions and situations where our weaknesses are in play. CARE is also the name of the model we can use as a source of inspiration when dealing with our weaknesses.

THE CARE MODEL

Compensate with a strength.

Ally yourself with someone who has the strength you lack.

Redefine and discover the upside of the weakness.

End activities that make you feel weak.

We need to look at our weaknesses and consider which strategy is best suited for each weakness.

1. Compensate with a strength

Practice using your strengths to compensate for your weaknesses. For example, if being systematic is one of your strengths, you may use this strength during a difficult conversation with a low-performing employee if this drains you. Sit down and use your systemizer gene to prepare for the conversation—prepare what you want to say, how to say it, and when to say it (remember timing and presence). Perhaps you can make up a word to remind yourself of what you want or need to say—in a systematic way.

Or you can use your natural capacity and curiosity when you find yourself in situations where you're feeling pressured because of the weakness of impatience. When you choose this strategy, you continue to engage a situation that may not appeal to you, but you're bringing a strength and thus energy and are then more likely to achieve success in the situation. Jane Johansen Pade, Head of Section at the Danish Ministry of Culture who was quoted earlier, recounted the following about her attempts to compensate for a weakness by bringing her strength of curiosity into play:

> *Previously, I had a very classic perception that weak sides are something that you're supposed to work on to make them go away. Of course, one is still obliged to do that if they cause serious problems. Weak sides in a leader can, of course, have quite a crucial impact on the person's ability to function as a leader. But the strengths-based mind-set has given me a more nuanced view of what I can do about my weak sides. I can compensate for them by using my strengths. For example, I have the weakness that I get impatient if things are not moving along or if others are not stepping up to take a responsibility. But I'm also very curious and interested in discovering the good reason that lies behind someone's behavior, and I'm good at setting clear conditions and discussing things openly. So I have learned that when I become impatient, I have to pause and bring one of my strengths into play: ask curious questions and uncover the core of the problem and then establish clear conditions. The interesting point is that subsequently I have asked for feedback to find out whether it works, and people were very surprised to hear that I had in fact felt impatient. They hadn't even noticed it in those situations. So the strength had in fact compensated for the weakness.*

Challenge yourself and carry out secret experiments to determine whether the strength actually compensates and pushes the weakness into the background or eliminates it completely. Find out what works for you.

REFLECTION

What strengths do you have that might compensate for each of your three most important weaknesses?

Why would that particular strength compensate for the particular weakness?

Have you already had positive experiences when using your strengths to compensate for your weaknesses?

What ideas do you have to bring these strengths even more into play in relation to your weaknesses?

2. Ally yourself with someone who has a strength you lack

When you begin to discuss your strengths and weaknesses with the people around you, something exciting happens. You discover important new things about your employees', your colleagues', and your superior's strengths. What do they love doing? Where do they experience success? The knowledge you gain through this dialogue is useful when you begin to work with your own weaknesses. In many cases, someone in your organization or among your friends and acquaintances has strengths in areas in which you are weak.

It might be difficult to imagine that someone loves doing the tasks that you loathe. Nevertheless, that is often the case. People's preferences differ more than they think. Sometimes these differences can become an advantage. Sometimes the differences lead to conflict because we want each other to do things the way we do them. The diversity that may at times lead to conflict can also be used as an asset in a team or an organization. Maybe your least favorite tasks can or should be taken over by others, but your colleagues may have possibilities that you haven't noticed because you haven't talked with them about strengths and weaknesses. Pick one of your weaknesses and consider the following:

REFLECTION

Which of my colleagues or employees likes this activity (which I find draining)?

How can I approach that person about working together on this or even turning the task over to him or her entirely?

Who could teach me a how to do the task in a way that is smarter, more fun, or faster?

Redefine and discover the upside of the weakness

In the previous chapter, you worked on your strengths. Part of knowing your strengths is knowing their pitfalls. Similarly, knowing your weaknesses involves knowing the upsides they hold. Your weak sides may in fact hold advantages—provided you are aware of them. In this instance, Ofman's talent pitfall model also can be used as a means of improving your awareness—this time around your weaknesses. Instead of putting a strength in the model, place a weakness in the talent pitfall box. Now the analysis can begin. What challenges does the weakness pose? To what actions, people, or situations are you allergic? Interestingly, any weakness will enable you to write about the advantages the weakness might hold.

Now the model looks like this:

THE WEAKNESS ADVANTAGE MODEL

WEAKNESS: This is the thing that you're not good at. It's something that you find difficult and that drains your energy.

UPSIDE: This emerges in situations in which your weakness comes into play in a positive way—where you manage to turn a weakness into an advantage.

CHALLENGE: This is what you must do to turn your weakness into an advantage or to make someone else take over a task that drains you.

ALLERGY: This may occur in relation to people who overdo the strength that is the opposite of your weakness or who do things that highlight your weakness.

A leader who was being coached described himself as "conflict-avoidant," a feature he considered to be a major weakness for him as a leader. Together he and his coach carried out an analysis of the weakness as illustrated below.

WEAKNESS: Conflict avoidance.

UPSIDE: People perceive me as approachable, likeable, and easy to talk to. They're not intimidated by me, and they think I'm a good listener.

CHALLENGE: To face confrontations when they're needed and to be more assertive in important situations.

ALLERGY: Confrontational and dominant people.

Naturally, the weakness is a challenge for him as a leader. Also, there were individuals on his team to whom he was allergic in particular situations because they were very confrontational. But his conflict avoidance gave him certain advantages, which he considered part of his strength repertoire. He was an excellent listener and was good at creating a cohesive team where everybody believed he or she was being heard and acknowledged. Being a good listener was an important strength for him, and it was helpful for him to recognize a strength in the middle of a weakness. By perceiving himself as a good listener and a good team player rather than being conflict-avoidant, he was able to add essential nuances to his self-image. He discovered options that he could use in the situations that drained him.

For example, he was now less worried about engaging in discussions that were characterized by conflict because his focus was on listening and understanding the perspectives of individual employees. His conflict avoidance gradually gave way to curious listening. The conflict avoidance will remain a factor throughout his career as a leader, but it has become less important. The hole has moved from below the waterline to above it.

For each of your weaknesses, consider the following:

REFLECTION

What advantages does this weakness give me (as a leader)?

What strengths does the presence of this weakness bring into play?

How might it affect me to reassess this weakness?

When is the difficult situation going to arise again, thus giving me an opportunity to take a closer look at the upsides of my weakness?

End activities that make you feel weak

People do many things because they think those things are expected of them. These are often considered to be organizational habits. No one knows why they persist, and no one knows how they emerged. But they continue undebated. Sometimes the situation is reminiscent of this anecdote.

CASE

The chimps and the trees

A team of researchers placed five chimpanzees in a cage that had three trees. The chimps had to climb the trees to collect their food. If a chimp climbed up the wrong tree (the tree in the middle), all the chimps were automatically sprayed with cold water (which they didn't enjoy). If they climbed up one of the other two trees, they were able to retrieve their food without the unpleasantness of a cold shower.

(continued on next page)

CASE (CONTINUED)

Quickly, all the chimps learned to use only the two "safe" trees to collect their food, even though the middle tree held food. Then the researchers replaced one of the chimps with a new chimp. Because the new chimp didn't know about the unpleasant effects of climbing the wrong tree, the chimp attempted to climb it. The reaction from the four other chimps in the cage told it in unambiguous terms that this behavior was unacceptable. With loud shrieks, arm gestures, and physical contact, they pushed the new chimp away from the tree. In this way, the new chimp soon learned to avoid the tree in the middle.

Then the researchers replaced the other chimps one by one, and each of the new chimps similarly learned to avoid the middle tree. At some point, all five chimps were newcomers to the cage. None of the chimps had ever been sprayed with water, and no one knew whether this would continue if they tried again. But the chimps never tested it or questioned the logic behind avoiding the tree.

The question is whether some of the draining things you do are still of value. Have you asked yourself or others why you do the things that drain you and whether your assumption of having to do them still holds? Does your engaging in this activity create anything of value for the company or the clients? Who finds it necessary and why? One way of testing this is to stop doing it and see what happens.

Consider the following if you are thinking about giving up an activity that drains you.

REFLECTION

Will I be dismissed if I stop doing it?

Will it affect my performance if I stop doing it?

Will anyone even notice or care if I stop doing it? (If so, on what do you base that? Have you tried?)

Can I spend less time on it?

With whom could I talk to find the courage or the necessary support to stop doing it?

Asking these questions can also be done as a team by making an explicit decision to abandon a particular practice.

CLOSING REMARKS

The goal of the first part of this book was to inspire leaders to apply the strengths-based paradigm and to start developing their strengths and dealing with their weaknesses. Part Two explores frequent management challenges, discusses how to meet them from a strengths-based perspective, and provides insight into questions leaders can ask and a process model they can apply in their day-to-day business.

PART TWO

STRENGTHS-BASED LEADERSHIP IN DAY-TO-DAY BUSINESS

When we're conducting leadership training, facilitating large-scale organizational development processes, or giving a speech (whatever it is we do), leaders usually ask for tools. That is understandable because it isn't enough to learn about a paradigm—leaders also need to be able to apply it in their daily lives.

As discussed in Part One of the book, it's essential that we understand the philosophy and perspective behind the tools that are presented in this second part of the book before we begin using them. Using a "tool" (such as a particular sort of question) in a leadership context requires a good sense of the situation, empathy, timing, authenticity—and in the strengths-based paradigm, a specific mind-set such as "looking for the good intention in others" or "reminding ourselves of people's strengths and resources before, during, and after talking with them."

But that should be clear by now.

The discussion of methods, processes, and tools in this part of the book gives us ways to apply a strength perspective and use this perspective step-by-step—via concrete methods, processes, and tools—to meet daily leadership challenges from a strengths-based perspective.

When we acquire new theories and methods, we gradually move from *holding a particular view of leadership* in the beginning of our learning process (in this case strengths-based) to *being able to practice that form of leadership*. At first, we proceed through trial and error because we probably haven't yet mastered the "tool" or the process we're testing or using.

Gradually, it will seem more natural to ask questions or to motivate others in a particular way. Then eventually we'll use the approach and the tools implicitly in our daily practices. We'll no longer think about the fact that we're using a tool from a particular paradigm. We just practice it.

When we reach that point, the strengths-based approach to management has become second nature. This journey of learning can be described as going from being (1) *unconsciously incompetent* in relation to practicing strengths-based leadership to being (2) *consciously incompetent* to being (3) *consciously competent* to being (4) *unconsciously competent* (www.gordontraining.com). Now we'll look at each step.

1. Unconsciously incompetent *in relation to the topic:* This refers to the time when we had never heard of strengths-based leadership. We didn't know we could learn anything about this approach to leadership, be inspired by it, or benefit in any way from learning about it. On this level, we need to know that this leadership approach exists (we need knowledge). Then we need to consider whether this management approach is of interest to us (acceptance of relevance). Once we've become aware that strengths-based leadership exists and that we might benefit from mastering it, we go from unconsciously incompetent to:

2. Consciously incompetent: Here we may think it's a shame that we don't know more about the approach and that we haven't fully mastered it. We understand that with this approach, we might achieve great results. On this level, we begin to search for knowledge and we start practicing the new tools we're presented with. If we keep training (using the tools, applying a strengths-based mind-set, etc.), one day we'll reach the next level and become:

3. Consciously competent: On this level in the learning curve, we use and master the strengths-based approach, but we still need to think about what we do. For example, others may not notice that we have to make an effort to ask questions in a certain way because we're now competent in using the approach. However, we still don't apply the approach automatically (that is, ask questions in a specific strengths-based way). We still need to think about what we do and to establish habits and routines related to our new management practices before strengths-based leadership becomes second nature. When we experience that we no longer have to think about using this approach—but just do it easily and unconsciously—we've reached the final level where we are:

4. Unconsciously competent: At this point, strengths-based leadership has become routine. We no longer think about the fact that what we're practicing is strengths-based leadership. We just do it.

We're likely to be inspired by the methods, processes, and tools presented in the next part of the book. We should begin experimenting with these specific and energy-raising leadership practices and go from being consciously (in)competent to unconsciously competent. This requires effort, at times we'll have doubts and revert to a fault-finding mind-set, and we'll sometimes find the tools difficult and awkward. The process of becoming a great leader who can apply a specific set of tools requires persistence. New tools must be tested many times before they come to us naturally and easily. That's the case whenever we want to learn something new. It takes time before we can master something new and no longer have to make an effort to do it. In fact, research has shown that it can take up to three months of daily practice before a new habit is established and feels natural. In fact, it may take even longer if the thing we're trying to change has been part of us for a very long time (Miller & Rollnick, 2012; Boyatzis et al., 2013; Covey, 2013).

Research has shown that it is easier to establish new habits if we share our efforts with others by telling about our goals and experiences during the process (Boyatzis et al., 2013; Miller & Rollnick, 2012). Others will then ask how the "training" is going and thus, directly or indirectly, remind us of the project we've embarked on. We'll benefit from finding a confidant who also wants to learn more about the strengths-based leadership approach and wants to use the tools with us or who is interested in checking up on us from time to time.

Along the way, we'll probably discover or find confirmation that we're already doing many things in a strengths-based way. Fortunately, it's fun to practice strengths-based leadership, and the results become evident fairly quickly. Employees usually respond positively to the strengths-based way of being asked, being involved, and receiving feedback for instance. So there's nothing to it but to do it.

5

STRENGTHS-BASED QUESTIONS

This chapter provides an overview of basic strengths-based questions that may be used in the many situations in which we find ourselves every day. When conducting one-on-one conversations, meetings, and change processes, for instance, we ask questions. When trying to understand and solve a concrete problem, we ask questions. It's paramount, though, that the questions we ask take us in a desired direction. Therefore, this whole chapter is dedicated to introducing strengths-based questions. Before digging into the different types of questions we can ask, we'll take a look at the benefits of asking questions at all.

CONTENTS

BENEFITS OF ASKING QUESTIONS

The strengths-based leader asks many questions, and there are many benefits of asking a lot of questions (see the following box). But as leaders, from time to time, we need to take a stand and state our view so that people around us know what we stand for, what we intend to do in various situations, what decisions have been made, and what topic is not up for discussion. The balancing act is to figure out when to ask questions and when to make a statement/when to conclude.

When dealing with this balancing act, most leaders are challenged by patience and the need for them to appear wiser and more knowledgeable. After all, why are they leaders if they don't know better? But in today's world, the leader is not necessarily the most knowledgeable person in the room or the one with all the answers. On the contrary, most great leaders know this fact and are able to surround themselves with people who are more clever than they are. The task for the leader then is to align the different strengths of and wisdom in people and bring them into play in a coordinated manner—as the illustration on the cover of this book depicts.

THE ADVANTAGES OF ASKING QUESTIONS	POTENTIAL DRAWBACKS OF MAKING A STATEMENT TOO SOON IN A PROCESS
Empowerment. You promote self-management (empowerment) and the individual employee's sense of strengths and of being the one with the answers. As a result, the person will not have to turn to you every time he or she encounters a problem. The person learns to turn to himself or herself and/or to colleagues before coming to you. That saves time and enables quicker and more decentralized action.	**Time consuming in the long run.** For the reasons stated in the box to the left.
Growth. You help the employee grow by encouraging him or her to reflect on his or her patterns of thought and action. In other words, you help the employee discover his or her inner potential by virtue of the questions you ask, such as "What drives you, where do you feel strong, where do make your greatest contributions?" All of these are aspects that you as a manager can guess at, but you can never know for sure. Helping your employee discover this increases the likelihood that he or she will bring his or her strengths into play—to his or her benefit, the benefit of the entire organization, and your benefit as a leader!	**Stagnation.** You do not learn anything new; the other person does not learn anything new.
Opens up the conversation and brings out many perspectives and points of view. Questions lead to reflection, both for you and the person you ask.	May **close down** the conversation before everything is on the table. Statements may lock the conversation into one particular perspective or track.
Your **understanding** of the other person's opinions, thoughts, and feelings grows. The risk of misunderstandings is minimized.	Possibility for **misunderstandings**. You try to make the other person understand you before the person believes that you understand him or her. When you forget to ask, you risk missing out on important information.
Learning. You might learn some brilliant solutions that spring from the employee's understanding and experience. *(continued on next page)*	

(continued) **Self-esteem and care.** The person you ask moves into focus and feels heard and valued.	**Risk of dominating and taking focus.** There is too much focus on you—you may seem dominating or uncaring.
Questions invite **new thoughts**.	**Statements conclude** and close down ideas.

BASIC STRENGTHS-BASED QUESTIONS

Now let's take a look at the many exciting and challenging questions we can ask as strengths-based leaders.

STRENGTHS-BASED QUESTIONS—IN SUMMARY

1. Follow-up questions
2. Questions aimed at clarifying a problem
3. Questions about a desired future
4. Miracle questions
5. Scaling questions
6. Exception questions
7. Questions about good experiences
8. Questions about progress and success
9. Proflection questions
10. Questions about decisions and actions.

1. Follow-up questions

Follow-up questions support all the other types of questions and can be used in any context in which we want to further explore someone else's perspective or simply want to better understand what the person is saying.

EXAMPLES OF FOLLOW-UP QUESTIONS

Can you tell me a little more about...?

What other things are important to mention?

Could you elaborate on that?

Can you give me a specific example?

What do you mean by the term/word...?

How do you explain the fact that...?

I am a little confused here. Could you try to tell me in different words what you mean?

2. Questions aimed at clarifying a problem

Questions aimed at clarifying a problem are not essentially strengths-based, but when properly framed, they can form the basis of a strengths-based process. We may need to examine a problem closer before we begin to ask questions about a desired future or positive deviances in the situation in which the problem occurs. An appreciative move is to listen to problems and complaints before we go down the strengths-based path. But we must not linger on a problem too long. As soon as the problem landscape has been outlined, we can move on to asking people what *they* want. Most people find it relatively easy to ask questions aimed at clarifying problems; nevertheless, here are a few typical examples.

EXAMPLES OF QUESTIONS AIMED AT CLARIFYING THE PROBLEM

What is the problem?

Why is this a problem?

How big is the problem?

Who is involved? (Is anybody else involved?)

What do you see as being the main challenge in this situation?

How long has the problem been going on?

What challenges do you meet?

3. Questions about a desired future

Questions about a desired future are useful for carrying out a plan that is essential in the strengths-based paradigm: the shift from problem focus to solutions focus. This was discussed in Part One with the axis model, which introduced the idea of focusing on the things we wanted to see more of. Questions about the desired future have the effect, so to say, of breaking the downward curve in the problem axis.

We can begin by asking where the other person wants to go rather than exploring how the problem developed in the first place. This is a minor detail that has a tremendous impact. It ensures a conversation that is constructive but not draining. Much of the inspiration for the phrasing of questions for the desired future comes from the systemic theorist Peter Lang, who has made the following observation, which is both poetic and razor-sharp:

Behind every problem hides a frustrated dream.

Remember to ask about the frustrated dream.

CASE

Adolescents with behavioral problems

Peter Lang has achieved amazing results with, among others, young people in Britain who have behavioral problems. The youths he worked with were used to being blamed for their lack of involvement in school and social activities. Through the use of a conventional approach, the emphasis was placed on finding the underlying cause of their asocial behavior, and attempts were made to convince the adolescents to change their behavior. The children defended themselves and refused to take responsibility for their problems.

Lang decided to take another approach and began the conversation with the children by asking about their dreams, hopes, and desires. He figured that there must be something they loved to do and that some resources must be hidden inside them waiting to unfold. He listened to their problems and then asked questions such as these: So when you have that problem, how do you want things to be instead? What do you dream of? If your wildest dream of your future came true, what would that be?

After first being startled by this kind man with his unusual questions, the young people softened and began to talk about their dreams and secret hopes for the future. Many of them had lost faith in themselves and their dreams, but with Lang's help, they considered the possibility that there might be something out there that could be exciting to engage in.

As a result of these conversations, many of the adolescents concluded that their schoolwork was an essential condition for their dreams to come true. Schoolwork became a means of achieving a goal rather than being a dull and useless chore. The students slowly started to take responsibility for their own destiny once again—or in some instances for the first time ever. (McAdam & Lang, 2009)

As leaders, we can use Lang's ideas every time we encounter a problem. It is called "breaking the curve," as illustrated in the preceding axis model.

Listen to problem talk, complaints, and negative stories. Complaints are a gift to us as leaders because they contain important information about what concerns the person airing the frustration. We should think of the "grumblers" as heroes who are not afraid to say the things that other people only say when we aren't around. That attitude will help us listen and be constructive.

We need to use our empathy and tact and then at some point begin to ask questions about what people want to see instead of the problem. There are many ways to ask these questions. The common denominator is that the question should lead people's thoughts toward something that can be created in the future rather than the negative things in the past that are impossible to change. Based on this desire, actions can then be established. Here are some specific examples of questions we can ask about the desired future.

EXAMPLES OF QUESTIONS ABOUT THE DESIRED FUTURE

How would you like things to be instead?

What is the dream scenario for the department from your perspective?

What do you hope to see in the department in the future?

If you could have your wildest dream come true in your current job, what would it be?

When you have these frustrations, this problem, it sounds as though you have an idea that something can be done differently/better. What is that?

The questions should direct people's thoughts toward something positive in the future, toward creating something new with others. The question should avoid leading to negative discussions of the past. For example, the question "What would you like to change?" might be well-intentioned, but by bringing it into the conversation, we might insinuate that someone has to change because what he or she did was wrong. And that risks leading to a discussion of who was right, who was wrong, and who did what and why. That might be interesting as long as it sheds a proper light on the problem (a prerequisite for us to even ask questions about the desired future). But in this part of the conversation, when we start asking questions about the future, our goal should be clear to everybody. If it isn't, we need to spend more time evaluating the problem, as described in the previous section.

REFLECTION

Consider one of the problems you are experiencing right now.

What is the underlying aspiration behind the problem? What is the frustrated dream? What do you hope will happen in regard to this problem?

Now we have a few ideas for asking questions about the desired future and may be ready for the next questions.

4. Miracle questions

The miracle questions should be asked when we want to challenge someone to take a radically different approach to future possibilities. It is often effective and makes people think along new lines. It turbo-charges the dialogue about the desired future. In its basic form, the miracle question has the following form and is expanded with follow-up questions.

EXAMPLE OF MIRACLE QUESTIONS

Introduction

(You may ask people to close their eyes): Imagine that you go to bed tonight and fall into a deep and heavy sleep. When you arrive at work tomorrow morning, a miracle has occurred overnight. All your problems have vanished like dew in the morning sun, and everything you ever wanted for the workplace has come true. There are no constraints. You can imagine anything you want. Can you envision that?

Questions:

What's the first thing you notice? (This is always the first question.)

What's the first thing you do when you get to work?

What is the mood like, and what is it that creates this mood?

How will your colleagues, your employees, your customers, the citizens, and your clients notice this amazing change? How are they interacting with and contributing to this new world of tomorrow?

How have they been involved in the change? What is their role in your organization now?

What is it possible for you to achieve now? How do you achieve it?

How do you impact the surrounding society in a positive way?

What other changes are worth mentioning?

What would be the smallest step you could take today that would bring you a little bit closer to the miracle?

The miracle questions bring the dialogue into a new dimension because it gives us permission to dream and to think outside the box. The funny thing is that the dream/miracle often isn't that far from the current reality or from what can be achieved or from the possibility of engaging and collaborating in the best possible way with people in and around the organization. In itself, it can be a major revelation to discover that the dream is not as distant as we may have thought.

When we ask the miracle question, we run the risk that people will look at us as if we're out of our mind and they may not be willing to play along. The introduction prior to asking the questions is very important. We may introduce the question as a mental experiment, which tends to put people more at ease. Or we may suggest that people try and see what happens instead of declining to participate. Of course, our relationship has a great deal to do with whether people are willing to answer the miracle question, but also how the questions are framed and what leads up to us asking them are important. If we haven't yet tried to understand the problem, people might think we're trying to sweep it under the rug or haven't really listened to them.

Finally, maybe we can take comfort in knowing that Albert Einstein is with us when we try to raise the dialogue to a new level. He said,

Problems cannot be solved on the same level of thinking that created them.

To bring it all back to reality, a type of question that is down-to-earth and specific, yet also highly effective, will be introduced: the scaling question.

5. Scaling questions

Scaling questions can be used in virtually any situation and at virtually any time in a conversation, process, or meeting. Scaling questions are simple, bordering on the trivial, and indeed are the butt of jokes in commercials and movies, where they are featured in parodies of therapists, for example. But in all their simplicity, scaling questions are effective and efficient. Most important, they can give us essential information about differences and variations in a situation, perception, or problem. According to the anthropologist and systemic theorist Gregory Bateson, information is a difference that makes a difference. Scaling questions let us discover the differences that make a difference, and then we learn from them. So let's take a closer look at these powerful questions.

INITIAL SCALING QUESTIONS

On a scale of 0 to 10, with 0 being poor and 10 being exceptionally good, where would you place your performance in this project so far?

On a scale of 0 to 10, with 0 meaning that you are completely drained of energy and 10 meaning that you are bursting with energy, where would you place your energy level in relation to this type of task?

On a scale of 0 to 10 how good are you at handling the challenge you are facing?

How serious is the problem on a scale of 0 to 10 (0 meaning bad and 10 meaning no problem at all)?

Affirmative scaling questions

What brings that high of a number? Why isn't the problem any more serious? Why are you not at a 0? (What activities, experiences, skills, or routines are contributing to the fact that the problem isn't bigger?)

Exception scaling questions

The number you just gave regarding your level of energy or the challenge or your problem is an average. Sometimes the number will be higher, meaning there is less of a problem or more energy, and sometimes it will be lower. On those days the problem is lower, perceived as less challenging, or the energy is higher, what is happening? How high is the number then? What is different in those situations? What do you and others do at those times and on those days?

(continued on next page)

INITIAL SCALING QUESTIONS (CONTINUED)

Imagine 10 on the scale questions

Imagine that the problem is gone and/or the level of energy is as high as it can be, meaning you are now at a 10 on the scale. What can you do when you are at a 10? What does it look like when the problem is gone? What do you do? What don't you do? What do others do? What do the people around you say? How do you and your organization collaborate with others at this level? How does it feel being at a 10? What steps have brought you here? How did you persevere? Who helped you?

First-step scaling questions

Now go back to the starting point and your starting number, symbolizing how you, on average, perceive your energy level or problem. What can you do to bring yourself one step closer to a 10/a solution? What could be your first step? To whom do you need to talk to take the first step? What do you need to talk about? Who and what might help you?

The scale gives us endless opportunities for asking questions. It can be used to discuss poor performance, energy levels, great performance, desired performance, and team performance. A strengths-based approach to low performance, for instance, will be based on the fact that despite the poor performance, there are probably things that are going well, even though it might be the exception: "So when you place your performance at a 2, why isn't it a 1?" "So you're at a 3 right now, which suggests average. I know your performance is sometimes at least a 7 or an 8. What do you do in those situations?"

The scale can also be used to explore differences between the employee's and our own assessment of the employee's performance. We may be familiar with the situation where the employee's self-assessment is higher than our assessment of his or her performance. That is a difficult situation, but the scale does offer some openings: "So when you assess your performance as a 7 and I put you at a 4, what might that reflect? What specific examples can we talk about to understand that difference?"

And the scale can be used to discuss good experiences from previous situations that are reminiscent of the challenge we are facing now: "At what times might we have had a team spirit that was as high as 9 or 10? In addition, what could we take with us from these situations to improve the present situation?" "You say that your energy level is currently a 5. Has there been a time when it was at the top of the scale? If so, what happened then?"

The scale also can be used to discuss goals and levels of ambition. The scale can help us specify our goals or raise the bar and the level of ambition: "So when your effort is at 5, how might you raise it to a 6?" "How high would you like to go?" "How would you have to work if you were to give yourself a 10?"

There is essentially no limit to the ways in which we can use the scaling questions. The number is simply a way of visualizing and calibrating our perception of a person, a performance, or a situation. The main point is our dialogue about why the number is as high or as low as it is.

What if the person's reply is all the way at the bottom of the scale, where things look really bleak? That's a relevant question. In that case, we may choose to abandon the scale and switch to exception questions to explore whether the situation is really as bleak as it seems. Often that will present an opening. The exception questions were briefly explored in the discussion about the scaling questions, but now we'll look at these questions in more depth.

6. Exception questions

Exception questions uncover nuances in an otherwise negative story. Exceptions are tiny glimpses of positive stories and hopes for the future in a difficult situation. When we hear stories about employees, leaders, departments, customers, or organizations that are negative and categorical, it's time to challenge them with an exception question. If we have a negative view of someone and believe that the person is being stupid, it's time to challenge ourselves with an exception question. This challenges 100 percent statements, which might sound something like this:

EXAMPLES OF 100 PERCENT STATEMENTS

He's always like that!

She never does anything right!

I always get it wrong!

It's the same thing with you guys every time we get near the deadline.

You are always so negative.

We never talk about the right things.

These 100 percent statements are rarely 100 percent correct. There are usually exceptions. And these exceptions can provide important information and help us focus and be constructive in situations where we might otherwise be dragged down the problem axis. When we encounter these statements or the chatter is generally negative, we might try some of the following "exception questions."

EXAMPLES OF EXCEPTION QUESTIONS

Are there situations where things are not like that?

In what situations is your teamwork pretty good?

Has there been an example where you achieved the results that you wanted?

Are there situations or tasks where you had a more positive view of your colleague (and people stuck to their 100 percent)? Has there been just a hint of a situation where things weren't like that?

Why is it important for a leader to challenge 100 percent statements and negative stories? It is important because no problems are permanent. These 100 percent statements and negative stories risk remaining unchallenged, in which case they can grow into accepted negative truths about colleagues, customers, the team, and the organization. Once something has become an accepted negative truth, curiosity stops, an impasse is reached, and the organization misses out on important possibilities. Many conflicts in organizations begin with 100 percent statements that judge other people negatively, so it is a good idea to challenge these statements to prevent conflicts. (Chapter 10 will discuss more about this.)

7. Questions about good experiences

Questions about good experiences also are an essential part of strengths-based leadership. Questions about good experiences are based on the assumption that some things have always worked well in the past, where strengths have been put into play and might be brought into play again in a new context. Asking about good experiences is the opposite of asking "What might you do differently?" where we assume that what the person does and has done is not good enough. So by asking "What good experiences have you had with handling this type of challenge?" we invite an exploration of the employee's or the organization's strengths and resources that we can draw on in the future. The clever and motivating quality of this approach is that it is easy to continue to do what we do well.

Development is not just about making changes. Development is also about doing more of what works. So let's look at some of the questions we might ask about good experiences from the past.

EXAMPLES OF QUESTIONS ABOUT GOOD EXPERIENCES AND STRENGTHS

What strengths were in play in that situation?

What did you do that worked well? What did others do?

What factors were at play that made you succeed at that situation?

How can you bring these experiences into your current situation?

What ideas does it give you to think back to the good experiences from then?

8. Questions about progress and success

Questions about progress and success are important to ask because they help us take the step from "just" *celebrating successes* to *learning from* successes. Here are some examples.

EXAMPLES OF QUESTIONS ABOUT PROGRESS AND SUCCESSES

What has improved since the last time we met? (Try starting a meeting with this question.)

What signs do you see that things are moving in the right direction?

What do you think has led to this progress?

What have you/we done to create this success?

What specific details have made a positive difference?

What did you do or say that worked so well at that meeting?

How can we use these good experiences in other contexts?

Asking the above questions is the strengths-based paradigm in virtually its purest form, and we can't do it too often. We need to keep an eye out for the success stories and highlight them. We need to amplify them to make them visible so that everyone can learn from them. Stories that involve the whole team are especially powerful and produce a sense of community. We should avoid highlighting our own role. We may want to downplay our role and let the employees take the glory. However, on our own, we may want to consider the following questions:

REFLECTION

What is going better for me as a leader these days?

What progress have I achieved personally lately? Why are things going better in this area?

9. Proflection questions

Proflection questions are about the emerging future. Inspired by Otto Scharmer and his "Theory U" (Scharmer, 2009; Scharmer & Kaufer, 2013), we should ask questions about the past—what we can learn from the past and what strengths we might build on from the past—as well as consider what new things we need to learn or do—ourselves, our team, or our organization. These questions require time to answer, probably more time than many of the other questions. They require that we take time to stop and listen to "what the future wants us to do" and use our intuition when answering them. Thus, we can't just download existing information; instead, we need to search for the answers from another source: our inner wisdom, intuition, and sense of what needs to be done in the future. Asking the questions starts this "proflection," not a reflection, meaning learning from the past but also learning from the future as it emerges, as Scharmer puts it. But we need to leave time in the conversation so that the other person can dig into new and different sources when trying to answer the questions. It might even be a good idea to leave more time than a normal conversation allows. For instance, we may want to consider asking the questions and then leaving the person alone before we ask for an answer. This is what typically happens at the bottom of the U in Scharmer's Theory U model, describing a profound transformational development cycle in individuals and/or organizations.

EXAMPLES OF PROFLECTION QUESTIONS

What does the future call you to do?

What is it in your life, your society, and your work that you need to change for a "future perfect" to emerge?

What do you need to stop doing? start doing?

Who could you learn from and maybe start working with for a new direction to take place?

What kind of partnerships, collaborations, and coalitions could you envision in the future, and to what might that lead?

There is some overlap between these kinds of questions and the miracle questions. But the proflection questions go a step further in terms of using a person's intuition. Therefore, these questions usually aren't asked at the beginning of a process. It will be too soon—the person who is asked the questions needs time to "warm up" before he or she can be expected to find great answers—answers that come from deep within.

10. Questions about decisions and actions

Questions about decisions and actions should be asked toward the end of conversations and meetings. They need to be asked, though, because far too often, people forget how important it is to end a good dialogue, meeting, or process by looking each other in the eye and agreeing to what each of them should do to follow up. Here are some examples.

EXAMPLES OF QUESTIONS ABOUT DECISIONS AND ACTIONS

What is the next step?

Now that we've talked things over, what do you think our decision should be?

In my assessment as a leader, it would be good if we.... How does that sound to you?

What do you feel like doing next?

Who will follow up on that?

What would you like from me in connection with this particular task?

What would you like me to start doing?

What is the smallest step you can take that would make a big difference?

In reviewing what each of us takes away from this dialogue, what will each of us commit to doing now?

What will you do?

We now have a general toolbox full of strengths-based questions. The chapters to come will discuss how we can use them in relation to specific leadership challenges. The challenge is to use them at the right time with the right timing. We'll begin with something that all leaders experience on a regular basis: one-on-one conversations with employees.

6

STRONG ONE-ON-ONE CONVERSATIONS

The topic of this chapter can be (and is) the topic of entire books. The goal here is to provide an introduction on how to conduct one-on-one conversations from a strengths-based perspective. One-on-one conversations refer to all conversations we have with our employees. This includes brief as well as long conversations, from informal dialogues taken in the hallway to more formal and planned dialogues where we agreed to sit down (or walk) and talk.

The informal conversations can be an important part of our dialogues with the employees, and we can use the same conversation and question techniques in informal talks as we use in more formal talks. Let's take a look at the more formal conversations in which leaders are frequently involved. The illustration below summarizes the terms that are frequently used with regard to dialogues that leaders and employees engage in at work.

CONTENTS

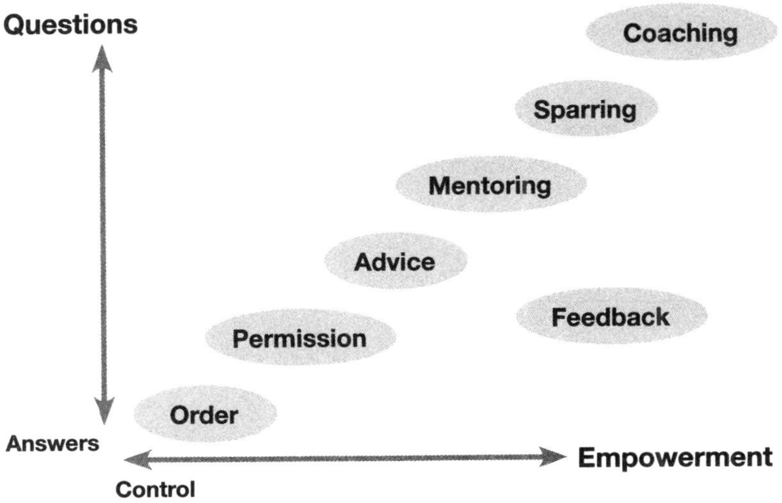

This chapter offers insight into our options for conducting the various types of one-on-one conversations using a strengths-based approach. Let's start with an introduction to five basic guidelines/tips for conducting strong conversations.

FIVE TIPS FOR A STRONG CONVERSATION

To get into the right frame of mind for the topic of one-on-one dialogues and "strong conversations," we may begin by having a strengths-based dialogue with ourselves based on the following reflection questions:

REFLECTION

What are some things that you do or say in dialogues that often have a good effect?

How can you tell that they have a good effect?

Where did you learn what you already know about good conversation techniques, coaching skills, or dialogue tools?

Who is your role model as a conversation partner?

What does your role model do in conversations that you find to be value-creating?

What challenges do you most commonly encounter when you have one-on-one conversations?

What would you like to improve in your performance with regard to future dialogues?

Which of your strengths can you bring into play when taking part in one-on-one dialogues?

There is no fixed recipe for the good conversation. But there are some basic ingredients that give us a good starting point. They are called "The five conversation tips"—the C-tips.

FIVE CONVERSATION TIPS—THE C-TIPS

1. **C**onsiderations and clarification
2. **T**imeout
3. **I**nvolvement
4. **P**resence
5. **S**trengths focus

1. Considerations and clarifications

Any good conversation starts with a clarification. Why are we having this dialogue? The conversation may have happened by accident; we met in the hallway of the building and started talking informally. But as soon as we have the opportunity to sit down with another person for a more formal conversation, we need to be well prepared. Consider the following issues before having a longer, more formal strengths-based conversation with another person.

The leader's preparation for a strong conversation

Before the conversation	• How do I want to invite the other person to have this conversation with me? • Where should the conversation take place? (It doesn't have to be in your office.) • How should I prepare? • Should the employee/colleague prepare? • What materials should we use? • What sort of provisions should there be? • What is the goal of the conversation from my perspective?
At the beginning of the conversation	• How do I create a safe setting? • How do we get off to a good start?
During the conversation	• What is it important for me to say? • What is it important to have the other person talk about? • What questions might give the conversation a good direction? • What questions can make the other person feel strong? • How will I make sure the energy continues during the conversation?
Conclusion	• How do I end things in a good way? • If the conversation goes well, from my perspective, what happens afterward?
After the conversation	• How do I hold on to the good energy from the conversation? • How can I support the other person in reaching his or her goals? • What do I need to add to my to-do list?

Once we have prepared ourselves for the dialogue and have invited another person, we're ready to get started with the conversation.

The first thing we need to do is set the framework and be clear about why the conversation is happening. That's the starting point. What follows is a more in-depth exploration of the topic being discussed, and then we end the conversation. Those are the basic ingredients in any great dialogue; they have a structure. In all its complexity, it is fairly simple: There is a start, something happens during the conversation where the topic is explored, and there is an end. It's called the **SEE model**.

THE SEE MODEL		
START	**EXPLORE ALONG THE WAY**	**END**
• Set the framework. Review the context, the goals, and your expectations for the conversation. • Ask about the other person's expectations of and wishes for the conversation. • Achieve as much agreement as you can about the purpose of the conversation. Is it just a chat, or do the two of you want to reach an agreement or make a decision? • Provide information necessary for the other person to be involved in the conversation on fair terms.	• Explore the topic. • Use the relevant types of questions. • Discuss the problem. • Say what you think. • Listen to the other person's thoughts and ideas. • Find new perspectives. • Explore resources, strengths, and good experiences. • Explore possible actions.	• Make sure you decide on the next steps. You need to state aloud what you have agreed to do and ask the other person to repeat it. • What do the two of you need to decide or arrange? • What needs to be written down? • Is it clear what specific steps the two of you should take now? • How do the two of you follow up? When do you meet again? • Conclude and summarize. • Ask for the other person's opinion of the conversation as a form of evaluation.

We shouldn't start a conversation without making sure the other person understands what is going to be discussed. Therefore, the start is very important. The end is also important, though. Far too many conversations end without any clear agreement about or a common understanding of what needs to be done and who should do what. So we need to remember to ask this as an open question every time: "So what do we agree to do?" "Did we make a decision, or were we just chatting?" There is nothing wrong with chatting; we just need to be clear about it.

2. Timeout

When there is confusion in the middle of a hockey game, the coach can call a timeout to discuss or explain the tactics, allowing the players to make the necessary adjustments to stay focused on the game and play their best. The same is true of a conversation. Any uncertainty or doubt should be cleared up to the benefit of both parties. Perhaps there is doubt about the topic of the conversation, or the conversation may change course and move in a different direction. Perhaps we have a feeling that our conversation partner is getting bored. Perhaps we believe the conversation is not value-creating. As leaders, if we have doubts about these issues during a conversation, we should call a timeout.

A timeout in a conversation is a "talk about the talk," also called a meta-dialogue. It's a useful tool for discovering what our conversation partner is thinking. Instead of trying to guess, we can ask. We also can use a timeout to share our thoughts with the other person to check whether our thoughts can help make the conversation more value-creating. Timeout questions are also a strong tool in managing meetings (discussed in more detail in Chapter 8). Following are some examples of the types of questions we can ask during a timeout in a one-on-one dialogue.

This kind of meta-dialogue also can be used to improve our conversations (or meetings). If we've tried it, we know that it can make a difference between a conversation or a meeting that is value-creating or a waste of time. It takes courage and the ability to improvise, though, because we don't know whether it will take the conversation in a new direction. But the payoff is usually worth the gamble. We make sure that our conversations are about the issues that matter most for the other person, for us, and for the organization. Another incredibly valuable benefit is that the timeout involves the other person, which is discussed next.

TIMEOUT QUESTIONS

- What are we focused on right now?
- I'm thinking that it's important to talk about.... What are your thoughts on that?
- Are we talking about the right things? Or could we be spending our time more productively by discussing a different topic?

(continued on next page)

TIMEOUT QUESTIONS (CONTINUED)

- What is the most important thing for you to address before the conversation is over?
- I had an idea while we were talking. Would you like to hear it now?
- I'm hearing three topics in what you are saying: X, Y, and Z. Is that correct? Which topic should we talk about first?
- If we had only 5 minutes left in this conversation, what would be most important for you to talk about?
- I sense we aren't talking about the most important things right now. In your opinion, what are they?
- Do you believe this conversation is adding value? Are we on the right track? If not, in your opinion, what should we be talking about instead?

3. Involvement

Everybody wants development. But few people want to change.

These wise words are often attributed to the Danish philosopher Søren Kierkegaard, who was already quoted in this book. The statement has a kernel of wisdom with which we're probably familiar from our leadership experience. When we try to persuade others to follow our directions, they may object and refuse our request. By contrast, when the same idea initially came from them, they're excited about it. This is a crude simplification, but nevertheless, it is often true.

There is a biological explanation for this phenomenon. A person's main task is to maintain his or her existence and integrity. If something threatens our physical or mental integrity, we become defensive (Maturana & Varela, 1987). Thus, a defensive response to input from others expresses a healthy sense of skepticism. Our task as leaders in any conversation is to be aware of this so that we can help the other person stay open—and that happens via involvement and a curious inquiry.

If we attempt to persuade another person or impose our opinion too forcefully, we'll disturb the other person and cause him or her to shut down. On the other hand, if we fail to challenge the other person with our questions and ideas, we're not providing enough of a disturbance and we'll fail to spark any development. This means that we should disturb the other person just enough to make him or her want to do something different and thus grow and develop. That is called a suitable disturbance, and it requires the other person's involvement to a point where he or she stays alert and awake enough to be engaged, but not too agitated to have put up a wall of defense.

We must use our own sense of the situation to determine whether we're providing a suitable disturbance. We should use our ability to notice the signals that tell us whether to tone down or intensify our constructive disturbance and involvement, and this requires presence.

4. Presence

This tip is both the easiest and the hardest—but maybe the most important—of all the tips. If we're not present in the situation, the other person will notice it immediately and the conversation will suffer. The art is being present during the entire conversation. When we're speaking with another person, that person deserves our full attention. Nothing is more annoying than talking to someone who isn't really "there." They're thinking about something else or aren't interested in what is being said. So we need to be present—set aside everything else that is on our minds and give our full attention to the other person for the whole conversation.

Our attention can be compared with a muscle. We can make it stronger if we exercise it. When we talked about presence as one of the main ideas in strengths-based leadership, we described how someone can train his or her attention and ability to be present. In addition to these ideas, the following guidelines might help improve the ability to be attentive and mentally present in a conversation.

SIX MENTAL STATES THAT HELP YOU STAY PRESENT DURING THE DIALOGUE

- **Discipline:** Harness your attention. Deliberately choose your focus and reclaim your attention immediately once you notice it beginning to wander.
- **Curiosity:** Examine and look for new, exciting angles in what the other person is telling you.
- **Openness:** Look for connections and patterns in what the other person is saying.
- **Nonjudgmental acceptance:** Accept the way things are and meet other people where they are.
- **Patience:** Master the pause and suspend your need to fix other people's problems right away. Give them time and see what happens.
- **Trust:** Loosen your need for control. Let the other person demonstrate that he or she has strengths and resources and the ability to master a situation. See what happens if you trust the other person to come up with great ideas, solutions, and angles.

Wherever we are and regardless of how we feel, we can train and challenge ourselves to become or remain present in the moment. When we catch ourselves being inattentive, we can bring our attention back to the moment. When we catch ourselves becoming impatient and wanting to provide answers, we can stop ourselves and curiously examine what happens if we stop our urge to do that. Every moment gives us chances to train our ability to be present—if we're aware of it.

5. Strengths focus

The last tip is the topic of this entire book. Briefly put, it is about making sure that we keep the strengths focus during a conversation by:

- Looking for the best intentions of and strengths in the other person.
- Harnessing the energy.
- Being aware that the way we frame our questions has a lot to do with the direction the conversation will take and thereby with our ability to find solutions to a given problem.

It is important to note that an appreciative and strengths-based approach does not mean that we as leaders should avoid bringing up those things that don't work. On the contrary, problems do need to be brought to the surface. But we need to talk about them in a way that is appreciative and strengths-based to keep the energy and morale high. It isn't the problems as such that cause problems, as was discussed previously. Often, it is the way we talk about the problems that causes problems.

If we follow the C-tips provided previously, there is every chance that the conversation will be as strong and constructive as it can be. But as strengths-based leaders, we should strive to get better, which we do only if we ask for feedback regularly.

ASK FOR FEEDBACK

Calling a timeout toward the end of a conversation to ask for feedback can be a great source of insight. For instance, you can ask the following questions:

- What did I say or do during our conversation that was helpful for you?
- Was there a particular time or question where I pushed my own agenda too hard?
- Was there a time or a question that made too small a difference or that you didn't find interesting?
- At what time was this conversation most engaging for you, and what created that energy?
- What good advice can you give me for conducting constructive conversations in the future—with you and/or with others?
- What else do you want to tell me?

By ensuring that we get valuable feedback regularly, we can gradually improve our ability to sense and pick the right questions at the right time and conduct constructive and even better conversations.

DEVELOPMENT CONVERSATIONS, PERFORMANCE CONVERSATIONS, AND THE DIFFICULT CONVERSATION FROM A STRENGTHS-BASED PERSPECTIVE

Now we'll look at some of the most common types of one-on-one conversations we can engage in as leaders and discuss how to give them even more strengths-based character. These conversations are as follows:

1. Development conversations
2. Performance conversations
3. Difficult conversations

1. Development conversations

Fortunately, recurring development conversations have become commonplace in most organizations. Whatever we call these conversations in our organization, it is a great opportunity to talk with employees about their development and contributions to the organization. We may find, though, that one annual development conversation is not enough. A lot can happen in a year, so three or four structured individual conversations a year is preferable. Having this number of development conversations each year lets us address problems before they grow big and unwieldy. These conversations do not have to last one or two hours; the point is that we set aside time to follow up on the agreements we reached in the "main" development conversation that might take place once or twice a year.

Some leaders do not like the formal, structured format of a development conversation. Many leaders have said that the relationship and the informal aspect is lost if things have to be formalized. "Can't we just have an informal talk and assume that everyone does his or her best on a daily basis? Do we have to follow up?" The answer is that if we have a good relationship and can handle the follow-up on an informal basis without necessarily setting aside time on the calendar, then everything is fine. However, many leaders fail to do this. They do not have the time, or they "forget" how important the follow-up can be for the employee. Leaders don't follow up to check on the employee; they follow up because they have a genuine interest in seeing whether the employee believes he or she is on track, has any questions, or needs any assistance. In that case, dislike for the formalized and structured character of the development conversation becomes a poor excuse for a leader to flout his or her responsibilities.

The purpose of a development conversation is *development*. A development conversation should serve to *align* the employee's development with the goals of the organization and to highlight to the engaged parties how the person is contributing to the common good of the company—and thereby to the common good in the world.

Traditionally, development conversations tend to focus on the holes in the cheese—on the issues the employee needs to improve to meet the standards. There will often be one box for the employee's strengths and another box for his or her growth and development areas (read "weaknesses"). However, in a strengths-based development conversation, both strengths and weaknesses are considered development areas. Both are important. In a strengths-based approach, most of the time is spent talking about the strengths and how the employee can develop them and bring them further into play. Let's take a closer look at how to conduct a strengths-based development conversation by using the framework of the SEE model described previously: how to start, explore, and end a meaningful development conversation. The discussion also will give advice on what to do before and after the conversation.

	STRENGTHS-BASED DEVELOPMENT CONVERSATION
Before the conversation	• Ask the employee to keep a strengths journal in the weeks leading up to the conversation. Talking about what is energizing and what is draining frames a focused and specific conversation about strengths and weaknesses and about how the strengths can be brought into play even more in the employee's workday. • Consider whether the conversation can take place outside your office. You may even go outdoors if the weather allows. Your choice of setting sends a signal. • Send an e-mail a few days before the meeting, outlining your thoughts about the meeting (perhaps with a few questions for the employee to consider in preparation for the meeting). • Take an extra look at the form the organization uses to structure the development conversation. Is it strengths-based enough? How is it phrased? What aspects of the form work well? What would you like to change, and what will it take to change it? (Do you need to align this change with someone from HR, perhaps, or your leader?) • Consider providing a snack for the meeting.
Start	• Spend a few minutes on small talk about children, family, and the weather. • Spend some time clarifying the conditions and your mutual expectations. • Ask about the employee's expectations and wishes for the conversation, following the guidelines in the SEE model.
Exploration during the conversation	• Show general appreciation of the employee's efforts. • During the conversation, examine how well the employee's goals and development match the organization's vision and strategy. • Review prepared materials. *(continued on next page)*

Exploration during the conversation *(continued)*	• Ask more in-depth questions about the strengths. – Back this up with positive feedback. – Work together to discover how the strengths can be brought into play even more and how the employee's workday can feature more of the elements and qualities that produce energy for the employee. • Ask more in-depth questions about the weaknesses. – Make a constructive contribution by stating your honest opinion. • Ask about the employee's progress and successes. – Back this up with positive feedback. – Discuss how successes can be repeated or amplified in the coming year. • Ask about the employee's challenges on the job. – Ask questions aimed at clarifying problems. – Ask questions about the desired future. – Ask the miracle question. – Ask scaling questions. – Ask questions about good experiences. • If there is a discrepancy between your assignment and the employee's, state your honest opinion and examine the difference (for example, use scaling questions). • For further inspiration, follow the guidelines in the middle phase of the SEE model.
End/conclude	• Make the necessary decisions together. – Ask questions about decisions and actions. – If something is not possible, say so frankly and clearly. • Ask about the employee's opinion of the conversation. • Conclude by expressing appreciation and thanking the employee for the conversation. • For further inspiration, follow the guidelines in the end phase of the SEE model.
After the conversation	• Ask the employee to send a follow-up e-mail with the agreements you reached, as well as his or her thoughts on the value the conversation created. It is important to have the employee send the e-mail, thus assuming responsibility for his or her development plan. • Keep your promises.

2. Performance conversations

In an age characterized by increasing demands for documentation, development conversations are often interwoven with conversations about goals and performance. The discussion here points to some of the possibilities that are open to the strengths-based leader in this type of conversation. Two scenarios are provided: a conversation with someone who is not achieving his or her goals (a low performer) and a conversation with someone who does achieve or exceed his or her goals (a high performer).

Conversation with a low performer

If we've conducted a conversation with an employee who, for whatever reasons, failed to meet his or her goals, we may have heard a little devil whispering in our ear "this is unbelievable" or "how hard can it be?" If the employee can tell from our eyes that this is what we're thinking, an unnecessarily difficult conversation may result. Usually, the employee is aware that there is a problem, so we don't need to shed too much light on it. Sometimes they don't know, though, in which case we need to address it up front.

There also may be situations in which the hole in the ship's hull is below the waterline, where the weaknesses of the employee are causing severe damage and we need to take drastic measures including, ultimately, dismissal.

But before we get to that point, there are plenty of possibilities for patching up holes and bringing the strengths into play to compensate for the weaknesses—strengths that we, as leaders, and the employee may have lost sight of in our focus on low performance. We need to remain open and frank about performances that are below par, though. Remember the Stockdale paradox and "Face the brutal facts," but also remember how important it is for the employee to believe that we still believe in him or her and still see his or her strengths. Only then can the employee perform well/better in the future (cf the Pygmalion Research on page 29).

When conducting a strengths-based conversation with a low performer, we should switch the conversation fairly quickly to the strength axis. This is where we're likely to find the answers for improving the employee's performance. The idea is that no problem is constant. So even if an overall performance is low, there will always be strengths and good examples of situations that worked better. We should explore these so that we can learn from them and, if possible, amplify them.

Below is a description of how we can approach a conversation with a low performer, using the same model given previously (the SEE model) and some good advice on what to do before and after the conversation.

DEVELOPMENT CONVERSATION WITH A LOW PERFORMER	
Before the conversation	• Ask the employee to bring his or her figures/goals. • Ask the employee to consider good examples of exceptions from the unsatisfying trend that occurred during the period in question. (Just doing this may surprise you and the employee positively). • Make sure you are certain about facts regarding the performance and gather concrete examples.
Start	• Be friendly and smile, but don't be frivolous or silly. This is, after all, a serious conversation. • Spend time clarifying the conditions and your mutual expectations. • Ask about the employee's expectations and wishes for the conversation. • Show general appreciation of the employee's efforts and examples of good performance, even if these are the exception. • Explain directly and respectfully what the problem is from your perspective, offering specific examples. Make it clear that growth and development are required. • Offer your support.
Explore during the conversation	• Talk about the best exceptions: – Intro: Your performance reflects an average of high and low performance. Let's focus on the situations or moments where you feel that you are performing well. – At what times during this period have you thought that you performed well? – What characterized that situation? – What characterizes you in these situations? *(continued on next page)*

Explore during the conversation *(continued)*	– How do others notice your performance in these situations? – How do you notice that you are performing well? • Talk about progress: – In your opinion, what has improved since the last time we talked? – What were the "keys" to these improvements? – What did you do that led to this improvement? – What can you do to move further in that direction? – How would you notice that you've moved 1 point up the scale? – At what times have you been higher? – What got you there? – Where on the scale do you believe you should be to achieve your goals? • If there are discrepancies between your experience and what the employee is saying, state your honest opinion and examine the discrepancy (for example, use scaling questions). • Talk about the desired future: – How would you like things to be instead? – What are you hoping for? What do you consider to be realistic? – Which of your strengths can you use to move in the direction of the desired future and to compensate for some of your weaknesses—some of the things that aren't going well right now? – What do you need to get there in terms of help, advice, resources, development courses, or something else? • Consider using the miracle question: – Imagine that a wave of a magic wand has made you the team's top performer. What would be the first thing you notice? – What would others notice? – How would the customers/users notice? • Talk about the numbers, using scaling questions: – On a scale of 0 to 10, where 0 is the worst performance and 10 is the best, where would you place your performance? – What is it that brings you up to …? – What could bring you one, possibly two, steps up the scale? *(continued on next page)*

End the conversation *(continued)*	• What is the next small step you can take to ensure positive development? (Preferably this is something the person has already shown as being capable of doing). • Confirm that you see this as a good plan. Be honest and frank if something isn't possible or if you don't think the plan is a good one. • Ask how you and your colleagues can help in this process. • Ask when the two of you should meet to talk about this again. • Thank the employee for the talk. Express your appreciation that he or she is willing to improve his or her performance and state that you think the employee can make it work (if you think so).
After the conversation	• Speak briefly with the employee from time to time and ask what you can do to help. • Ask the employee to send an e-mail that summarizes your conversation and clearly states what you agreed on.

Our goal as leaders is to send a motivated and strengthened employee out the door. With the questions and dialogues provided here, we have a good chance of achieving that objective.

Conversation with a high performer

The second scenario in this section is a conversation with an employee who is doing well—perhaps even performing above expectations. Here the challenge is to maintain the positive aspects of the employee's performance and to preserve the person's spirit and motivation.

This type of conversation offers an opportunity not only to celebrate the success of the employee, but also to learn from it so that the employee (and perhaps others) can repeat and amplify the success. As strengths-based leaders, we have a particular interest in learning from success stories and in asking ourselves this question: What are the conditions that enable high performance?

Below are some tips for the conversation with a high performer.

STRENGTHS-BASED CONVERSATION WITH A HIGH PERFORMER	
Before the conversation	• Ask the employee to bring his or her figures/goals. • Ask the employee to answer some questions about the explanation for the good performance. • Find your own examples (exemplified by numbers and concrete situations) of the employee's high performance. • Think about how you can make this employee feel like the important and valued employee he or she is.
Start	• Spend some time clarifying the conditions and your mutual expectations for the conversation. • Use specific examples to express your appreciation of the employee's work. • Offer your help and support.
Explore during the conversation	• Express your assessment of the employee: If things have gone so well that it's time for the employee to take a break to remain a high performer, that should be your advice. • Look at the employee's strengths using questions about progress and success: – Please tell me about a situation where your performance was particularly good. – What did you do, specifically, that was good? – What effect did that have on others or on the outcome of the task? If there are discrepancies between your experience and what the employee is telling you, state your honest opinion and examine the discrepancy (for example, use scaling questions). – What strengths did you bring into play in that situation? – How can you transfer the use of these strengths to more situations? – What were the "keys" to reaching these improvements? – What did you do to achieve these improvements? – How can you move farther in the same direction? *(continued on next page)*

Explore during the conversation *(continued)*	• Use scaling questions to raise the bar: – On a scale of 0 to 10, where 0 is the worst performance and 10 is the best, how would you rate your performance? – What capabilities and actions bring you all the way up to...? – How high on the scale do you believe you can go? • Raise the bar with the miracle question: – Think about this: you wake up tomorrow and notice that a miracle has occurred—that is, your performance level has suddenly gone even higher along with the fact that you and those around you flourish. – What is the first thing you notice? – What has changed? – What will you/your colleagues/leaders/customers/other stakeholders be doing differently? – What is the first thing others notice that convinces them that a miracle occurred? How does it feel and look? What happens?
End the conversation	• Conclude with the following questions: – What dreams, ambitions, and goals do you have for yourself, the organization, and the company's vision/mission for the future? – How can the organization and I as your leader assist you on this journey toward your future goals? – What will you focus on in the future? – What will be the next small step you take to ensure positive development? (You may want to contribute your own ideas about initiatives.) • Confirm that you see this as a good plan if you really think so. • Once again, express your impression that the employee is already doing well.
After the conversation	• Ask the employee to send an e-mail summarizing what you talked about and agreed on in the conversation. • Speak briefly with the employee from time to time and ask if there is anything you can do. • Speak favorably of the employee to others.

Now we turn to conversations that are about a heavier topic—difficult conversations. In Chapters 10 and 11, we provide ideas for managing stress and conflicts. The following section deals with general topics of which we need to be aware when we're speaking with an employee who, regardless of the cause, is having a hard time.

3. Difficult conversations

The difficult conversation is similar to the conversation with a low performer. An important difference, however, is that in the difficult conversation, the precise nature of the problem and the desired future may be more elusive. In the difficult conversation, there may be no specific figures or ratings to relate to, but instead more or less clearly acknowledged issues that we as leaders need to discuss with the employee. Maybe the employee is sad and not himself or herself. Maybe there are issues in the employee's personal life that affect his or her situation at work. Maybe the person has been out on sick leave. There may be a hidden or open conflict between the employee and a colleague. There can be many causes.

The difficult conversation may also spring from the fact that the low performance has now become so problematic that the next step is dismissal unless there is a big improvement in his or her behavior. In this case, the situation shouldn't come as a surprise to the employee because he or she should have had some warning before the conversation. It's important that we set the right conditions for the conversation before the conversation takes place and make it clear to the employee what he or she can expect from the conversation. If the employee expects a nice talk, he or she will be astonished and possibly defensive when we introduce the severity of the problem.

As leaders, we must find the right way to begin the conversation based on the employee's situation. But there are certain general aspects we should be aware of if we want to bring a strengths focus into a difficult conversation.

THE DIFFICULT CONVERSATION	
Before the conversation	• Consider whether the conversation is optional or whether it is mandatory for the employee. Voluntary participation is preferable, but you are entitled to demand a conversation if the employee's behavior or performance has had a negative effect on the workplace. • Explain before the meeting what it is you want to discuss so that the employee is not left feeling uncertain. For the same reason, you should generally conduct difficult conversations on short notice. • Carefully consider where the conversation should take place. Neutral ground may be preferable. • Prepare what you want to say, especially with regard to beginning your introduction and establishing the conditions. • You may want to write it down. • You may consider bringing a third party to the conversation. *(continued on next page)*

Start *(continued)*	• Generally, the same introduction is used as with the low performer. • If the employee is going through a difficult time and the conversation is intended as purely supportive, you should use questions to involve the employee fairly early in the conversation. • If the employee's difficult situation affects results, quality, cooperation, etc., you may also, as with a low performer, offer direct feedback about your perception of the situation before you ask questions. To reiterate, the same rules for good feedback apply here. The more specific, kind, constructive, etc., you are, the better (see Chapter 7).
Explore during the conversation	• Acknowledge and explore the problem using questions aimed at clarifying the problem: – What is the problem? – What is your biggest challenge in this situation? – Who, if anyone, is involved? – How long has the problem been going on? – What obstacles do you encounter? • Talk about the problem using scaling questions: – On a scale of 0 to 10, where 0 is the worst and 10 is the best, how serious is the problem? Despite everything, why is it not as low as...? – How would you notice that you had moved 1 point up the scale? – At what times is the situation better? – What happens when the situation is better? • Talk about the desired future: – How would you like things to be instead? – What are you hoping for? What do you consider to be realistic? – What might be the first small step you and/or others could take in that direction? • Talk about good experiences: – What experiences do you have from managing similar problems? – What did you do then that worked well? – What strengths did you utilize that helped you meet the challenge? – How can these experiences be useful in the current situation? – When you think back on positive experiences in managing similar problems, what ideas come to mind that you can draw on or use in the current situation? *(continued on next page)*

Explore during the conversation *(continued)*	• If there are discrepancies between your experience and what the employee is saying, state your honest opinion and explore the discrepancy (for example, use scaling questions).
End the conversation	• What might be the next step for you? • Confirm that these are good steps. Be honest if something is not possible. • How can your colleagues and I support you? • What, if anything, requires further effort that would benefit from outside support? • When should you and I sit down to talk about this again? • Thank you for this talk. Was it an okay experience for you?
After the conversation	• Speak briefly with the employee from time to time and ask if there is anything you can do. • Ask the employee to write a summary of the conversation—what you talked about and what you concluded. • Follow up with another meeting (typically after one or two weeks).

CLOSING REMARKS

No two conversations are alike. For us as leaders, the key is to choose the right focus, the right questions, or the right statements at any moment during a conversation. That is a big challenge, and it requires our full attention. We will benefit from using some of the ideas in this chapter as inspiration for future conversations.

7

STRENGTHS-BASED FEEDBACK

CONTENTS

As we discussed in Part One of the book, the following is a fundamental assumption in strengths-based leadership:

> *We need other people's eyes on us to bring ourselves into play optimally. The eye cannot see itself.*

In other words, we need feedback. The importance of asking many questions as a leader and encouraging others to do the same should not be underrated. But often, employees and our superiors are also curious to hear what we have to say, what we think the best solution is, and how we assess their contribution to the team or the project. And we need to hear their opinion and ask for it. This is especially important the higher we move up the management hierarchy because research shows that the higher we are, the less frank the feedback we tend to receive (Boyatzis et al., 2013)—unless we create an atmosphere where giving and receiving honest feedback is valued, wanted, and expected and is thereby part of the daily life of the organization.

As a leader, we have a responsibility to create this atmosphere and to communicate and give feedback in a manner that is appropriate for the context and to check whether the other person grasped our intended message. If an employee believes that we're criticizing him or her when in fact we're trying to be constructive, we must accept his or her perception and try again. It's not okay for us to say, "You don't get me! Why don't you listen!" and reject responsibility for the misunderstanding. Instead, we could say, "I don't think I expressed myself clearly enough. Let me try to put it this way...."

Essentially, we must assume responsibility and try to modify our communication and feedback to the person we're talking to. Of course, the other person has a shared responsibility for listening carefully, but unfortunately we can't change others. We must begin with ourselves if we want to ensure proper communication and feedback in our team; department; organization; and, yes, society.

Communication and feedback are tools that can be used to influence others in a particular way. In a sense, all communication can be regarded as manipulation. What we say has an effect on others. And what we hear from others has an effect on us. Thus, in many ways, using strengths-based communication and feedback is an ethical choice of making that influence count in a positive direction. Strengths-based communication and feedback motivate, strengthen, elevate, and promote confidence, empowerment, and responsibility. By contrast, conventional fault-finding communication and feedback is often draining, undermines motivation, and diminishes people's sense of confidence and their desire to act and take responsibility.

Think of the axis model. When we move along the negative axis (the problem axis), focusing on mistakes, shortcomings, and weaknesses, we can feel the energy draining out of us and the people we're talking with. When we move along the positive axis, looking forward to the desired future and focusing on strengths, resources, and past successes, we can feel the motivation and the energy level increase in us and in others. It is easy to tell the difference by listening to the language and the words that are used in a conversation. Consider the two sentences in the box below. The statements say the same thing—and then again not.

It's important to avoid shooting down each other's ideas.	**It's important to maintain a free flow of ideas.**

The statement on the left has a potentially skeptical, reproachful, and draining effect, and by stating this, we risk turning people off. The statement on the right evokes an image of everybody working together to create a free flow of ideas. It suggests a more energetic and trusting line. All communication has a value charge.

Now let's dig deeper into how to give and receive feedback from the strengths-based perspective. But first, we need to think back to a time in life when we received feedback that was positive and helpful for us.

- What happened?
- Who gave you the feedback?
- How was it given?

By thinking of and remembering this time, we dig into some of the key elements of providing feedback in such a way that something can be learned and we acquire more insight. And that may lead to a change in behavior in a desired direction.

And the whole purpose of giving and receiving feedback is to ensure learning and continued development (Serge, 1999).

Strengths-based feedback strengthens and generates learning, development, change, and transformation—in individuals and in the organization as a whole.

Traditionally, the thinking has been that we stand to learn most from our mistakes. Thus, the emphasis in giving feedback has been about negative features—things that need to be changed or eliminated. Strengths-based feedback takes another approach. Because we know that we learn not only from our mistakes, but also from our successes, we shouldn't focus only on offering feedback about the things that don't work.

Thus, a tenet in strengths-based feedback is this:

Highlight and comment on the things that others do well. That will help them to continue doing it. Focus on what the person should be doing differently instead of only pointing out the things that are not good enough.

Many people have had bad experiences with getting feedback because the focus was solely on their faults and mistakes. Then feedback is associated with something unpleasant and anxiety-provoking. It is crucial to deal with these negative associations and build new ones by highlighting and offering positive feedback on the behavior that we want to see more of. This might help build the expectation that feedback can be (and within the framework of the strengths-based approach should be) associated with learning, developing, and improving an individual's strengths and dealing with an individual's weaknesses. Feedback should be considered to be other people's perceptions and perspectives, and those should be seen as gifts and a valuable source of learning and insight for the person and/or team. When given in the right way, feedback can boost a person's confidence and self-esteem and create and generate positive spirals of learning, sharing, and growing in the organization.

Of course, feedback must be realistic. If a performance was predominantly poor or maybe even disastrous, there is no point in highlighting only the one thing the person did well in his or her overall performance. (For example, it's great that you showed up.) If a person receives positive feedback that he or she knows is far from reality, the feedback loses credibility. The person will stop listening and begin to think, "Does he even dare to face the facts? Can I use this for anything? Is he completely conflict-avoidant or a starry-eyed optimist?" And obviously, that is not constructive.

The goal in establishing a feedback culture within the strengths-based paradigm is to enable people to learn to listen and begin to learn from the things they do well. At the same time, they should also develop a realistic image of how others perceive them. As a result, they can consider what they should deal with/eliminate/change in a presentation, a behavior, or some other aspects that are included in the feedback.

THE 5C AND 3F MODELS FOR ESTABLISHING A STRENGTHS-BASED FEEDBACK CULTURE

As leaders, we can do a great deal about our communication to establish a culture of open, frank, and constructive feedback in the workplace. Next, we'll review, step-by-step, how this can be approached. These suggestions can be summarized in the 5C model.

THE 5C MODEL FOR STRENGTHS-BASED FEEDBACK

The feedback should be:

1. Continuous
2. Caring
3. Constructive
4. Concrete
5. Concise

1. Continuous feedback

You should lead by example in giving and receiving and requesting feedback.
Do it more often than you normally do.

From the moment we realize the importance of giving and receiving feedback, we should lead by example. We should request feedback after a meeting, after a presentation, and after a one-on-one dialogue. Also, we should practice giving feedback more often than we're used to. Initially, it may seem strange or awkward, but gradually, everyone will discover that requesting and giving more feedback than usual facilitates learning.

2. Caring feedback

Remind yourself and others about the intention of feedback: generating learning. The intention is kindness—helping others to grow, develop, and learn.

It is much easier to receive the feedback openly if we keep reminding ourselves that the feedback is given so that we can learn. As strengths-based leaders, we should make sure the feedback that is given and received under our leadership is based on helping people improve. It should be caring.

We should also remind others that the feedback given and received is only one perspective among many. Another person's perception of us is one perspective *in a specific situation*. And this perspective can offer some hints, but not necessarily the whole truth, about us. Other people may have a different perspective. By reminding others of this in our position as leaders, we increase the likelihood that they (and we) will be able to receive what others are saying with an open and curious mind.

3. Constructive feedback

Notice whether others are ready to receive the feedback.

Regarding this point, timing is everything. It is important to give the feedback as close as possible to the perceived incident. But there is no point in barging in with feedback if the other person is upset, unhappy, or overly excited. If the person receiving the feedback is "wound up" emotionally, there is less of a chance that he or she will be able to remember and thus learn from what is said. In an emotionally charged state, people devote all their energy to the issue that set off their emotions; consequently, they have less energy to devote to learning and remembering. It also can make a difference when other people are present. In many cases, it is more constructive to offer feedback one-on-one unless we want others also to learn from the feedback. Remember, though, to be ethical concerning these issues if they're personal. Also, if the feedback we're about to give is negative, we're better off sharing it with the individual one-on-one instead of in a public setting.

4. Concrete feedback

Concrete feedback is based on observations and assessments of one's own experience of something that someone else does, says, writes, etc.

The more specific the feedback, the better. Superficial comments such as "great" or "try again" are difficult to operationalize. The more specific the feedback is, the easier it is for the person receiving the feedback to change his or her behavior (or to continue doing more of or even amplifying what worked).

We can make sure the feedback given and offered in the organization is specific by teaching ourselves and others to ask questions about the situations. This is especially helpful if someone makes a superficial or judgmental comment that we don't understand.

QUESTIONS ABOUT FEEDBACK

- Exactly what was it I said that worked well?
- How did I do it?
- What did I do that didn't work well?
- What did I say?
- What do you think I should continue doing?
- What should I stop doing, and what can I do instead?

It's important that we ask the questions in a curious way, showing that we're looking for additional information. Curiosity is a crucial aspect of giving and receiving feedback.

When we're giving feedback, we should remember to ask the other person why that person chose to do what he or she did in the situation the feedback is about, possibly *before* we give the feedback. This may result in an explanation that makes our feedback superfluous or gives it a new angle. It also prevents misunderstandings. Maybe the other person had a very good reason for doing what he or she did or for behaving/reacting the way he or she did. Remember, this is one of the key elements of the ideal pit: to look for good explanations in others' behavior.

There is always a good reason people choose to do what they do.
Be curious about the underlying motivations and intentions of people's behavior
before you "judge" them or offer feedback.

Just as we see only the top 10 percent of an iceberg, we don't see everything when we're looking at other people. What we see (and what our specific feedback can address) is behavior and signals. What people do and say or don't do and say is what we see. What isn't apparent is the basis of the behavior: thoughts, feelings, needs, and intentions. When we interpret a signal and give feedback based on this, such as "I can tell you're nervous," we risk overstepping the other person's personal boundaries and mistakenly attributing feelings or intentions that aren't present.

Instead, concrete feedback can sound something like this: "Your voice is trembling a little, and you're speaking very fast. This gives me the impression that you're nervous. Is that correct?" We offer concrete feedback but don't judge prematurely.

To make sure we continue providing concrete feedback, the model of the three Fs might help.

THE THREE Fs

Facts: What actually happened in concrete terms (as factually as possible—that is, avoiding interpretations)? For example: You walked in a little late. People were becoming restless. Then you stood facing them, your arms were akimbo, and you began to whisper. All the attendees stopped what they were doing and began to listen, and you really got their attention. They forgot that you had been late. You kept their attention for the first 10 minutes, but you probably kept at it a little too long; after that, it seemed as though the energy left the room.

Feelings: What did I feel, specifically? For example: It had a very strong effect on me that you were whispering. I think the others felt the same way. You seemed confident and calm. It was contagious, so I was calm too. But it was hard for me when you didn't stop sooner. I became nervous and lost my energy.

Future: What should you continue doing or do differently another time? For example: I think you should show up on time. It worked out fine this time, but generally, it's an uphill battle from the start because people find it unprofessional. I know I do. And then you shouldn't continue to whisper quite as long. I also think that you should present fewer slides after the introduction. There were too many. You should reduce them by half. But the whispering in the beginning was cool—really surprising. Keep using that.

5. Concise feedback

We're unable to deal with lengthy explanations, models, theories, or input when we receive feedback. Therefore, the feedback should be brief and to-the-point.

Cut your feedback to the bone.

FEEDBACK IN THE TEAM, THE DEPARTMENT, AND THE ORGANIZATION

The 5C model presented above can be used when we give feedback to another person, but it also can be used when we provide feedback to each other in the team, in the department, or across the organization. The fact that feedback promotes learning is true not only in relation to individuals. We must draw inspiration from the feedback model to highlight what the team or department does well in a continuous, caring, constructive, concrete, and concise manner. There's tremendous potential for learning in situations in which we create extraordinary results together.

Give feedback on and examine with curiosity the times you achieved extraordinary results together.

Normally, our performance is just above or just below average. We have some red days where we're below average and some green days where we're above average. Often we tend to talk a lot about the red days, the days when things are not going so well, and about what we should do to make those days green. But today we'll do something else. Today we'll examine and learn from what happened on Monday—where we didn't just turn green, but crashed through the ceiling.

- What actually happened? What was it that made Monday such a great day?
- Who did what and why?
- I'd like some feedback about what I did that day that helped us turn green.
- Now turn to the person sitting next to you and tell him or her what you did that helped us go to the top of the green scale?
- What did the person sitting next to you do?
- What can we learn from this day that we can use on the days we're in the red?

In the situation mentioned above, together with the team, we examined what happened on a day or in a situation where we did far better than normal. We should try to make it a habit to pause regularly to examine how we're doing as a team. For example, we can introduce the following feedback session after every meeting or team effort. The exercise is simple; all it requires is five of our fingers.

Evaluate and give feedback on your meetings and/or team efforts.

Regarding the meeting we just had (or the team effort we just gave to Project X), how would you assess it on a scale of 0 to 5 (with 5 meaning it was an incredibly productive meeting or project that created value and 0 meaning it was a waste of time)?

Count to three and ask everybody to silently indicate the score he or she would give the meeting by holding up the relevant number of fingers.

Then ask one of the people who is indicating the highest score:

- What brings you all the way up there?
- What did we do that was good in this meeting?
- What did you do? What did others do?

(continued on next page)

Now ask one of the people who is indicating the lowest score:

- What keeps you from giving it a 0 (or a lower number than the one you indicated)?
- What makes you hold up this number of fingers?
- What would it take for you to give the meeting a higher number of fingers?
- What could you have done? What could I have done? What could others have done?
- Summarizing question: What went well at the meeting? What should we do differently or more of next time?

The questions in this feedback exercise are similar to the scaling questions introduced in Chapter 5. In all forms of feedback, we can draw further inspiration from these ways of asking questions. The goal is to learn. We need to make a habit of learning from the things we go through together—the good as well as the bad.

THE 3:1 FEEDBACK RATIO

Research has documented that teams that perform well above average compared with teams that work under similar conditions are characterized by having a 3:1 ratio on the following communication parameters (Losada & Heapy, 2004; Fredrickson, 2009):

3	1
Positive statements about the project and/or other team members and their ideas	**Negative statements** about the project and/or other team members and their ideas
Inquiry. Question marks/explorative statements. Could we do things like this? What do you mean? Can you elaborate on that?	**Advocacy. Exclamation marks/argumentative statements.** That's the way it is! That's the way it's going to be! That's the way it has to be!
Focus is on other team members	**Focus is on oneself**
Engagement and energy in the project	**Reservation and caution**

Research shows that teams that have more positive communication, ask more questions, focus on each other, and are passionately engaged in the project are more high-performing. Every time they make three positive statements (on average), they make one negative statement. Every time they ask three questions, they offer one conclusion.

The interesting thing about this ratio in relation to feedback is that in high-performance teams, the members make three positive comments about other team members' good contributions and ideas for every negative thing they highlight. That illustrates what you should be emphasizing in your feedback. If you still aren't convinced about the justification of highlighting and amplifying the positive aspects of other people and your team, these research findings should eliminate any doubts. Predominantly highlighting the good things that other people do when we give feedback pays off.

Note the word *predominantly*. The formula does not indicate a ratio of 3:0, but of 3:1. If that one negative statement is missing, the team is conflict-avoidant and does not voice the negative aspects at all. That isn't nuanced feedback. Teams also need to talk about the things that aren't working. And from time to time, someone needs to make a statement instead of only asking questions.

REFLECTION

How often do you give feedback?

Is the feedback you give predominantly positive or negative?

How do you feel about giving feedback? Do you think it should highlight the positive or the negative aspects (or both)?

What type of feedback do you believe produces the best results?

What type of feedback do you typically receive? Why?

Do you have a tendency to forget to give positive feedback? Many people do. And it's human nature to notice those things that are missing and that prevent us from reaching our goal. The focus on shortcomings has helped us secure our survival as a species, but the world has changed. It's no longer only caution and a focus on shortcomings that help us progress. Instead, it is an awareness of everything that has taken us this far—and the awareness of those things that will help us progress even further (at least as long as the talk is about social systems, as mentioned in the first part of the book). With regard to machines, it still pays off to look for the underlying cause of a problem. But as soon as we want to engage others in solving a problem, we should bring some energy and positivity into the situation because this makes us "work better."

So to deal with a tendency to focus on shortcomings and negative aspects, we must remember the 3:1 ratio the next time we give feedback.

REMEMBER 3:1 WHEN YOU GIVE FEEDBACK

- Tell your colleague what you appreciate and respect about them.
- Provide specific examples of the last time you noticed your colleague making a contribution—for example, something that helped the team's development.
- Practice noticing what your colleagues do that is constructive and positive so that you can give them feedback on it. Find at least five things in one week.

What is one thing the other person should change, do differently, or stop doing?

You may want to offer suggestions as to what the other person should be doing instead.

This chapter concludes with some interesting research from the Gallup Institute, which found that the 3:1 ratio also counts in happy marriages—almost. The researchers studied the communication style in couples and found that couples who are happily married and will be for many years to come don't have a 3:1 ratio in their communication; they have a 5:1 ratio! Married couples should think about how often they complain or express negativity about their spouse or about what they're doing together—how often do they express positivity, are they engaged, and do they ask curious questions?

8

STRENGTHS-BASED MEETINGS

Good meetings are one of the driving forces in organizations. Bad meetings drain people of energy and agency. Good meetings create energy and the desire in people to make a difference; establish clarity about direction and agreements; and provide a growth medium for valuable ideas, innovation, and creativity. This chapter focuses on how we as leaders can chair and create strengths-based meetings that make a positive difference and bring the organization closer to its overall goals.

We begin by discussing point by point what we can do to prepare for, plan, hold, and anchor strengths-based meetings in the organization.

CONTENTS

BEFORE THE MEETING

Reflection before the meeting

The first thing we should do before hosting a meeting is to consider the following:

REFLECTION

Think of a meeting in which you participated that was efficient, inspiring, and value-creating—a meeting that made a difference for you and the department or organization and thereby for the product you were offering.

What did the host of the meeting do that contributed to making the meeting value-creating?

What did the participants do?

What was your own contribution?

What other factors had a positive impact?

(continued on next page)

REFLECTION (CONTINUED)

Considering those points, what would it be helpful to do before, during, and after the next meeting to make it a success?

What kind of atmosphere should characterize the way the meeting is conducted?

What is the most important thing to achieve and to follow up on after the meeting?

Now imagine that the meeting went really well.

What happened at the meeting?

What did you do that helped make the meeting a success?

What did the employees do?

How did you reach decisions and conclusions?

What was the best thing that happened at the meeting?

The considerations and reflections outlined above should provide some input as to what we can do to prepare for, carry out, and anchor the meeting to make it a success. We need to keep these points in mind as we continue and as we prepare for the next meeting.

Now we need to sort out the formalities around the meeting. The formal framework of the meeting doesn't ensure a good meeting. But it does affect the meeting—perhaps more than we realize. Besides, the formalities allow us to chair the meeting without unnecessary "noise" or distractions in the form of uncertainty among the participants about why, how, where, and how long this meeting will take place. The most basic formalities to address are listed below.

The following formalities should be in place before the meeting:

A. Invitation

B. Agenda

C. Distribution of roles

D. Preparation questions for the participants

E. Venue and table arrangement

F. Mental preparation

A. Invitation

Depending on the circumstances and the type of meeting, the invitation to a meeting may include the following information:

- Who will participate
- Time frame and venue
- Meals/snacks/beverages
- Agenda
- Process description—the format of the meeting. Will it be based on information, involvement, activities, or other formats?
- Expectations, tasks, and/or preparation questions for the participants

Calling a meeting may be seen as a trivial formality that deserves only minimal attention. But the invitation is important. It sends the first signal about what the participants can expect from the meeting. As discussed in Part One, the expectations that people have or are faced with are vital. These expectations affect the outcome of the meeting.

The wording of an invitation should match the target group. We should remember the idea of suitable disturbances that was discussed in Chapter 6, but try to make the invitations more sparkling and colorful without losing the professional quality.

B. Agenda

The agenda outlines the theme and goal of the meeting. Like the invitation, an agenda can be formal or "sparkling" in wording depending on the target group. An agenda shouldn't include too many items. A point that involves dialogue requires more time than an item that requires standard information. We need to be realistic about what we can achieve in an hour or two. It's more satisfying to cover all the points at a comfortable pace and finish early than to rush through the points without covering them in depth.

An agenda can be presented as a classic bulleted list, which makes it easy to understand. Alternatives to the bulleted list include models that link more directly to the organization's goals, strategy, or other aspects. For example, an agenda can be presented like a balanced score card. The individual points are placed in the matrix to provide an overview of the relevance of the points for the department. Here is an example of that type of agenda.

Clients	Economy
• New clients • Trends within the X industry • Ways to serve clients even better and make sure they're happy	• What the figures are right now • How to increase earning per client • How to change incentives based on numbers to value
Business procedures	**Growth and learning**
• Ideas for the communication strategy • Implementing LEAN in the department • Ways to make collaboration with stakeholders flourish	• Department seminar in June • Education/training budget for next year • Those who will interview the most valued customers about their experience with the company

The agenda is general and indicative of the overall direction, and it is an important tool to help us stay on track during the meeting.

C. Distribution of roles

A clear distribution of roles is essential. It should be clear from the beginning of the meeting who does what and how it should be done. It can be difficult to keep track of the people who have asked to speak while taking notes and presenting the latest turnover figures. Therefore, the following roles should be delegated:

- **Chairperson.** The chairperson keeps track of who wants to speak and makes sure that everyone who wants to speak has the opportunity to do so. Thus, the chairperson also looks for small signs from people who may not say much or raise their hand but who are sometimes on the verge of doing so. In those cases, the chairperson could say, "Would you like to say something?"
- **Note-taker.** This task is often delegated to an assistant, but it can be rotated. Keep the minutes brief, simple, and clear to improve the probability that people will read them afterward. Consider whether just stating the decisions will suffice.
- **Timekeeper.** The timekeeper focuses on making sure that the agenda points are finished within the time allotted and lets the participants know if the schedule is slipping.
- **Energy-keeper.** Just as someone should be responsible for keeping time, someone should be tasked with keeping an eye on the energy level during the meeting. The energy-keeper calls for a break if one is needed (or asks, "Do we need a break? You all look like we do."), opens windows, fetches more coffee, and does other tasks. The energy-keeper's specific task is to check whether people are still on board and have the necessary energy and engagement in relation to the meeting—and to intervene if that doesn't seem to be the case.

D. Preparation questions for the participants

It can be helpful to ask the participants a few focused questions a few days or weeks prior to the meeting to initiate their reflection on the topic of the meeting. There are clear benefits to using this method to encourage the participants to get a head start before the meeting. For instance, the attendants will be better prepared because they've already spent time thinking about the topic. And when these questions are asked as a means of preparation, people begin to reflect. Thus, even before a course or a meeting, the participants may begin to think or act differently in certain situations. For example, questions such as "When do you think our teamwork is at its best? What happens in these situations? When did you last experience good teamwork with one of your colleagues?" will influence the employees and make them notice situations characterized by good teamwork. This awareness may cause them to be more curious than normal, which their colleagues will sense and respond to positively. A positive cycle has been set in motion even before the meeting takes place, simply due to some focused questions.

E. Venue and table arrangement

The next step is to consider where the meeting should take place and how to arrange the room for the meeting (if it takes place in a room at all). The meeting doesn't have to be held in the same room with the same table arrangement as is normally used. In fact, studies have demonstrated that meetings improve if the venue and the table arrangement are changed regularly (Axelrud, 2014). It's simply a matter of being able to keep the participants' attention. If people sit in the same seat in the same room for every meeting, they're more likely to stop paying attention. The participants tend to switch to "autopilot" and fall into a rhythm of not being focused; instead, their mind wanders. During a strengths-based meeting, nodding off should be impossible. Here the energy takes center stage because learning is maximized when energy is maximized. A simple way of boosting the energy level is by changing the meeting venue or the table arrangement. For example, we can do the following:

- Move the meeting to the corridor.
- Hold the meeting in the kitchen.
- Borrow a room somewhere else in the building.
- Hold the meeting outdoors, maybe even on a walk.
- Remove the tables from the room in which meetings are usually held.
- Sit somewhere else in the room (fixed seat assignments imply fixed thought patterns).
- Turn the horseshoe around.
- Hold the meeting standing up or alternate between sitting and standing.
- Rent or borrow a room outside your building.

Another good idea is to make sure the room is inviting and cozy. The conditions in the room have a significant impact on the mood. For example, we can put flowers or candles on the table or nicely lay out the table for coffee. These are the little things that make people feel welcome and thus more inclined to engage in an open and frank dialogue and put in the extra effort necessary to contribute to a value-creating meeting.

F. Mental preparation

As leaders, we must show up for the meeting prepared and focused. We know best how to prepare for meetings. We know what to read and deal with. What can be difficult is the mental preparation. It is about walking in the door and being fully and wholly present. It is about bringing our full attention to the meeting and leaving our concerns and other tasks at the door. If we fail to do this, our lack of focus will spread to the participants. They can tell that we're not fully present, and they too may begin to drift off in thought and action (Goleman, 2013). Therefore, we must lead the way and do our best to oversee the details before the meeting so that we can concentrate fully and be present at the meeting. If we can't be fully present, perhaps the meeting should be canceled. The following ideas help us walk in the door for a meeting with enhanced attention and focus.

TIPS TO STAY PRESENT AT MEETINGS

1. *Always* leave time between meetings. That gives you time to get from one place to another and to refocus mentally.
2. As the chairperson, you should be the first person to show up. That makes it easier to focus while appearing calm and well prepared.
3. Check the technical facilities and the design of the room ahead of time.
4. Use mental focusing tools, such as awareness training, to ensure that you're 100 percent present in the moment (see Chapter 2).

Here's an example that illustrates how we can prepare mentally before the meeting.

MENTAL PREPARATION FOR A MEETING

1. **Be aware and focus in a broader sense. Slow down.**
   - Get comfortable someplace where you can sit undisturbed for a few minutes. You may want to close your eyes. Begin by anchoring yourself in the moment without doing anything other than paying attention to yourself.
   - Ask yourself, "What am I experiencing right now? What thoughts are on my mind? What am I feeling? How does my body feel?"
   - Note and acknowledge the experiences even if they're unwanted.
2. **Be centered.**
   - Focus your attention fully on your breathing on every inhalation and exhalation. Do nothing for a full minute other than simply breathing and being present in the moment.
3. **Expand.**
   - Expand you awareness away from your breathing and ask yourself these questions: "How does my body feel now? What am I feeling? What thoughts do I have?"
4. **Be aware and focus. Prepare to chair the meeting. Ask yourself these questions:**
   - What is my goal for the meeting?
   - Who is going to be there, and what are my good experiences with them? What do I respect in each of them?
   - What have I previously done to make this type of meeting a success?
   - What should be the first thing I say or do at the start of the meeting?
   - When the meeting ends and it has been a success, what will have happened?
5. **Get up and get started.**

Now let's turn our attention to the actual meeting and learn what we can do to make it strengths-based.

DURING THE MEETING

Kick-off

There are many ways to kick off a meeting. Only our imagination sets the limit. We should do something different and surprise people. The main thing is to establish the focus of the meeting from the beginning and to maintain that focus throughout. If people are unfocused, we're wasting our time. We should make sure that people show up on time and that they're mentally present from the beginning—just as we've prepared mentally for the meeting.

If we want to use a method that sharpens the participants' focus and presence, we can consider using an awareness exercise as the meeting begins.

MEETING KICK-OFF WITH PARTICIPANTS' FULL ATTENTION AND AWARENESS

Introduce the exercise as a way of sharpening the participants' focus on the meeting that is about to begin.

- State the instructions below using a calm voice. Pause briefly between each instruction.
- Sit down or stand comfortably with your feet planted firmly on the ground. Keep your back straight and widen your chest to allow the air to pass in and out of your lungs freely.
- Close your eyes or focus on a point in front of you.
- Focus on your breathing and nothing else. Feel the breathing in your body. Feel the air passing in and out through your nostrils. Be fully and calmly present here and now with your breathing (short pause with silence).
- Turn your attention to the other participants in this meeting. What strengths and potentials do they have? What good experiences do you have from working with them? (short pause with silence)
- Turn your attention to the meeting that's about to start. What sort of a meeting is it? What do you hope the meeting will accomplish? How will you contribute? Take a minute to think about this before beginning (1 minute of silence).
- Turn your attention back to the room and begin the meeting.

This is unconventional and highly effective. Some people might be skeptical, but most are more focused after this exercise. All the questions in the exercise are strengths-based. They point toward a desired future or ask about the colleagues' strengths. The point is to generate constructive thoughts from the beginning. Even if the meeting deals with heavy and difficult challenges, it's important to keep an open and curious mind.

If the participants haven't met before, we can ask them to introduce themselves or each other. Following is a successful kick-off exercise. It's a presentation round that creates a good atmosphere and a good energy level. It can be time-consuming: between 10 and 30 minutes depending on the number of participants. But especially in meetings that are about starting up a team, a project, or other long-term partnerships, this is time well spent.

INTRODUCTION EXERCISE

Ask the participants to interview each other one-on-one for 6 minutes based on the questions below. Tell them ahead of time that they will be retelling each other's stories.

- Talk *briefly* about yourself (name, company, department, function, tasks, accomplishments in the past, or whatever else is relevant).
- What is the main contribution you can make to this team (this workplace, this department, etc.)?
- What are you most looking forward to in terms of (still) being part of this workplace/this team?

After the interview, the participants introduce each other to the whole group.

A meeting is usually more focused and productive when the participants know each other a little better and when there is an emphasis on each individual's strengths and possible positive contributions.

As leaders, we should try these exercises and find an unconventional way to kick off meetings. The main point is to set a good framework and create a focused atmosphere. Participants should not be allowed to look at their computers or phones, so we should ask them to put these aside. People often use the screens as a wall to hide behind, with the excuse that they are taking notes. (What they're really doing is reading their e-mail.) If the meeting has a note-keeper, no one needs to look at a screen. Instead, we can encourage them to look into each other's eyes.

The meeting itself

To make the meeting as constructive, forward-looking, and solution-oriented as possible, we can use the following four elements as a guide:

Remember the following elements during the meeting:

A. Promote positive emotions and a solution-oriented language throughout the meeting.

B. Find, amplify, and learn from successes.

C. Initiate constructive disturbances to focus everyone's attention.

D. Involve the participants.

A. Promote positive emotions and a solution-oriented language throughout the meeting.

If there is a good feeling in the meeting along with positive, solution-oriented people, it is much easier to create value and progress. It is a proven fact that once people have shared laughs and generally get along well, they're quicker to reach agreement about important results and what it takes to achieve them (Boyatzis et al., 2013; Fredrickson, 2009). As discussed earlier, research has demonstrated that people who are charged with positive emotions are more creative and innovative and better at finding alternative solutions to problems. A strengths-based meeting culture facilitates value-creating meetings.

The key to maintaining a strengths-focused direction throughout a meeting looks relatively simple on paper, but it can be hard to accomplish in practice. We must keep the axis model present in the back of our mind. The strength axis is often characterized by good energy, innovation, and responsibility. The problem axis is often characterized by negative emotions, unconstructive dialogues, and a lack of responsibility. To check where we are at any given time, we can listen to the language and the choice of words. Below are a few examples of what we can listen for.

Language on the problem axis	Language on the solution axis
The problem is that...	What we want to achieve is...
It's outrageous that they haven't...	We have to make it our responsibility to...
We have bad experiences with...	We have good experiences with...
We're too small to do that. (We're too big to do that.)	It's an advantage for us that...
We can't do that because...	We've done something similar before, and we can do it again.
If only we had...	What should we do in the future?
It seems overwhelming.	What small steps can we take as a start?
Management doesn't give us any information.	We'd like more information about ...
We don't normally...	Maybe we could try...

Both types of language are likely to be used at a meeting. It's natural for people to vent their frustrations as well as their hopes. Our task as managers is to facilitate and amplify the strengths-based and solution-oriented language. The best way to do that is to ask for specific examples and ask follow-up questions about the points and observations that people share. We can use affirmative statements and feedback, leading by example with our language.

We also should acknowledge and challenge the language on the problem axis. It's crucial, though, that we don't suppress problem language or negative language. If we hear a negative statement, it would be a mistake to say, "Let's put the negative stuff aside and focus on the positive." That would be perceived, correctly, as a lack of acknowledgment (that is, not seeing, hearing, or understanding) and make people lean back, cross their arms, and withdraw from the process.

However, an important element in the positive atmosphere at meetings is that the participants help maintain a solution- and strengths-focused approach. When and why is the energy level high? When and why is the energy low? The energy level can't be high all the time, but if it's been low for a long time, the reason may be that the language and the dialogue have become too problem-oriented. In that case, it's time to "break the curve"—to see the other side of the story. We might let the energy-keeper help in noticing and addressing excessively long problem-oriented and draining discussions.

B. Find, amplify, and learn from successes.

A direct way to create a high-energy level, momentum, and thus value in meetings is for the participants to spend time talking about shared successes. Many tend to dismiss their own positive results, as in "I'm just doing my job!" But there is a benefit in a person talking about what he or she did, individually or collectively as part of a team, in specific cases in which he or she did better or perhaps excelled. The participants can use questions about good experiences and successes to elaborate on the factors that led to the success. That turns it into shared learning and a shared source of inspiration at the meeting.

FIND AND AMPLIFY

It can be an advantage to do this in an interview format, one-on-one, or in small groups prior to the meeting.

- What progress have we made lately, in your opinion?
- What have you done that made a positive contribution to this? (Feel free to give specific examples.)
- What have your colleagues done that contributed to the progress?
- How has management contributed to the progress?
- What is the wisest or smartest thing a colleague or a manger did lately?
- What can you do to maintain and strengthen the positive trend in these areas?

In addition to generating learning, participants are almost guaranteed to have a positive experience at the meeting because of the examples that are brought up in this sort of dialogue. They should extract shared learning from it and identify small steps they can take together or individually to keep the trend moving in the right direction. They can use this exercise whether they are doing well or poorly. Even when things are at their worst, there are still examples of progress and positive exceptions. This knowledge shouldn't be lost in difficult times.

Participants should spend time at meetings learning about how they work when they achieve their best results. What was it that put them in the green zone on Monday? How did they land that assignment? Why did they take hardly any sick leave last year? Briefly, attendees should ask about it, investigate it, and be curious.

Another effective approach is to ask about the participants' best experiences in handling a situation such as a difficult one the group is currently experiencing. To do this, we as leaders can ask questions about what takes place when something happens in spite of the circumstances. These experiences can serve as inspiration and help the group identify things they can do to deal with the situation now as well as in the future.

Regardless of the magnitude of the problem, there is help and energy to be found in learning from past and/or other people's successes and in co-creating/envisioning a desired future state of the team, department, or organization.

As strengths-based leaders, we're constantly look for a good story that describes the positive trends in the organization. By asking about the best experiences, we're digging up the best stories. Of course, we also are looking to achieve resonance—an emotional rapport with the team or department. If the mood is predominantly negative, we probably shouldn't ask the members to focus on positive stories from the past, the key word being *probably*. This is where our sense of the situation comes to the test.

Now let's turn to the next element we can use when chairing strengths-based meetings: constructive disturbances aimed at sharpening everybody's attention.

C. Initiate constructive disturbances to focus everyone's attention.

Disturbances arouse attention. They make people sharpen their senses. The term *constructive disturbances* means that we should consider what we can use before, during, and after a meeting to make the meeting varied, exciting, interesting, strange, focused, and fun. Routine often leads to boredom, boredom implies a lack of focus, and a lack of focus means less value (Goleman, 2013). So we should look for every opportunity to vary the means we are using at meetings and create quirky disturbances (that is, be surprising without being contrived). We know best how to achieve that. It depends on who we are and who the participants are.

DURING THE MEETING, THE LEADER MIGHT USE THE FOLLOWING TO CREATE CONSTRUCTIVE DISTURBANCES:

- Music
- Color
- Quotes
- Flip charts instead of PowerPoint slides
- Video clips
- Physical activity
- Space outside the meeting room or outside the building
- Guests (many people outside the team/department would gladly share their positive experiences in a particular context)

Another way we can introduce a disturbance, an attention grabber, or a surprise is to whisper, to open windows, or to ask people to leave their computers outside the meeting room, turn off their phones, or switch places halfway through the meeting. There is nothing as draining as a three-hour meeting where attendees sit in the same seat across from someone who appears to be checking e-mail rather than paying attention to the meeting. That behavior drains people's energy and destroys their focus. If someone isn't paying attention, we should ask that person to leave. Doing so is also a potentially value-creating disturbance.

D. Involve the participants.

How much of the time do we speak in meetings with our team? Twenty percent of the time? More than 50 percent of the time? Ninety-nine percent of the time? How tightly do we manage the dialogue? How strong a focus do we have on involvement and the process compared with simply carrying on a monologue?

If we're serious about adopting a strengths-based leadership approach, involvement and a focus on process management/facilitation of meetings are essential elements. Of course, the way we involve people and manage the process during a meeting depends on what's happening at the meeting, what's being discussed, and what the purpose of the dialogue is. Most meetings contain different types of dialogue. The following illustration offers ideas about the degree of involvement and control that various types of meeting dialogue require.

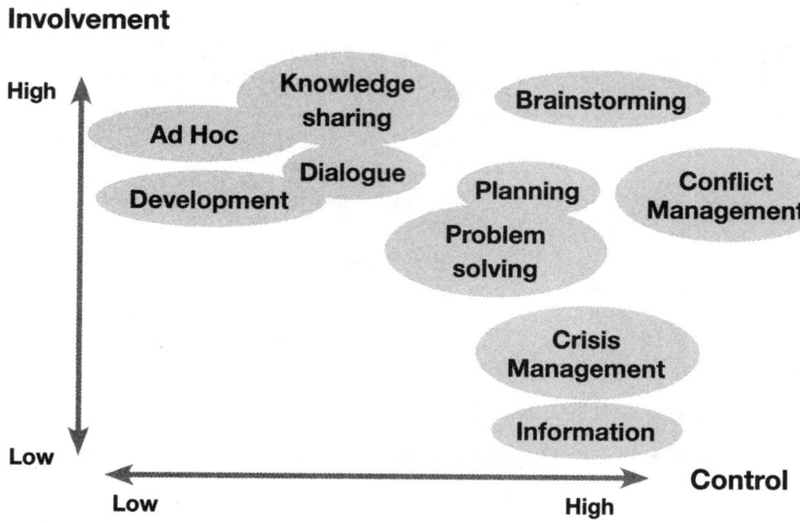

As illustrated above, in most meetings, we should try to involve the participants as much as possible. The key is to bring everyone's heart and mind into play.

The need for control is more complex. It can vary considerably from meeting to meeting. But generally, brainstorming, conflict management, crisis management, and information meetings call for a high degree of control. Brainstorming requires control to prevent the creative process from disintegrating into discussions about the merit of ideas. Conflict management necessitates control because it is necessary to keep the parties' communication and emotional outbursts on track and to ensure constructive dialogue. Crisis management requires a visible manager who leads the way. And with information, it is then necessary to control the time factor to keep the meeting from dragging on.

The degree of involvement, on the other hand, varies. In regard to brainstorming and conflict management, it's important to involve the participants because that produces the best solutions and ideas. With crisis management and information meetings, our input and indication of direction is essential. But we must ensure that participants are involved even if that involvement is limited. At the very least, we must remember to ask the participants whether they have questions.

To use involving techniques properly and timely, we need to hone our ability to notice what is required and helpful at any given moment. Timing and sense of the situation is crucial. We must be able to pick up on signals from the participants during the meeting while noticing our own thoughts and feelings. That requires us to switch off "autopilot" permanently so that we're fully aware and present in the moment. In an almost literal sense, we need an "eye in the sky" monitoring ourselves and the participants from above.

Below is a review some of the techniques we can use to involve the participants during the meeting.

> INVOLVING TECHNIQUES DURING A MEETING
>
> - Use time-outs and meta-reflection
> - Initiate one-on-one conversations
> - Have the participants break up into smaller groups
> - Use brainstorming

Use time-outs and meta-reflection

Chapter 6 briefly touched on the concept of time-outs. During a meeting, a time-out gives us an opportunity to engage in a dialogue about the meeting and have the participants talk about whether we talk about the right things. We ask ourselves: "Is the meeting creating value? Are we talking about the right topics?" A time-out is a good addition to our own reflections and hunches about whether the meeting is creating value and staying on track.

It's brave to call a time-out because we must be willing to change course if that's what the participants call for. Thus, if we call a time-out, we must have the ability and the courage to improvise and to involve the participants in deciding the direction of the meeting. On the other hand, the reward is substantial.

We get a chance to turn a trivial and slightly dull meeting into an energized and value-creating event, and we appear to be a flexible and effective chairperson. It gives us an opportunity to get everyone on board.

The method consists of pausing at some point during the meeting and asking for the participants' immediate feedback on questions such as the ones that follow.

TIME-OUT QUESTIONS (DIALOGUE ABOUT THE MEETING)

- How is the meeting going right now?
- What is on your mind right now?
- What have been the best parts so far?
- Are we talking about the main topics/the right topics?
- What are we aiming for right now (for example, an idea or a decision)?
- If we had only 10 minutes left, how could we make the best use of that time?
- On what issues do we need to reach an agreement?
- What is the most inspiring thing you have heard a colleague say in the meeting so far?
- How can we/the meeting sharpen the focus even more?

Initiate one-on-one conversations

Imagine that we've given a presentation about something and now, immediately after the presentation, we are asked whether there are any questions. We encounter a wall of silence and fear that no one has been paying attention. The energy is sucked out of the room. This is also known as "death by PowerPoint" (Sibbett, 2010; Axelrud, 2014).

There are at least four reasons people remain silent when they are asked a question such as this in a large assembly.

- It can be hard to be the person who breaks the silence.
- Some people have a hard time speaking in front of a group.
- The question is too general.
- The participants need some time to digest what they heard.

Instead of addressing the general group, we could ask the participants to reflect in pairs for a few minutes before we open the debate about our presentation in the larger group. That creates a safe space where the participants can determine whether their immediate response to the presentation is completely off the wall or whether someone else might be thinking the same thing or at least understands the point of view/reflection. By asking the pairs to discuss specific questions, we help the participants reflect on what they heard and relate to the points we raised. We're *not* giving them a chance to be distanced and indifferent, which is the purpose: to involve and activate the participants.

We can use reflection in pairs to address many different aspects (for example, the participants' thoughts about a particular topic, their input on the topic of the meeting, or their ideas about the next point on the agenda).

Reflection in pairs on themes and presentations at the meeting

"Face each other one-on-one. Briefly (2 to 4 minutes) discuss..."

When the pairs have had a few minutes to discuss, ask them what they talked about.

Ask the question of two pairs, three pairs, or all the pairs or only those who volunteer. That depends on the situation.

Most pairs will have an answer; after all, they did talk about something. But if a pair asks us to skip them, we should do so. We should consider whether it's worth the trouble to apply more pressure. Silence often means that a person has nothing new to contribute. It's valuable in itself that the two talked with each other, even if they don't want to share their discussion with the rest of the group.

We can introduce this exercise several times during a meeting. We also may introduce it as a *walk & talk*, where we set aside more time for a walk. We also should consider a *walk & think,* which is good way for the more introverted and reflective people to think things through before they return with the input/ideas they reached in their individual reflection process.

Have the participants break up into smaller groups

If we have a little more time and want a slightly more in-depth discussion, an old-fashioned group activity still has merit as an involving method. We should keep the group activity relatively brief, however (15 to 45 minutes). We should ask specific questions to keep the dialogue on track and consider allowing people to go outside or at least leave the room. We should make the meeting brief and concise, asking participants to cut to the bone unless the details are crucial for the remainder of the process or for the decision.

The procedure is simple. We should do the following:

- Frame some questions for the groups to work on.
- Ask the groups to return with a flip chart, a PowerPoint presentation, a drawing, or something else that illustrates and summarizes what they discussed and the result they reached.

- When the groups return, ask them to take turns presenting their discussions. We can skip this or keep it brief if time is an issue.

Use brainstorming

If a meeting requires the attendees to develop ideas, a guided brainstorming session may be a good method. A good brainstorming session is characterized by the following points:

GUIDELINES FOR BRAINSTORMING

1. Set aside your prejudice and experiences.
2. Encourage wild ideas. Do not shoot down any ideas. Say yes.
3. Build and expand on other people's ideas.
4. Stay focused on the topic.
5. Offer one idea at a time.
6. Be visual.
7. Remember that quantity rules. It's better to have many crazy ideas than a few dull ones.

A brainstorming session should be tightly managed to avoid any discussion of the ideas during the brainstorming. In a brainstorming process, the ideas are not up for discussion. Discussing the merits of an idea is a kiss of death to creative thinking. The process should flow freely without interruption. The group can assess the ideas later.

A guided brainstorming session can be based on the following simple script:

GUIDED BRAINSTORMING PROCESS

- Define the theme or the challenge for which you need to come up with ideas and the time frame for the brainstorming process.
- Have a flip chart, markers, and sticky notes handy.
- Instruct the participants on the process and the seven brainstorming guidelines listed previously.
- Ask each participant to provide one idea, write it on a sticky note, and put it on the flip chart.
- Don't allow anyone to block an idea at this stage. Say "yes" to all the ideas, build on them, and think out of the box.
- When the session is over, sort the ideas into themes and proceed from there.

Here's a different approach to brainstorming. The participants reflect on their own for 10 minutes, write down their wild ideas on sticky note notes, and place them on the flip chart. The whole group then reviews the ideas. The advantage of this approach is that a person can think for himself or herself, making introverts happy. The advantage of taking turns is that one person's idea might spring from something another person said. Both approaches are fine, and the guidelines apply in either case.

We can now choose whether to contribute to the brainstorming process by adding our own ideas. The advantage of not contributing is that we can focus on the process. The advantage of contributing is that we can help set the standard for how wild, crazy, or ambitious the ideas can be (as long as we don't drag the process down by not being ambitious enough).

The goal of this section was to provide inspiration to experiment with different ways of involving the participants in meetings and thus getting everyone on board. We need to find our own style and do it in a way that is appropriate for the organization. But we must not let ourselves be held back by our assumptions about what is permissible at the meetings in our organization. We must break the habit. Ultimately, it is up to us to try new things. Involvement is welcomed.

Regardless of how good a job we did with the invitation, the preparations, the kick-off, the release of positive emotions, and involvement in connection with the meeting, when we chair a meeting, we're responsible for bringing the meeting to an end on time and with the necessary decisions in place. The next section discusses the issue of closing meetings and the movement toward decisions and action.

AT THE CLOSE OF THE MEETING

Often the main challenge with regard to a meeting occurs when ideas and thoughts have become decisions. When it's time to conclude the meeting and delegate responsibility, things get serious. At that point, everyone has a stake in changing the state of affairs. And once it comes down to distributing tasks and launching initiatives, the problem is that everybody already has a full schedule. There are no shortcuts or any conclusive answers about how to close a meeting well. Some is warranted, however. But first, we reflect on the following:

REFLECTION

Think of a meeting in which you took part that ended with clear and transparent decisions and/or action points that were actually implemented.

What did the chairperson do that helped close the meeting in a good way?

What methods did the chairperson use during the closing stage of the meeting?

What contributions did the participants make?

What other elements in the setup and framework of the meeting played a positive role?

One of the most important aspects of our role as managers is to indicate toward the end of the meeting that we're moving toward closure—the first suggestion of what it takes to close a meeting well.

Indicating the shift from dialogue to concluding decisions/agreements

The shift from dialogue to concluding decisions/agreements is crucial. Often the way in which we handle this shift determines whether the meeting was successful.

We can let the group know it's time to make decisions or involve the employees in choosing the time, considering their energy level and readiness to close the discussion. Not every meeting has to end with concluding decisions/agreements, but it should be clear to everyone in attendance whether a decision is/was the goal and that if nothing is concluded now, the point at which something will be concluded (if a conclusion is needed). Conditions that are necessary for any decision to be carried out are clarity and a common understanding of what was decided.

When the agreements are in place, our responsibility is to close the meeting in a good way. We should thank the participants for their contributions, their energy, and their involvement. If possible, we should end the meeting early. That gives a feeling of good process management and of things having been wrapped up in a calm manner.

The last topic in this chapter briefly touches on thoughts about following up on and implementing the things that were agreed upon and decided at the meeting.

AFTER THE MEETING—FOLLOW-UP AND IMPLEMENTATION

The following scenario is a familiar one: The chairperson had a great meeting with a good energy level and good agreements. Unfortunately, after the meeting, few of the initiatives were carried out. When the topic is brought up, people look at the floor, trying to come up with excuses as to why their initiative hasn't been completed.

But here is the opposite scenario.

REFLECTION

Think of an example where agreements from a meeting were carried out and initiatives were implemented as planned.

- *How do you explain the fact that the agreements were implemented?*
- *What motivated the participants to take action?*
- *What did the chairperson do at the meeting to ensure that the agreements would be implemented?*
- *What did the chairperson do after the meeting that had a good effect?*
- *What other factors were relevant?*

We may have ideas for how to anchor and ensure the implementation of decisions. For additional inspiration, more ideas follow. Strengths-based tools for follow-up are based on the assumption that everyone is doing his or her best and is generally happy to take action and assume responsibility for the long term. If someone hasn't taken action, he or she probably has a good reason. That good reason may be that the person did the opposite of the following recommendations:

> **FIVE PIECES OF ADVICE FOR ANCHORING MEETINGS**
>
> A. Take small steps.
>
> B. Send a follow-up e-mail.
>
> C. Establish a buddy system and networks.
>
> D. Post agreements as reminders where people can see them.
>
> E. Use regular follow-up.

A. Take small steps

In their everyday work, most people are busy and focus quickly shifts from an exciting development project to mundane tasks. Therefore, there can be a real advantage in identifying small steps that will take someone in the right direction rather than aiming for grand, impressive plans that don't make it out of the desk drawer. There are many advantages to identifying small, clear steps before the end of the meeting.

- Small steps produce quick and clear effects. It's satisfying when someone can check off a contribution that makes a difference in a larger context. If it takes six months or a year before someone can do that, the action plan is too broad.
- Small steps are manageable. As an old proverb says:

  Any journey, large or small, begins with the first step.

- Sometimes it's possible to take small steps before the meeting is over, called "Do it now." We ask the participants to do something at the meeting. Why wait before calling a client if that phone call can be made right now? Why agree to e-mail each other tomorrow to arrange a meeting if the group can pick a time right now?

By taking small steps *at the meeting*, the participants can walk away with the feeling that they've already begun. That makes it much easier to continue.

B. Send a follow-up e-mail

A follow-up e-mail can be a good way to maintain the focus and momentum of a productive meeting. The e-mail can contain the following elements:

- Minutes of the meeting
- A greeting, thanking people for a good and productive meeting

- Acknowledgment of the participants' efforts
- Thoughts about your benefits or the common benefits of the meeting
- Questions for the participants' consideration
- Pictures, quotes, or anything else referring to the themes discussed at the meeting

C. Establish a buddy system and networks

It can be helpful to establish a buddy system or a network among the colleagues before they leave the meeting. This gives the colleagues an opportunity to help each other stay focused on implementing the initiatives. Having a buddy or a network obliges, and it's nice to have someone with whom they can talk things over.

D. Post agreements as reminders where people can see them

A simple way of reminding each other of agreements and decisions on a daily basis is to post them somewhere visible in the office. This may be in the form of a poster in the kitchen, a funny little note stuck on the mirror in the restroom, or a reminder that pops up on the intranet. Our imagination is the only limit; the idea is to remind ourselves and others regularly what everyone agreed to do.

E. Use regular follow-up

Regular follow-up gives the participants help to move on, to clear obstacles, or to provide whatever else is needed to make sure the agreements are implemented. We also can delegate the task of reminding people of their responsibilities and thus receive reminders ourselves from time to time. Of course, people are responsible for doing what they need/promised to do. On the other hand, it can be easier to get things done if there is regular follow-up on the tasks at hand.

CLOSING REMARKS

A meeting is a forum where people in the organization can bring their strengths into play, coordinate their efforts with each other, and find the inspiration and energy to act. The chapter closes with a story from a leader who embraced some of the ideas from this chapter and didn't just think about them, but lived them.

CASE

For the last team meeting of the year, which took place in a hectic period in December, I thought we ought to pause and take a positive breather together. So I did the following:

The setting:

- We met in a large meeting room where the tables had been removed and the chairs were placed in a circle to create a shared, open space.
- The lights were out, and battery-driven tea candles had been placed on the floor.
- Around the candles, I had placed cookies.
- In the background, a computer was playing music.

The meeting:

The employees came in and sat down, somewhat startled but excited, and the atmosphere was good from the start.

I wanted the meeting to have an exclusively positive approach, with the end of the year in mind. So I planned to have 5 to 10 minutes of silence while everyone used the small slips of paper that had been handed out to write down what went well in the year that passed and what would be cool to focus on in the year to come.

After a few minutes with some shushing from me, everybody immersed themselves in the task, with the music in the background, the dimmed lights, and some sweet treats—a powerful experience; I also completed the task.

When everyone was finished, I asked one person to go first and said that afterward that person had to pick the next speaker—so I could lean back and be present and focus on the statements the employees were offering.

Finally, the employees remarked that I had not been picked. I was then asked to make my statements. I thanked everybody for their participation and their input and thanked them for their effort this year. I closed by handing out postcards with personalized greetings to all 16 team members.

All in all, it was an amazing meeting, as many remarked in addition to offering praise for the postcard.

Conclusion: Thinking a little differently works. Just do it!

It's courageous for a leader to shake up the framework of the team meeting for the benefit of all the participants. Some people think about doing it. Others do it!

9

STRENGTHS-TRAINING YOUR TEAM

CONTENTS

Putting together and developing a strong team is one of the primary tasks of leaders. In this context, a strong team is defined as follows:

> *A strong team consists of a limited number of people (five to nine) who have complementary strengths and a common foundation and who cooperate with dedication toward a common goal and the creation of meaningful results for which all the team members take considerable responsibility.*

Tom Rath and Barry Conchie (2008) describe a strong team as the "collective talent of the team." A strong team can achieve more than the sum of the individual members' achievements. The team has more latitude in operational decision making than does the individual employee. In a strong team, all the members use their strengths most of the time. The challenge is to coordinate direction, decisions, and actions to make sure the team pulls in the same direction and covers for each other's weaknesses.

To be identified as a team, certain fundamental issues need to be in place. Based on the work of Katzenbach and Smith (1993, 2005) and French and Bell (1995), these issues are summarized next.

SIX FUNDAMENTAL COMPONENTS OF A TEAM

1. **Small number:** The team must be small enough that a manager has a sense of all the members. Typically, a team consist of five to nine people and is most efficient with six to eight people.
2. **Complementary strengths, skills, and personality types:** There should be sufficient diversity within the team in terms of complementary strengths, skills, and personality types. The strength of the team should be bigger than the sum of its parts because of these complementary elements.

(continued on next page)

SIX FUNDAMENTAL COMPONENTS OF A TEAM (CONTINUED)

3. **Meaningful purpose:** The team should have a common, defined purpose that goes deeper than performance goals.
4. **Specific goals:** The team must work toward common goals that are simple, specific, and measurable. There must be consensus about the goals, which can be pressure-tested by checking that everybody talks about them in the same terms.
5. **A clear approach to the task:** All team members must know what the approach is to solving the task and what is expected of each of them in solving the task. The values and methods that underlie the approach in addition to well-defined cooperation terms should be transparent.
6. **Reliability, discipline, responsibility, and a degree of "we feeling":** The team members should assume a shared responsibility for the purpose, the goals, and each other's well-being and development, and they should work in a goal-oriented and disciplined manner. The team members must be reliable and loyal, and the individual members are expected to do what has been agreed upon and to comply with norms and regulations. The distinction between individual responsibility and team responsibility should be clear and transparent. The "we feeling" and the joy of accomplishing something together should be a top priority.

This chapter introduces some basic theory about team development and discusses what characterizes strong teams. It then addresses how we as strengths-based leaders can put together and strengths-train our teams—the team we might be leading/supervising right now and any team of which we are members. We'll offer inspiration for putting together and strengths-training a team from scratch and/or for learning how to restructure or bring out the best in the members who are already on the team. We'll also discuss what we can do as leaders in a specific step-by-step approach to help our teams achieve a level of high performance.

To be and qualify as a high-performance team, the team must possess and promote the components mentioned in the preceding box. If any of these components are missing or if they're present only to a limited degree (for example, the degree of "we feeling"), we're probably dealing with a working group, not a team.

FROM WORKING GROUP TO HIGH-PERFORMANCE TEAM

In 1993, Jon R. Katzenbach and Douglas K. Smith (1993) presented the following model. It describes the development from being a mere working group to being a full-blown high-performance team.

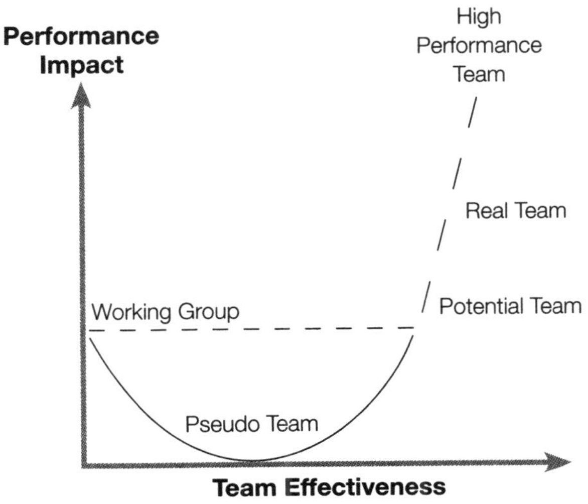

Team Development Curve

A **working group** is a unit without common performance goals. Its internal cooperation works fine, and it exchanges information and methods to enable the individual members to complete their tasks. But it lacks a common goal for which everyone feels a shared responsibility. The working group can improve its performance, but its potential is limited because the individuals work on their tasks separately.

A **pseudo-team** is the weakest of all the units. There may be a document defining common goals and tasks, but the members lack the skills and the willingness to pursue them. They call themselves a team but do not possess any of the characteristics that define a team. The team delivers less value to the organization than the working group because although the individual members have meaningful interactions with their colleagues, everybody pursues his or her own goals and motives without being open and honest about it.

A **potential team** is characterized as a unit that has common goals and tasks and puts in a common effort to achieve its goals. However, it often lacks greater clarity about specific values, goals, tasks, and a teamwork approach. A working group that wants to redefine its cooperation to become a team must go through this phase before its performance can exceed its capacity as a working group.

An **actual team** is the basic form of team. It's a unit where the members have complementary skills and strengths and are committed to a common purpose, goal, and task approach. The team feels a common responsibility for managing the tasks and the teamwork. Here the performance can become markedly better than in the working group.

Finally, the **high-performance team** has all the hallmarks of an actual team. In addition, the team members have a strong commitment to everyone's personal growth and success. This commitment permeates the team. The team members use their strengths most of the time and make up for each other's weaknesses, rendering these weaknesses insignificant. A high-performance team exceeds expectations on every parameter; thus, the team can be a role model for other teams both inside and outside the organization. Here the whole is clearly greater than the sum of its parts.

Gallup studies of management teams support Katzenbach and Smith's definition of a high-performance team in some areas and supplement it in others. Rath and Conchie (2008) summarize the characteristics that strong teams have in common according to the Gallup study.

CHARACTERISTICS OF STRONG TEAMS

1. **Conflict does not destroy strong teams because strong teams focus on results:** There can be a heated debate about important issues, provided the team members don't make the debate personal. There's a sense that team members are on the same side, regardless of differences in opinion.
2. **Strong teams prioritize what's best for the organization and then move forward:** The team keeps the larger common goal in view. The team members put the organization's needs and goals above their own. The team members help each other.
3. **Members of strong teams are as committed to their personal lives as they are to their work:** Most of the surveyed managers in strong teams believed that they had a good balance between their work life and their personal life.
4. **Strong teams embrace diversity:** According to the authors, the key is to find individuals who demonstrate a balance of strengths and to put together a team with a high degree of diversity in terms of strengths, personality, gender, age, ethnic background, etc. The team members in the strong teams look for each other's strengths rather than each other's flaws and shortcomings.
5. **Strong teams are talent magnets:** This is the team of which everybody wants to be a part. The most ambitious people in the survey sought the challenge of being part of a top-notch team with other talented people because they considered it stimulating and developing.

REFLECTION

Are the six fundamental components of a team present in your team (or working group)? If so, to what degree?

Where would you place your team on the performance curve? Are you in a working group or a high-performance team?

Is your team a strong team?

What can you see in your team now that would be useful to strengthen and promote?

THE STRONG TEAM

As previously described, Buckingham and Gallup have used statistical data to determine what separates high-achieving teams from mediocre or bad teams/working groups (Buckingham, 2007). The Gallup researchers were puzzled by the fact that teams that were working under the same conditions could have such marked differences in performance. A closer examination revealed the following:

The best teams consist of individuals who bring their strengths into play as much as possible and whose strengths supplement each other.

As discussed earlier, another study found that only 17 percent of the surveyed team members used their strengths most of the time. What a waste!

How many of our employees bring their strengths into play most of the time? What if we as leaders could enable them to do that? Imagine the results they could achieve together! This requires that we highlight the employees' strengths and help them discuss strengths and weaknesses of the team. The following offers a guide to this form of dialogue and then turns to the issue of what is expected of us as leaders if we want to strengths-train our team further.

GUIDE TO A DIALOGUE WITHIN THE TEAM ABOUT STRENGTHS AND WEAKNESSES

1. Ask the employees to chart their own strengths and weaknesses over a two-week period (as described in Part One of the book) and to do a strengths test.
2. Set aside time for the team to share their strengths and weaknesses with each other.

(continued on next page)

GUIDE TO A DIALOGUE WITHIN THE TEAM ABOUT STRENGTHS AND WEAKNESSES (CONTINUED)

3. Make an overview of each member's top three strengths and weaknesses and give it to everyone on the team.
4. Ask each team member to tell a story about a situation in which he or she brought one of his or her strengths into play. Let the other team members express whether they see this as a strength in the person.
5. Ask each team member to talk about a specific situation in which he or she was drained of energy, which meant that the team member was using one of his or her weaknesses. Let the other team members express whether this situation might be energizing for them and whether they would be willing to take over the task that the other person finds draining. If not, use the approach described under point 7.
6. Are there tasks or situations that everybody loves to do? How can you as a team build a reputation that lets you solve more of those tasks or be in those situations more often?
7. Are there tasks or situations that everybody finds draining? In that case, draw inspiration from the CARE model and explore whether you can compensate, ally with others (outsource perhaps), take a different view of the task, or give it up entirely. Would anyone notice?

The life stages and development of the strong team

In 1965, Bruce Tuckman presented a model for the development stages of a team. Tuckman based his model and sequential theory on studies of teams in various contexts. He argued that these stages were necessary and natural in the development of any team. Many leaders have found his model a great source of inspiration, and countless studies have validated the model and found that it offers a summary of the development that a team normally undergoes (West, 2004; Katzenbach et al., 2005). So even though the model is 50 years old, it still holds knowledge and insight for anyone who wants to understand what takes place in a team.

Tuckman's model involves five stages (the fifth was added in 1977).

TUCKMAN'S MODEL OF THE DEVELOPMENT STAGES OF A TEAM

- Forming
- Storming
- Norming
- Performing
- Adjourning/transforming

As indicated by the name, the **forming** stage is when the team is formed. The team meets and initiates a collaboration. There is a clarification of tasks and roles, and the actual work of carrying out the tasks begins. The team members generally have a strong focus on their roles and act independently. People generally behave in a polite and low-key way. People try to get to know each other and to determine what is acceptable behavior on this team. During this stage, experienced team members are often trying to influence the culture and tone of the team. The tasks are being done, but the team has not yet achieved top performance, as there is a strong focus on members getting to know each other and to understand the tasks.

The **storming** stage is when the members' diversity can create conflicts. Different ideas, opinions, personalities, and working style may be problematic but also a source of energy and spirit. Dialogue takes place regarding wishes and expectations about management style and cooperation and about the content and approach to the tasks. There is a big difference in the amount of time the team spends in this stage. Some teams spend a short amount of time in this stage, whereas others don't move past it. Due to disagreements, this stage may be troublesome to some people. But it is a necessary stage, as this is where the team members get to know each other. The team manager's primary task is to bring the team through this stage by instituting a culture of open and constructive dialogue and by emphasizing the importance of bringing different opinions and ideas to the table.

The **norming** stage is when the team roles fall into place. The members adjust to each other's personalities and habits. A consensus begins to emerge about the team's values, guidelines, methods, and professional conduct. A mutual trust has been established, which builds a sense of security, particularly important when the team must deal with disagreement. In the best teams, the knowledge of each other's strengths begins to bear fruit and tasks and responsibilities flow to those members who have the particular strengths, especially if the issue is discussed on an ongoing basis. The team begins to be more efficient, and performance goes up. If disagreement grows too pronounced, creativity and innovation (and hence development) suffer; however, this is why it is important to take advantage of the team's diversity.

The **performing** stage is the period in the team's life when everything runs smoothly, both in terms of the task and the relationship among the team members. The team members rely on each other in the sense that the team handles its tasks better than the individual members could have done on their own. The whole is greater than the sum of its parts. Motivation is high, and the goal of the team members is to create something together. Disagreements and differences are used constructively in the development of tasks and cooperation, and everybody uses his or her strengths.

With the performing stage, the team has reached its peak. Most teams go back and forth between the stages. A conflict or a new team manager can quickly bring a team back to the forming or storming stage. Long-term teams often repeat the life cycle stages.

Adjourning/transforming. In 1977, Tuckman and his coauthor Mary Ann Jensen added a fifth stage to the model. At this stage, the team either disbands or is transformed into a new team. This may occur because a task has been completed, as is typically the case with project teams, or it may occur in connection with restructuring or other events where the team breaks up, is merged with other teams, or is otherwise reshaped. This stage can be threatening or anxiety-provoking for an individual. But it also can be seen as an exciting journey toward new destinations surrounded by new people. In any case, it is important that the leader and the organization take this separation stage seriously and mark a shift by saying good-bye to the old and welcoming the new.

The figure below illustrates how team performance typically develops over the different stages.

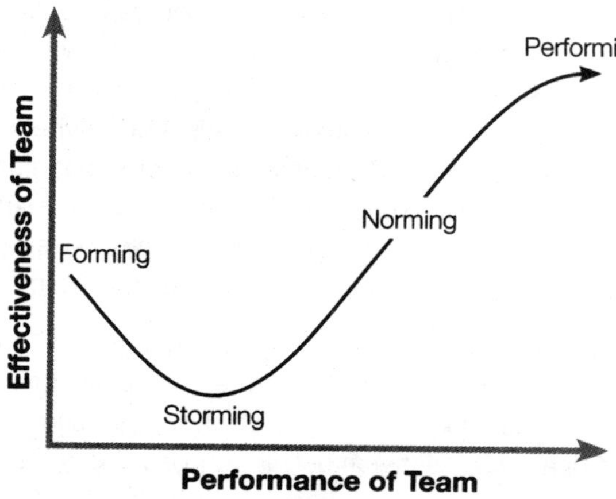

Tuckman's Team and Group Development Model

The storming stage often leads to a drop in the performance curve, as a great deal of energy is directed at the discussions that take place before the norming stage is in place. On the other hand, well-managed storming and norming stages can form the basis for creating a high-performance team for the long term.

There is a striking similarity between the team performance curve from Katzenberg and Smith and the performance curve in Tuckman's stage model. It's possible to draw a line between the two, illustrating that a group that is working toward becoming a high-performance team may have to go through a stage where its performance drops because it needs to devote time and energy to build the foundation for the strong team. However, Katzenberg and Smith include a dotted line from working group to potential team to indicate that the path may be direct if the team members *choose* to work on becoming a team. And they describe it precisely as a choice. Do the team members want to choose to focus on increasing the efficiency of their group with the limited potential that lies in being a working group? Or do they want to take a chance and work toward becoming a team with the possibilities this entails?

REFLECTION

Do you recognize some of the stages from the time with your current team?

How have you worked as a manger in the different stages?

In what stage is your team right now? What indicators tell you that?

Below is a review of the possibilities that can be achieved when we work as strengths-based leaders in the different stages of our team.

GUIDE TO STRENGTHS-BASED LEADERSHIP IN THE LIFE STAGES OF A TEAM	
Forming	• You have an active role in securing a good start. Bring the team together often. Speak, ask, and listen. • Be clear in your communication about the team's goals, tasks, and role in the organization. Spend time on both the big picture and the details. Talk about roles, strengths, and preferences. • Set the course and involve everybody as much as possible. • Focus on achieving results in relation to the goals. • Help the members to get to know each other. You can use one of the test and type indicator tools mentioned later in the chapter to give people insight into each other's preferences, strengths, and weaknesses, but include informal social activities as well. • Ask everybody to keep a strengths journal and then have dialogues about strengths and weaknesses to clarify what each team member is passionate about and what he or she finds draining. • Take the time to clarify expectations about the teamwork, roles, and ground rules. • Be aware that the individual team member is focused on his or her own tasks, goals, and roles. • Spend time on team-building activities. *(continued on next page)*

Storming *(continued)*	• Use your presence and sense of the situation to notice moods and signals. • Be visible and make yourself available. • Set the course, make the necessary decisions, and involve everybody. • Do what you can to ensure that tasks, roles, and responsibilities are distributed in a way that is fair to everyone. • Discuss values, guidelines, agreements, tasks, and methods. • Have conversations and meetings on an ongoing basis. Ask the team members individually and as a group how things are going. • Deal with conflicts as soon as you become aware of them. • Continue to underscore the importance of seeing diversity as a way to creating value. • Be the culture you wish to see: Be open and solution-oriented in your approach and in your language.
Norming	• Withdraw more, but continue to be visible and to make yourself available if anyone needs you. • Continue to focus on diversity and bring the strengths into play even more. • Offer specific feedback on achieved results. Learn from the successes together. • Continue to focus on creativity, ideas, and innovation. • Raise the bar and find new goals.
Performing	• Find more inspiration for this stage in the section "Becoming a High-Performance Team."
Adjourning/ Transforming	• Know that your actions depend on whether the team members experience the transformation as exciting or threatening. Often it will be a mix. • Make the process meaningful by placing it in a larger organizational context. • Provide information about formal, informal, and practical details that might lead to concern or doubt. • Mark the change with an official act (for example, a meeting at which you say good-bye to the old and/or welcome the new). • Pay attention to each team member's reactions and ask how the person is doing. • Share your own concerns and thoughts in connection with the change. • Ask each team member about his or her thoughts and possible role in connection with the change.

Throughout the process, we as leaders should remain authentic, focused, and self-aware in our leadership approach. This requires that we have an eye for risks, development potentials, and individual strengths in the complex life cycle of a team.

The following discussion focuses on the specific steps we can take as leaders to help our team become high performing. We begin by considering the makeup of the team.

BUILDING A STRONG, COHESIVE TEAM

Putting together and leading a team is a challenge. The strengths-based approach to putting together a strong team places priority on introducing diversity to the team to make sure different strengths and personality types are represented. That renders the team members' weaknesses irrelevant or less relevant because one colleague will have a strength when someone else has a weakness.

Diversity and complementary strengths

Tintin and Captain Haddock. Laurel and Hardy. Calvin and Hobbes. What makes these partnerships so fascinating that they hold people's interest for decades? The answer is diversity. The legendary stockbroker and multibillionaire Warren Buffet once said that he makes his best decisions with his long-standing business partner Charlie Munger. Buffet is an enthusiastic yea-sayer; Munger is a skeptical nay-sayer. Together they have formed a strong team for decades due to, not despite, their differences (Wagner & Muller, 2009).

What sets individuals apart is a mix of strengths and weaknesses, personal preferences, style, and temperament. A strong team should be made up of people with different strengths, competencies, and personalities so that they carry out their task well.

One person doesn't have all the strengths and competencies that are necessary to carry out a task or all the personal styles (personalities) that are necessary to communicate both internally and externally with different people and via different media. We as leaders must accept that every individual has one or two of the necessary strengths and competencies as well as a unique personality. We also must make sure that the team members cover for each other's weaknesses. That lets an individual team member focus on bringing his or her strengths into play without having to worry about learning something that he or she is not passionate about or has the abilities or personality for. That's what is unique about teams—the individual's weaknesses become insignificant because other team members have their strengths to offset the individual's weaknesses. In a team that has the right makeup, a member can rest assured that others will compensate for his or her weakness with their strengths and competencies.

In a strong team, the whole becomes stronger than the sum of its parts because the strengths complement each other. This renders the individual's weaknesses insignificant.

Thus, to maximize synergy, we should compose and develop a team based on the idea of strength through diversity. We can ensure diversity by hiring people from different backgrounds (profession, ethnicity, culture, and country), gender, personality style, and strengths. Because this book is about leading from a strengths-based perspective, it will take a closer look at the latter.

Rath and Conchie (2008) describe how they've discovered, through years of studies, that four domains of complementary strengths are represented in high-performance teams. Therefore, we should make sure that at least these four strengths are present when we form a team. The four strengths in question are as follows:

Four strengths that often lead to high performance when they're present simultaneously in a team

- Execution
- Influence
- Relationship building
- Strategic thinking

Managers rarely search deliberately for people who are the best addition to the strengths that are already present on a team. Typically, managers look for people with specific professional qualifications rather than people who would create a more balanced team in the form of complementary strengths.

REFLECTION

Have you ever looked for a colleague or an employee whose primary qualification would build stronger relations among the members on your team, considering their professional qualifications only secondarily?

Have you ever looked for a team member who would be good at influencing the outside world in support of your team's ideas (and maybe not much else)?

Have you ever looked deliberately for a colleague or an employee who was different from you? Why or why not?

Can we compose a perfect team? No, but we can put together a team that has an interesting and challenging element of diversity. We can do our best to avoid falling into the trap that many managers fall into, which is to look for employees who resemble us and the existing team. This is a normal human inclination: to surround ourselves with people who share our views and display a similar behavior and mind-set. We probably do this to avoid conflicts and to simplify the working process. (After all, it can become tiresome to discuss everything all the time.) But as was discussed earlier, development can take place only if there is a suitable disturbance. Differences provide a disturbance and add fresh, new perspectives—they generate development and enable high performance; they are the cornerstone of a strong team.

We should take this into consideration when we have to recruit new team members or compose or restructure a team. We should build the best ship with the tools and materials that are available.

The next task is to launch the ship and set its course. And only once the ship is launched will we find out what sort of ship we built. What sections are strong and robust? Where are the leaks? What drives the ship forward? How is it steered? What maintenance and improvements does it require? And in what sort of waters does it travel best? The following discussion takes a closer look at what it takes to create a high-performance team.

BECOMING A HIGH-PERFORMANCE TEAM

A high-performance team is more than just a group of people brought together around a task. It's a team that achieves results faster and better than the individual members would have done on their own.

Following are some of the most importance ingredients we as leaders will need to build a high-performance team.

INGREDIENTS THAT CAN LEAD TO HIGH PERFORMANCE

- The individual members know their strengths and weaknesses and are able to bring their strengths into play most of the time.
- The members have a profound interest in each other's growth and development.
- The mood of the team is permeated by passionate commitment and a sense of shared ownership in regard to completing the tasks and achieving the goals.
- The goals are desirable and attainable.
- There is a high degree of appreciative feedback and exploratory and curious questions within the team as well as positive statements about the project and the other team members (in a ratio of 3:1).
- There is a strong "we-feeling" and a strong sense of reward and satisfaction from the achievement of common results.

(continued on next page)

INGREDIENTS THAT CAN LEAD TO HIGH PERFORMANCE (CONTINUED)

- The individual team members display reliable, responsible, and loyal behavior.
- There are many examples of innovative approaches and experimentation within the team based on a culture of tolerance of first-time mistakes.
- There is a high degree of openness, respect, and affection among the team members.
- The primary focus is on amplifying successes, building on and learning from the things that already work well, and talking about what will/can work in the future, secondary to learning from mistakes and taking precautions not to repeat them in the future.

The following discussion provides inspiration for using strengths-based methods in a step-by-step process to help current teams become high performers.

Team development is a long and demanding process that requires persistence. If we encounter resistance, we should listen to it and welcome it as an expression of healthy skepticism. We should ask questions about the resistance and uncover the underlying wish.

Strengths-based steps to go from a working group to a high-performance team

Level 1. From working group to a potential team

- **Clear communication and optimism:** Make it clear that this is, in your opinion, a working group more than a team. Explain that you would like the group to develop and that this is the beginning of a journey toward high performance. Talk about the potential rewards. Create optimism without making unrealistic promises. You should express a sense of realistic optimism that can spread to the employees. This optimism is the oil that greases the engine when the group begins to gear up. It ensures that you and the employees remain open-minded, curious, and creative throughout the process. Once the optimism is present, the other points are easier to deal with.

- **Create a burning desire:** Often the journey begins from a burning platform, a huge problem that forces the members of the group to "pull themselves together," or a restructuring in the organization. Using the break-the-curve tool, you can help frame a dream, a burning desire that all members of the group can help articulate and about which they can feel passionate striving for.

(continued on next page)

Level 1. From working group to a potential team (continued)

- **Sort out team basics:** These are the purpose, goals, tasks, roles, responsibility, and work methods and approaches. Involve the employees as much as possible in these processes. Find inspiration for involvement and active meetings in Chapter 8. Allocate the necessary time for these processes.
- **Clarify expectations:** Describe your expectations and ask about the employees' expectations. In addition to this dialogue, have the employees discuss their expectations of each other.
- **Build trust and a sense of security:** It is essential to make room for dialogue and team building to enable each team member to see his or her position on the team, to sense the other team members' acceptance, and to discover the other team members' strengths.

In connection with the early stages of establishing a team, the importance of the following four essential elements is often highlighted:

The CORD model: essential factors in establishing the team

Conditions: Timelines, task brief, etc.

Overall direction: Determine the overall vision, purpose, and goals for the team and the individual members.

Relations:

- Internal relations—roles and interactions. How do you cooperate to optimize the way you handle your tasks? What are your ground rules and values, or what should they be?
- External relations—How do you best cooperate with external partners, other teams in the organization, customers, management, the community, society, NGOs, etc.?

Decision-making competence: What is up to you to decide? Where do you need others' approval? How do you broaden your scope of decision-making competence?

Many key issues must be sorted out in this phase, and the process may be time-consuming. It is important to allow the necessary time—if any of these issues remain unclear, it will take time to sort them out later.

Level 2. From a potential team to an actual team

- **Focus on achievements and performance:** This is where you begin to focus on creating a performance culture. Ensure daily follow-up on measurable goals.
- **Provide information about key figures:** The team members should know the key figures so that they understand and can help achieve results.

(continued on next page)

Level 2. From a potential team to an actual team (continued)

- **Regularly discuss each other's strengths, weaknesses, and preferences:** Share with each other what you are passionate about and what you find draining. Be honest. There will be remaining tasks that no one is passionate about. Be open about it. No one can engage their strengths 100 percent of the time. Seventy-five percent of the time is a good number. Supplement each other's weak sides with strengths whenever possible.
- **Evaluate and improve on an ongoing basis:** Purpose, goals, handling of tasks, and work methods should be reevaluated regularly and refined. This will enhance the sense of a shared responsibility.

Level 3. From actual team to a high-performance team

- **Discuss each other's strengths and preferences in depth:** Ask the team members to complete a strengths test and keep a strengths journal. Use these tools regularly to improve the mutual understanding within the team.
- **Give and receive feedback:** Feedback is an important element in becoming a high-performance team. That point has been made repeatedly in this book, and in this context too, that feedback is an essential aspect of a team's and an individual's development. As a manager, you have a special responsibility for giving and requesting feedback. Schedule it so that it occurs regularly in a structured form.
- **Catch each other doing the right thing:** Look for strengths that come into play. Look for initiatives that worked better than expected. Generally focus your attention on all the great work your employees do every day. Every day something important and value-creating is going on around you. There are no ordinary moments.
- **Learn from your successes:** It is not enough to celebrate your successes; you have to learn from them. Use every opportunity to ask strengths-based questions about the results, progress, and successes that will be apparent if you check. Even at a time of crisis, some things go right. Find and emphasize the things that work.
- **Raise the bar:** Enjoy seeing the things that work and keep asking each other what the team can do better. You cannot rest on your laurels. High performance requires constant innovation and development.
- **Be an innovative manager:** Innovation and room for new ways of doing things requires that you have the courage to let go of your own ideas about what to do and instead involve the team members in innovative experiments. In the next section, this topic is addressed in greater depth, as innovation has proved to be one of the keys to creating and maintaining high-performance teams.
- **Organize social events:** Knowing each other on a personal level is an important factor on a high-performance team. Why? Because one of the main characteristics is a strong commitment to each other's personal growth and success, and this commitment is easier to achieve when you know each other personally. Also invite the families of your team members to these events to increase everyone's understanding of the whole person. In a high-performance team, the members are happy to spend their free time with colleagues.

CLOSING REMARKS

As in level 3, innovation on the part of management is one of the main ingredients in bringing a team up to the high-performance level. The American management professor Gary Hamel describes how certain fundamental principles can help pave the way for what he calls "management innovation." Hamel (2007, p. 19) defines management innovation as follows:

Management innovation is anything that substantially alters the way in which the work of management is carried out, or significantly modifies customary organizational forms, and, by doing so, advances organizational goals.

Hamel (2006, 2007, 2012) offers countless examples of how management innovation enhances performance and makes the impossible possible. So when we as leaders set out to create a high-performance team, we should consider whether to introduce a few innovative management initiatives. We'll have to escape the limitation of thinking that we know how things work simply because they've always been done a certain way. Hamel (2007, p. 161) offers an example from the world of aviation:

In 1900, it would have been accurate to say that human beings couldn't fly, but it would have been wrong to say they would never fly. What kept humankind earthbound for so long wasn't the law of gravity, but a lack of inventiveness. And so it is with management.

To create a high-performance team, we must create the conditions needed to think outside the box and enable an unconventional view of management, team, tasks, and organization. Following are a few general principles to support that (based on Hamel, 2006, 2007, 2012; Hamel & Prahalad, 2010).

HAMEL'S PRINCIPLES OF MANAGEMENT INNOVATION

- **Experimentation is better than planning:** You cannot plan your way to high performance. It occurs as the result of many small and large experiments, where you try things out with your team members and evaluate whether the idea should be scrapped or developed into a new practice. Give the team members the freedom to experiment and view failures as a necessary source of learning.
- **Markets are more dynamic than hierarchies:** In a hierarchy, decisions are made at the top and then move down the chain of command. In a market, decisions are made in a vaguer manner, as many people "vote with their feet." The "wisdom of the crowd" means that decisions are sometimes best made as a team and that sometimes the team may know better than you the best way to proceed. Let things go with the energy flow.
- **Everyone has the right to disagree:** Create a culture where you promote disagreement and differences of opinion. One way to do that is to listen to criticism even when you consider it unfair. By encouraging everybody to speak his or her mind and listening to the input with an open mind, you facilitate a democratic and open organization where everyone can speak freely. This brings the necessary information to the surface, and the necessary questions are asked during the decision-making processes.
- **People change if there is something worth changing for:** What you do must be meaningful, and everybody has to believe that it makes a difference. There has to be a mission and a set of goals that contain a deeper value than simply making money. If an organizational change makes sense to the individual, he or she will be willing to play an active and responsible role in bringing about that change.
- **Diversity fosters creativity:** A creative and innovative organization has room for diversity. Daily operations must be stable; otherwise, there is no room for innovation. And without creativity, no development of new products with an earnings potential will take place. It is all connected. And the greater the diversity within the team, the better. This means that separating R&D from Production and Quality Assurance is a thing of the past. Bring the departments together and give them a chance to talk to each other, understand each other, and learn from each other.

10

STRENGTHS-BASED CONFLICT RESOLUTION

CONTENTS

Conflicts are a part of life in the workplace as well as our personal lives. Conflicts are a source of energy and force us to rethink. Conflicts promote dynamics and movement in a system. But conflicts also can be too numerous, too intense, or too destructive for us to use them constructively in our individual and common development.

Conflicts essentially consist of two components: specific problems and frustration. Typically, a specific problem will need to be solved. And at least one of the parties in a conflict will believe that the other party is preventing him or her from reaching a solution or a personal goal. The frustration arises because one party sees the other party as an obstacle to doing what seems necessary. A brief definition might be this:

A conflict is a disagreement involving one or more individuals in which at least one party is frustrated due to the feeling of being prevented from reaching a goal.

Conflicts are a special challenge for the strengths-based leader. In difficult conflicts, it can be challenging to engage people in constructive and strengths-based dialogues. If we initiate an attempt to deal with a conflict by asking the parties to describe what they perceive as each other's strengths, they will be justified in feeling that they aren't being taken seriously. We have to begin somewhere else and use a variety of tools to turn the dialogue in a strengths-based direction. Therefore, it is important to understand the dynamics of conflicts to be able to choose the right strategy and to time initiatives appropriately. The following discussion provides a brief introduction to the fascinating and complex dynamics of conflicts and possible explanations for why they arise.

CAUSES OF CONFLICT

As human beings, we are in constant conflict with ourselves because we must adapt to our environment so that we can function optimally. (Those who are unwilling or unable to adapt ultimately risk being ostracized or arrested or losing their mind.) Our relationships, which include our workplace relationships, spouse/partner, and friends, are a source of joy in what we can achieve together. But at the same time, they can be a source of frustration due to the constraints that are placed on us with regard to what we can achieve given our current conditions. In interactions with others, this internal conflict may result in conflicts with anyone we perceive as being obstacles for us in realizing ourselves and/or in achieving a goal.

The Norwegian conflict researcher Terje Hotvedt (1999) points to six basic explanations for the occurrence of conflict when people encounter each other in organizations.

1. Problematic diversity
2. Choices and decisions to be made between two evils
3. Lack of freedom and autonomy
4. Limited resources
5. Mutual dependence
6. Lack of awareness of the conflict

1. Problematic diversity

Diversity occurs wherever people, nations, and cultures meet. In addition to defining ourselves by our differences with others, we also define ourselves by our similarities with others. We seek the safety of similarities and seek to distance ourselves from people who are different from us. In intergroup relationships, classic sociopsychological experiments show that we are quick to find similarities internally within a group and differences in relation to members of other groups (Sabini, 1992). As one of the consequences of this, we are likely to attribute more negative features to the members of another group than to the members of our own group. Diversity risks turning into condemnation or rejection.

In the relationship among individuals, differences are perceived as particularly problematic when another person's character and the actions that express it generate negative emotions such as irritation and frustration. Even the people we love the most are different from us, which may make us happy, help us develop, or annoy us.

REFLECTION

Think of your siblings, your friends, or some of your colleagues.

- *How do they differ from you? How is that expressed?*
- *Which differences might you perceive as problematic?*
- *Which differences do you learn from?*

2. Choices and decisions to be made between two evils

When we face a difficult decision, we often feel the tension between what we want and the expectation or demands that our surroundings have of us. We make many decisions on a daily basis that have consequences for us and for others. In a conflict, we may believe that we're faced with a choice between two evils. We choose to suppress our own needs (or to let others down), or we pick sides between two parties who expect or demand different things of us.

REFLECTION

Think of a situation in which you had to make a tough choice.

- *What made the choice difficult?*
- *What factors ultimately determined your choice?*
- *What possibilities did the choice involve?*

3. Lack of freedom and autonomy

As human beings, we have a deeply felt need for freedom. When our freedom is threatened, we are willing to fight for it, sometimes to the death. Organizations and human relations often have a built-in disparity, which may give some people a sense of not having the freedom and influence they want. The feeling of not having the freedom to make the choices we want is a source of frustration that often results in conflicts.

REFLECTION

Think of a situation in which you experienced constraints on your freedom.

- *How did you respond?*
- *What did you do to reclaim control?*

Think of a situation in which you experienced a feeling of freedom and autonomy.

- *What did you do that helped bring about that situation?*

4. Limited resources

One of the most powerful sources of conflict is a struggle over scarce resources. When we're faced with an existential threat, whether it concerns food, land, pay, interesting job tasks, security in employment, status, time, or other resources, our will to fight may kick in. Consider the conflict that may emerge when a top position in a company or political party must be filled.

We expend a huge amount of energy in competing with other people and groups. This energy can benefit both parties, but it also can trigger a conflict that may be harmful to both parties. We all strive to fulfill our own needs, and if we believe that someone gets in our way, the seed of conflict has been planted.

REFLECTION

Think of a situation characterized by scarce resources in which you had to cooperate with someone else.

- *What happened in the group?*
- *How did you respond?*
- *How was the situation resolved?*
- *What was the best thing that came out of the situation?*

5. Mutual dependence

We depend on others to fulfill our needs and make our dreams come true, and others depend on us. Managers depend on their employees' goodwill and ability to do the job. Employees depend on their manager's ability to structure and show direction. In our personal lives, we depend on our loved ones for affection and a sense of security. The closer we are to someone, the more emotional we are about our mutual dependence. Conflicts arise if we believe that others take advantage of our dependence on them and they fail to deliver what is expected or help us attain our goals and dreams.

REFLECTION

Think of a close colleague.

- *In what ways is your mutual dependence expressed?*
- *What conflicts can that cause?*
- *In what ways does this person enable you to fulfill your dreams?*

6. Lack of awareness of the conflict

When one party is unwilling to acknowledge his or her active role in maintaining a disagreement, that will be a major source of frustration for the other party. It may be a conflict in its own right if one party refuses to accept his or her share of the responsibility for resolving a problem/disagreement. If one party brushes aside the issue and says, "It's not my problem if you think I'm annoying," the stage is set for an intractable conflict simply because mutual acknowledgment of the disagreement is a precondition for finding an effective solution.

REFLECTION

- *Have you ever encountered someone who was unwilling to accept his or her share of the responsibility for a disagreement or a problem?*
- *Have you ever refused to acknowledge your share of the responsibility for a problem?*

Think of the most responsible and self-aware person you know.

- *What could you learn from this person?*

In a given conflict, the six basic explanations of conflicts may be present on their own or in various combinations. A conflict in one area will have a tendency to intensify conflicts in other areas.

Conflicts typically have one or more of these conditions as their underlying cause. At times, it may be hard to identify the source of an emerging frustration. Deliberately or unconsciously, we may direct our frustration at the people around us. In a sense, the conflict can be said to be looking for a cause. If we don't determine what it is that frustrates us or the parties involved, it can be difficult to manage the conflict constructively. Understanding and being aware of the six conflict explanations is the first step to understanding and managing conflicts better.

A strengths-based approach to conflicts is based on the assumption that everybody does the best he or she can with the resources that are available, and that makes it essential to search for the motivation behind the seemingly incomprehensible actions that sometimes occur in conflict situations.

The Norwegian conflict researchers Ståle Einarsen et al. (2010) describes four levels that may be useful for understanding conflicts.

GUIDE TO ANALYZING CONFLICT IN AN ORGANIZATION	
Organizational level	• Physical conditions • Culture • Ambiguous structures • Lack of common goals and direction
Group/department level	• Relationship between manager and staff • Ambiguous roles • Ambiguous distribution of competencies and resources • Focus on mistakes and shortcomings
Interpersonal level	• Bad chemistry • Personal style • Competition • Mistrust
Individual level	• Focus on individual mistakes and shortcomings

Most conflicts can be described and managed on all four levels. It may be useful to expand our understanding of an intractable conflict by considering whether we missed anything on one of the other four levels. Might there be other explanations for the conflict than the one that's apparent? Often the focus tends to be on the individual level and interpersonal level. We tend to explain the conflict with regard to what is staring us in the face: the other person's mistakes and shortcomings. As leaders, we may fall into the trap of explaining a conflict between two employees by referencing their poor mutual relationship exclusively. We might forget that the structure of the team or the culture that permeates the organization also plays an important role in the combatants' behavior. And how might our own behavior affect the situation?

Often there are many useful perspectives on all four levels. Efficient solutions rest on a combination of initiatives and agreements that support each other. It is essential that we promote dialogue and reach joint agreements that everyone can get behind. In some cases, we may need to introduce sanctions to make people stick with the agreements, but that it is only an option once the potential for dialogue has been exhausted.

The unique characteristic of the individual level is that it is up to the person to reflect on his or her options. We can't force people to change against their will. Authentic personal development has to come from the inside.

As strengths-based leaders, we are constantly on the search for nuances, and the distinctions between the four levels can help us see crucial distinctions in the conflict.

REFLECTION

Think of a conflict you have had in a workplace.

- *What explanations can you think of on the different levels?*
- *What limitations and possibilities can you see in the various explanations?*

THE SLIPPERY SLOPE OF CONFLICT

Another conceptual framework that is helpful for understanding our own and other people's conflicts is the slippery slope of conflict. Inspired by the original model of conflict escalation (Glasl, 1980), it offers a guide for understanding the severity or intensity of a conflict. Different levels of conflict have their distinct characteristics and should be handled using different methods. Here the image of a slippery slope is used because a lack of active management typically results in the conflict worsening and moving gradually down the levels.

The introduction of this guide also discusses the options we have as leaders when intervening and dealing with the conflict.

Separating the issue and the person is crucial in any conflict situation. The more intense the conflict is and the more intense the emotions are, the harder it is to accomplish this. Already on levels 2 and 3 of the slippery slope, parties involved in a conflict may begin to find it hard to make this distinction. As leaders, we can avoid mixing up the issue and the person by listening carefully to what is being said. If one of the parties says that the other party is the problem, we should ask about that immediately. If the language being used judges the other person, such as "He is being disrespectful," that also is a clear signal that the parties have begun to confuse the issue with the person. As leaders, we can ask the following key questions at an early stage in the process:

- *What* is this about? (shedding light on the matter)
- *Who* is involved? (shedding light on the people involved and their mutual relations)

On levels 7–9 of the model, we find the very difficult conflicts. This is also where we find severe bullying, harassment, and psychological and physical terror. Conflicts descend to these levels too often. A 2014 survey from Workplace Bullying Institute showed that 27 percent of employees had current or past direct experience with abusive conduct at work. Bullying and harassment won't be addressed specifically in the context of this book. But very briefly, bullying and harassment require conflict management and dialogue. In its extreme, that type of conflict also requires that a leader take a hard stand and *demand* changes in people's behavior. In extreme cases, this may involve disciplinary measures or written warnings and the involvement of health and safety, Human Resources, and trade union representatives.

<table>
<tr><th>CONFLICT LEVEL</th><th>CHARACTERISTIC</th><th>MANAGEMENT</th></tr>
<tr><td>1. Disagreement</td><td>Beginning disagreement
Irritation and frustration</td><td rowspan="3">Levels 1–3:
• Cooperation is possible.
• Focusing on the issue is possible.
• The leader may be able to manage the conflict on his or her own.
• Involved parties may be able to manage the conflict on their own.</td></tr>
<tr><td>2. Rejection</td><td>See each other as opposites
The other person's fault
Compromise is difficult</td></tr>
<tr><td>3. Combative</td><td>Minimal understanding
Poor communication
Attributes negative intentions to the other party
Old stories being told</td></tr>
<tr><td>4. Formation of alliances</td><td>Extreme attitudes
We want to win
Them and Us</td><td rowspan="2">Levels 4–6:
• Management has to send clear signals and demand a proper tone.
• Dialogue and trust must be reestablished.
• Clear, written agreements are needed.
• An external mediator may be called for.
• The leader's superior is involved.
(continued on next page)</td></tr>
<tr><td>5. Stereotyped hostile perceptions</td><td>Counterpart lacks morals
Counterpart lacks sense</td></tr>
</table>

<table>
<tr><th>CONFLICT LEVEL</th><th>CHARACTERISTIC</th><th>MANAGEMENT</th></tr>
<tr><td>6. Open hostility</td><td>Open attacks
Threats</td><td></td></tr>
<tr><td>7. Attack is the best defense</td><td>Responds to attacks with escalation
Undermines the other person's weapons and position</td><td rowspan="3">Levels 7–9:<ul><li>External mediator is required.</li><li>Physical separation may be necessary at first.</li><li>Space for listening must be established.</li><li>The leader's superior makes clear decisions.</li><li>Demands must be clear.</li><li>Sanctions must be unambiguous.</li></ul></td></tr>
<tr><td>8. Anything goes</td><td>The ends justify the means</td></tr>
<tr><td>9. War</td><td>Victory is the objective
Counterpart is to be destroyed or eliminated</td></tr>
</table>

On all nine levels, the involved parties justify their own actions as self-defense or as necessitated by external circumstances. Other people's actions are explained by the assumption that they have lower morals or ethics compared with the average person. The justification of one's own actions and the condemnation of other people's actions is a key factor in the escalation of many conflicts.

Knowing how a conflict evolves and noticing the level of a given conflict allows us as leaders to pause and reflect on our own role if we're part of the conflict. We can then talk to the relevant parties and contact an external consultant, a mediator, or another leader in the organization to ask for help in turning things around. Maybe our superior needs to be involved, and perhaps a competent shop steward would be a good sparring partner. We can use the model to consider our approach or the next step to take. The only thing that might stop the downward slide is active intervention that pulls in a constructive direction.

REFLECTION

Think of a tough conflict you have been involved in.

- *How far down the slope did that conflict go?*
- *What did others do during this process that you thought was wrong or reprehensible?*
- *What did you do that you normally would not have done?*

Think of a conflict that was defused.

- *What did the other involved parties do that helped defuse the conflict?*
- *What did you do?*

Now the conflict dynamics have been analyzed. This analysis gives us an understanding of what conflict management tools to use. But we can't find the solutions by only looking to the past and analyzing it. We must take a more forward-looking approach to the conflict in order to handle it.

The next step is to look at the tools that might help in managing conflicts and raise them to a level where the parties can work together or find a common solution that is acceptable to everyone.

STRENGTHS-BASED CONFLICT MANAGEMENT

From conflict to resolution—breaking the curve

To some extent, understanding and analyzing a conflict rests on a mind-set that is based on identifying mistakes or shortcomings. We examine what is wrong so that we can understand the perspectives of the two parties. If we dwell too long on what is wrong, we risk driving the parties into a dead end of blame and guilt and excuses from which they will never escape. On the other hand, it is important to make all parties feel as if they have been seen and heard in the analysis of the conflict. Making them believe that they are being taken seriously and are being listened to is part of the solution, and it is a prerequisite for the subsequent stages of conflict management. If people do not believe that they are understood and have been heard, they will resist being part of the solution. Our first step as leaders, therefore, is to analyze and uncover the problem.

The next step in a successful conflict management process is to turn the focus away from causes and mistakes to solutions and resources.

Identifying the wishes and dreams that lie behind the conflict makes it possible to set goals that point toward constructive solutions instead of pointing back to causes and blame. Thus, it is not the analysis of the history of the conflict per se that creates the dialogue about solutions, but rather the dialogue about the future. The emphasis switches from the transgressions of the past to the constructive actions of the future (see axis model 2, Chapter 5). The following guide provides the sorts of questions and interventions that can come into play in this crucial shift in focus.

Note how we don't find solutions by exploring the issue of disrespectfulness or by asking follow-up questions about the misunderstandings. We find solutions by focusing on where the people want to go. The energy lies in the dreams and the solutions. Looking at the other side of the coin leads to a constructive language that enables the parties to talk about the future rather than being stuck in the mistakes and shortcomings of the past. Our task is to provide the safe space and the energy that enable others to "proflect" about the future possibilities.

GUIDE TO "BREAKING THE CURVE" IN CONFLICTS		
Conflict/problem **Past**	**Dream/wish** **Future**	**Solution/goal** **Steps that enable us to reach the desired future**
• What is the problem? • How do you experience it? • What do you find frustrating? • How do you think others experience the situation?	• What is your hope? • What is the best way we can cooperate, communicate, and work together in the future? How would you like it to be?	• What agreements can we reach? • What would be a good solution? • What steps can you take?
"I believe that my colleague takes a disrespectful tone with me when we disagree on something."	"I would like us to have a constructive and frank dialogue about our disagreements in the future."	"It would mean a great deal to me if we could discuss disagreements in specific terms without pointing out each other's personal flaws."
"We sometimes misunderstand each other, and that leads to poor decisions."	"If we create better understanding, we can create better results together."	"Let's agree to ask each other more questions when we doubt something."
"We wind up arguing when we distribute the tasks of the day."	"It would be nice to have a clear distribution of tasks."	"Let's make a monthly schedule together with the manager."

Constructive language

It's crucial to stick to constructive language when we try to resolve a conflict. To use constructive language, certain conditions must be in place. Only when we have a firm grip on our own communication can we begin to affect the dialogue in the right direction. The following discussion reviews three key areas of constructive language:

- Maintain self-aware and constructive language.
- Distinguish between observing and interpreting other people's actions.
- Use assertive communication.

1. Maintain self-aware and constructive language

To remain constructive, we must be able to see our part in the conflict. Unfortunately, in a conflict, people often—consciously or unconsciously—slip into a language that is judgmental toward others' mistakes yet forgiving of their own. In a conflict context, this phenomenon is called deception and self-deception. It can be summarized in two simple sentences:

- I do what I do because I have to!
- You do what you do because that's what you're like!

An important task for us as leaders is to challenge that type of language in a respectful way. To be able to behave constructively, the leader must help the employees develop a more nuanced understanding of why others do the things they do. In all likelihood, the counterpart also has an explanation to justify his or her actions.

With questions and guidance, we can encourage the parties to look for additional explanations of each other's behavior. We must take responsibility for our own actions without hiding behind self-deception and justification. If we're being criticized as leaders, we also are put to the test and risk being drawn into the conflict. In that case, language takes on even greater importance. Constructive and confident language sounds like this:

- I do what I do because I think it will have a good effect!
- You do what you do because you have a good reason to do so!

2. Distinguish between observing and interpreting other people's actions

As in any other context, it is important in a conflict situation to focus more on one's *observation* of other's actions and less on one's *interpretations* of these actions. The following guide helps in making this distinction.

By having the parties talk about their perceptions of the counterpart's actions without resorting to negative interpretations and judgments, as leaders, we ensure that they will be less inclined to feel as though they're under attack and misunderstood.

The easiest way for us to avoid misunderstandings is to ask the parties to tell each other about their observations and interpretations based on concrete examples of when they got off on the wrong foot. Conflicts are often a sign of insufficient information. When the constructive communication and the open dialogue have been reestablished, the missing information can be incorporated to improve the parties' mutual understanding. That may be one of the strengths-based leader's most important tasks when managing conflicts.

GUIDE TO DISTINGUISHING BETWEEN OBSERVATIONS AND INTERPRETATIONS	
OBSERVATIONS	**INTERPRETATIONS**
Behavior Actions Words Body language Facial expressions	Personality Values Needs Intentions Thoughts Emotions
Visible	Not visible
Facts and information "What do I know?"	Guesses and sensations "What do I think?"
Example of an observation: I see that my colleague is yawning and looking out the window when I'm talking to him.	Negative and judgmental interpretations: • He's arrogant and indifferent. • He doesn't care about anyone else. • He finds me boring. • He wants to show me that he finds me incompetent. Curious and nonjudgmental interpretations: • Maybe he's just tired. • He listens but forgets to show it. • Maybe he spotted something interesting out there. • Maybe he really isn't interested but doesn't want to hurt my feelings by saying so.

3. Use assertive communication

Assertive communication means equal and respectful communication with impact. The concept has been described and applied for many years, but it remains a challenge to make the counterparts in a conflict choose this form of communication. The following section should inspire us on how to guide others in the use of assertive communication.

Assertive communication aims to enable the sender to speak his or her mind without making the counterpart feel under attack or the target of blame. Assertiveness is contrasted, on the one hand, with aggressiveness (attacking) and, on the other hand, with submissiveness (being compliant, hiding frustrations).

To be assertive, we must rely on the facts we have access to about the other person's actions. When we aren't sure how to interpret a given situation, we have to acquire more information. We do that by presenting our perception of the situation and then asking about the other person's experience. We stay in our corner without judging, but offer the other person insight into our thoughts and emotions. Being assertive means respecting the other person as well as ourselves and our boundaries. It takes both honesty and courage to be assertive.

The previous example where the colleague was yawning and looking out the window while someone was talking to him is used below to illustrate the difference between assertive communication and a more aggressive communication style.

The aggressive form of communication is easy to resort to when both parties refuse to budge. As leaders, we should provide guidance and ask questions to drive the conversation in the right direction.

To use constructive communication in any situation where we feel we're under attack or we feel angry or frustrated, we need to have a high degree of self-control and openness so that we can see many interpretations of the other person's signals. We have to weigh our words carefully. We can't change other people, but we can have a constructive effect on the conversation by using careful communication. If we allow our anger to control us, we're not likely to reach a good solution or goal, where both parties are happy afterward.

	AGGRESSIVE COMMUNICATION	ASSERTIVE COMMUNICATION
Initial choice of words to indicate one's perception of the situation	Generalization: "I can't stand that you always ignore what I have to say."	Fact: "I see that you're yawning and looking out the window."
Interpretations	He is uninterested and disrespectful.	Maybe he is uninterested, or maybe he's just sleepy and not thinking about the negative signal it sends to be yawning and looking out the window.
Emotions	Frustration Doubt Uncertainty	Confusion Doubt Uncertainty
Thoughts	Judgmental: "He doesn't respect me." "He's arrogant."	Nonjudgmental: "I feel confused and frustrated. It makes me wonder whether what I'm saying is of any interest to you."
Focus	On blame and on judging the other person	On wishes and on conveying one's hopes for the future
Consequence/ summarizing dialogue	"It's your fault that I get angry and we can't work together." "You have to respect me!" "You really ought to pay attention!"	"I'd like it if you indicated a little more clearly that you're listening or if you'd let me know explicitly that what I'm saying doesn't interest you."

In the words of Winston Churchill:

Speak in anger and you will deliver the greatest speech you will ever live to regret.

Conflict mediation

As leaders, we have a substantial influence on the collaboration, efficiency, and culture in the workplace. Hence, when things go wrong, we should step in quickly to help straighten things out. Leaders who are unable or unwilling to recognize a conflict are not living up to their responsibility. Below is a summary of some of the things that we should focus on when conflicts occur.

LEADERSHIP IN CONFLICTS	
Be loyal and constructive.	You must show exemplary behavior. Speak well of others. Do not blame anyone. Give your employees frank and specific feedback on good as well as poor results.
Put the conflict into words.	By putting the conflict into words, you make sure everybody speaks in the same context. That makes it easier to understand each other and to avoid misunderstandings.
When in doubt, ask.	You must show your uncertainty and ask questions if things are not being said and you sense that something is up.
Acknowledge the issue if you're involved.	If you're part of the conflict, you won't be able to remain neutral. In that case, the most appropriate course of action is to introduce another mediator.
Create clarity using the "T-S-R model."	In a conflict, before a stable solution can be achieved, it is often essential to provide clarity and structure. Address the three main categories below in the order shown. 1. What is our task? 2. What is the nature of our structure and organization? 3. What is the nature of our relations and communication?
Define the scope.	Define the scope of the dialogue. The framework may be individual conversations, conversations involving both/all counterparts, or conversations involving the entire team. As a manager, you are responsible for defining a scope that facilitates a constructive and effective dialogue. *(continued on next page)*

LEADERSHIP IN CONFLICTS (CONTINUED)	
Make demands.	Violations of regulations and inadequate results should have consequences. As a manager in a conflict, you demand that the parties cooperate. But you have to do so in a sensitive and respectful way to avoid undermining the parties' motivation. You should insist that the parties speak to each other in a constructive manner and work toward a common solution.
Consider seeking outside assistance.	There is no shame in acknowledging that a conflict has become too difficult to handle. In many cases involving conflict management, it's wise to request outside assistance. Also, you may have access to coaching or be able to ask the advice of more experienced managers.

Below is a good example illustrating how a strengths-based leader can take a constructive approach to handling a conflict.

> *If I can tell that there is a problem in my department that isn't just going to disappear (sometimes it does, of course, so there is no reason to barge in right away), I explore the specifics of the situation as it appears from both points of view. There are two sides to every story. Then I invite the counterparts in, and we sit down for a talk. I make them talk about the issue. We had a conflict involving two employees who were very different people. They were both competent and wanted things to be done right. They had a difference of opinion about certain issues, and the disagreement had grown. We managed to resolve the situation in such a way that they both felt that they had made some concessions. We agreed that we would try a certain approach for two weeks, and then we would talk to see how things were going. I defined the scope, enhanced the dialogue, and made sure they both gave an inch. They were both decent and conscientious people, so it wasn't hard, especially when they both realized that the other person was trying to do things well. It is important to avoid a one-sided view. Preferably, they should both have to make concessions. And then time worked in our favor. The situation calmed down. They felt that the issue had been addressed, and they both became aware of their share in the conflict and of the other person's good intentions. They will never be the best of friends, but that's not the point. They just have to be able to work together in a constructive manner.*
>
> —Jannie Funch, Department Manager, D&S Regulatory Affairs, Novo Nordisk A/S

As leaders, we must ensure a balanced approach and hear both sides of the story. Our leadership can make the difference in the next conflict our employees must deal with. Below is a guide with specific steps for structuring a mediation process involving two parties.

GUIDE FOR MEDIATION MEETING	
Take the necessary time to define the scope and conditions.	• Establish the ground rules for the dialogue. Involve the parties by asking whether they have any requests in this regard. • Explain how you view the situation from your position as a manager. • Underscore that finding good solutions is important for both the parties and the larger organization.
Unfold everyone's perspectives.	• Use a variety of question techniques to uncover the various perspectives. • Remember that when one person is speaking, the other listens. • Remember that when one person has been allowed to speak, the other person can give his or her version of the same issue. • Sense the person's mood and ask about frustrations.
Catch the counterparts doing the right thing.	• During the process, when the parties do or say something that's constructive, helpful, or solution-oriented, mention it as an example of movement in the right direction. • Listen for openings where the parties reach out to each other. Seize that opening and ask what the other person thinks of it.
"Break the curve."	• Direct the conversation to the topic of the future when the parties are ready for it. Ask about wishes and possible solutions.
Use specific written agreements.	• Remember that the interests of the organization are the top priority. • If possible, let the parties define the solutions. • Make specific demands concerning the nature and content of the agreements if you find it relevant. • Support the agreements, but be honest if they aren't feasible. *(continued on next page)*

GUIDE FOR MEDIATION MEETING (CONTINUED)	
Devise a follow-up plan.	• Include a specific timeline. • Define your role in the ongoing dialogue between the parties.
Thank the participants.	• Look the parties in the eyes and ask how they experienced the process/meeting. • Thank the parties for their effort. Mention what you appreciated in the process (for example, that they were frank and that they listened to each other and to more specific points). • Offer your continued support as their manager. • Follow up with meetings with each party before the next group meeting is held, where both parties are present again.

A conflict mediation process may contain nuances that are impossible to predict. Conflict mediation is a difficult but exciting challenge. The tools outlined in this chapter should provide ideas that we can use the next time we have to mediate between two parties in a conflict. The sooner the issue is addressed, the better.

CLOSING REMARKS

Conflicts are relations that have become temporarily derailed. Sometimes it is impossible to reestablish the good relationship, and in that case, the relationship must end. But in many cases, people can reach an understanding. The goal of this chapter was to outline the steps that can help bring the relationship back on track. Strengths-based conflict management begins with us. We can't change other people. We can only change our own thoughts and actions in relation to the conflict we've become a part of or must mediate in. By assuming responsibility and engaging constructively in the dialogue, we may come to serve, directly or indirectly, as role models.

As leaders, we can make the parties in a conflict point a finger at themselves and accept their responsibility. We can help them rebuild broken trust by introducing the necessary reflection and information. And we should remember to look for these principles constantly. Mahatma Gandhi called for nonviolent demonstrations against an oppressive British rule, but he was not a man who shied away from conflicts. In one sentence, he summarized what is needed for people to (re)establish the bond of trust:

Be the change you wish to see in the world!

11

STRENGTHS-BASED STRESS MANAGEMENT AND IMPROVEMENT OF WELL-BEING

CONTENTS

As strengths-based leaders, we're involved in setting the agenda in a number of areas. We lead by example, and our employees take note of our behavior and our way of dealing with situations, including the pressures of work. As discussed earlier, the initiatives we introduce to our team or to the organization have an impact on the mood in the workplace—for example, on whether the employees are thriving and enjoy going to work and on whether we're cocreating a flourishing or withered workplace.

Of course, the employees, our colleagues, and our customers play a role too. Their reaction to the activities, dialogues, and initiatives we introduce is crucial. We're not alone in this responsibility, but we are responsible for taking the initiative to achieve a high level of well-being and success in the workplace. It is a fact that people pay more attention to our behavior than the behavior of other employees. That means how *we* handle our situation when we're under pressure and what initiatives we take to prevent and manage stress and enhance our own well-being are very important.

The emphasis of the book on bringing our own and our employees' strengths more into play should serve as a process that enhances well-being and helps prevent stress. People's experience of stress is often directly or indirectly related to their experience of being able to use their strengths (or not) and to pursue their passion (or not).

Stress, well-being, and strengths-based leadership are closely linked.

This chapter presents some basic knowledge about stress—what it is and isn't—and how we can detect it in ourselves and others. We need to use this basic knowledge to see if stress is beginning to sneak up on us and our team. Then the chapter looks at the steps we and the employees can take to prevent and manage stress in the workplace. The third section of the chapter provides insight into the form of management that should be used in relation to the employee at different stages—from calm to burnt out. In closing, the chapter reviews some recommendations for promoting well-being within the team.

FROM CALM TO BURNT OUT

Being busy and hurrying are not the same as being stressed. In everyday speech, the term *stress* refers to the whole spectrum. We may have experienced stress, but technically speaking, stress is a fairly severe condition. Therefore, we shouldn't overuse the word because once we reach a point where we are stressed, we need all the strength we can muster to let others know that we need help. It's hard to express the severity of the condition if we use the word all the time and if we are simply busy or experiencing an unusually heavy workload.

As leaders, we influence the dialogue and the way issues are addressed in the organization. It may be helpful to distinguish between being calm, being busy, being under strain, being stressed, and being burned out. We should introduce these distinctions in our everyday speech.

Being calm: These are the times when we have the mental energy necessary to develop and learn new things and to handle our daily tasks. We thrive and have the mental energy to grow and to relate to and assist our colleagues. On this level, we believe there is a match between demands and resources and between being efficient and being able to perform well. We have a good overview and may be able to spot new trends, and we take a proactive approach to new methods and procedures. We are happy to cooperate with others, including external partners.	
Being busy: We hurry, but we manage to complete our workload without putting in extra hours. On most days, we leave on time, but we haven't had the time to engage in preventive or developing activities during the day as we would under calm conditions.	
Being under strain: We work faster than normal and put in extra hours. We are still productive and efficient, although we're beginning to experience symptoms such as headaches and dizziness. However, it's a temporary phase, and we are still convinced that things will sort themselves out.	

Being stressed: At this point, we have been under so much pressure that many persistent physical symptoms begin to appear, and we are beginning to lose faith that things will improve. Productivity drops. We lose our focus and may have more sick days than normal, have a shorter fuse, and make more mistakes.	
Being burned out: Burn-out occurs when we have attempted in vain to adjust to a situation over a period of time. The body's defenses are depleted, and we are no longer able to handle the situation. Eventually there is an emotional withdrawal and physical exhaustion where energy and engagement are gradually reduced. A person who suffers burn-out has "broken down" and must take sick leave. This results in serious consequences not only for the individual, but also for the colleagues who are left to shoulder an even larger workload because their colleague is absent.	

Later, the chapter will present ideas as to what we can do to deal with employees who are in these stages—from being calm to burned out. The following discussion will dwell briefly on what characterizes the condition of stress, which has received so much attention lately. As mentioned earlier, the purpose of spending some time on providing an understanding of the condition is to enable managers to recognize it more easily when it occurs in them or in one of their employees so that they can intervene.

What is stress?

Stress is a reaction to strain on the body and the mind that is severe enough to produce physiological reactions such as heart palpitations and muscle tension.

If the strain is temporary, we speak of **acute stress**. Acute stress occurs, for example, when we're startled and have to respond quickly. In acute stress, our body rapidly enters a state where it is ready for fight or flight, which is helpful, for example, when someone yells at us so that we don't step in front of a car. In that situation, we don't want to think about whether the car that's about to hit us is a pretty color or has a nice driver; instead, we have to respond promptly to avoid injury. In acute stress, we rapidly mobilize the energy needed to deal with the situation—and when the situation has been resolved, we return to a normal state of physiological alertness. Our pulse slows down, our blood pressure is stabilized, and our muscle tension decreases. This natural response to stress allows us to take quick action in situations in which there is no time to think.

If the strain is persistent or recurring, however, we can suffer from **chronic stress**. If we're under any kind of pressure for a long time, we're in a constant state of alertness. Physiologically, we're not designed to maintain this state of alertness over the long term. We're designed to respond to acute stress when we encounter a danger and then quickly switch to recovery and relaxation. However, in modern society, we often trigger this stress response with thought patterns such as "I'll never make it/I can't do it/I'm no good /I don't want to…." In these cases, the signals sent to the body are the same as if we were facing life-threatening danger. Even if we aren't facing a physical threat, the body perceives it as such. That's why chronic stress is described as stress due to worries because worrying about a future event can kick the body into a state of alert.

Briefly summarized, stress can be defined as follows:

Stress is the body's response when internal/external strains (stressors) exceed our resources and our capacity—physically as well as mentally.

This means that we're stressed when we can't handle the strains we're faced with. This strain also can be about dealing with boredom and the lack of challenging tasks or dealing with tasks that seem meaningless or unsatisfying. Thus, although stress is the result of "excessive outside pressure," it also occurs whenever a mismatch takes place between demands/expectations and the amount of strain. This involves situations in which the body/person is struggling to achieve equilibrium but is constantly thrown off balance so that proper adaptation doesn't occur.

Symptoms of stress

Below are some of the typical symptoms of stress; they can also be seen as warning signs or consequences of stress. These are the things to notice in yourself and others if you suspect the presence of stress. Some things are clearly visible from the outside, others you can sense, and some you can uncover only if you ask (yourself or others).

Behavioral symptoms	Mental symptoms
• Reduced capacity to perform • Encapsulation • Indecisiveness—unable to complete tasks/make decisions • Conflicts with others • Lack of dedication • Increased use of stimulants	• Poor ability to focus • Impaired short-term memory • Confusion • Excessive attention to details • Learning difficulties

Physical/somatic symptoms	Emotional symptoms
• Headaches	• Mood swings
• Dry throat and mouth	• Irritation
• Tension	• Impatience
• Heart palpitations	• Restlessness
• Dizziness	• Anger/aggression, cynicism
• Indigestion	• Guilt, anxiety
• Sleep problems	• Sadness/depression

When we're on the lookout for stress symptoms and want to know whether we or someone else is suffering from stress, we should look for changes. Major or minor behavioral changes may be a sign of stress. If someone (you or an employee) is usually extraverted and cheerful and suddenly begins to keep to himself or herself, snaps at others, and/or becomes introverted, that person may be suffering from stress. If someone who usually juggles multiple tasks or projects at once suddenly finds himself or herself incapable of doing that, he or she may be suffering from stress. As a manager, your main option is to observe how the people around you are feeling. When you notice warning signals, you should ask about them to give the individual employee a chance to engage in a dialogue with you. And you should pay careful attention to your own signals. Listen with an open mind if someone tells you that he or she is concerned about you.

If we sense that the strain we're experiencing may be excessive, we should react promptly and deal with the issue. A discussion of the specific steps we can take to deal with stress at different levels appears later in the chapter.

General stressors

We need to be familiar with the basic stressors, which trigger a negative reaction in practically everyone. The effect these factors have on individuals varies considerably. If two people are exposed to the same stressor, their respective experiences may be very different.

REFLECTION

Have you ever seen a colleague experience something as being stressful that you perceive as being interesting and exciting?

Do you know someone who stays calm in situations that you find stressful? or vice versa? What do you make of that?

Goal frustration

Feeling as though we're prevented from reaching a goal (because we lack the resources to attain it or because an outside factor prevents it) will trigger stress in most of us. If we're aware of this, we can help ourselves by finding the resources and the solutions required to reach the goal or by adjusting the goal (for example, by lowering our level of ambition). Goal frustration causes many conflicts, which can be a stressor in itself.

Conflicts

Conflicts in the workplace are a stressor that most of us have experienced. It is the knot in the pit of our stomach when we go to work knowing that a person with whom we're having a conflict will be there. Conflicts are straining and stressful because we devote our energy to dealing with the issues when we should be focusing on work-related tasks. But we can't perform at our best until the conflict has been resolved. The previous chapter outlined some ideas for conflict management that are also relevant as a way to reduce stress. On the other hand, stress can produce conflicts simply because we have a shorter fuse and a narrower perspective.

Unpredictability

The inability to predict the future is a fundamental aspect of the human condition, and yet we constantly try to change that. We attempt to create situations that are predictable and under control. We do this so that we can switch to "autopilot" and free up energy for other tasks. There is nothing fundamentally wrong with this. However, it becomes a problem when we experience a change that we don't know how to deal with or we deal with negatively and fail to embrace. The change may be that a good colleague is dismissed. In that situation, we might miss the colleague while wondering who will be fired next. Or the change may involve new management or changes in the organization that leave us doubting or own position. We're off balance, and we spend energy trying to reestablish the familiar pattern.

Lack of clarity

Another stressor related to unpredictability is a lack of clarity about what is expected of us. If we've failed to establish clear roles and expectations for our employees, they're justified in feeling pressured and stressed. Because nobody wants to perform poorly or fail to live up to expectations, people devote their energy to figuring out what is expected of them. Almost all of us want to meet other people's expectations, but in some cases, we don't know what's required of us (due to a lack of dialogue). That's stressful. We should create as much predictability as we can and clarify conditions and expectations for ourselves and our employees—and learn to "surf the waves" over which we have no control (in other words, not worry about those things but "go with the flow" instead).

Too much or not enough influence and responsibility

Having influence on and responsibility for our work (for example, in relation to priorities and when and how the tasks are carried out) can provide a sense of freedom as well as an extra burden. To many of us, the flexible workplace has made the job never ending. There's no freedom; we just bring our computer with us and log on wherever we are. But if we don't draw the line, we have a problem. Flexible hours and the delegation of responsibility might lead us to put in more hours, which can develop into a significant stressor. On the other hand, studies show that a lack of influence and responsibility can have similarly negative effects. We thrive when we believe that we can influence our environment. That gives us a sense of being in control, in charge. When this sense is missing—when we believe we don't have any influence or any responsibility—we experience a sense of helplessness and powerlessness. (A thorough review of research on the role of influence and responsibility in relation to stress can be found in Karasek & Theorell, 1990.)

A mismatch between demands and control

As mentioned at the beginning of the chapter, stress can stem from having too much work—when we lack the resources (such as time) to get the task done—and from not having enough work (too many resources in relation to the demand). If we aren't challenged enough, our body responds with symptoms of stress. Again, the key is to strike a balance. The body perceives it as a sign that something is wrong when we can't bring our abilities into play because time pressures keep us from doing things properly (living up to our own standards) or because we're not challenged enough. This balance differs from one person to the next.

Stressful life circumstances/events

Finally, certain life circumstances or events affect the degree of balance we experience and thus whether we experience pressure/stress. Circumstances in our personal lives that act as stressors include a death in the family or in a close circle of friends, divorce, marriage, changes in our financial situation, a pregnancy, a birth, a move, renovation of our home, our spouse finding a new job, loss of a job or retirement, holidays, and vacations. A common feature of all of these personal stressors is that they can throw us off balance in the short or long term. As leaders, we should consider an employee's personal life when he or she speaks of feeling pressured. Naturally, we should respect the boundaries between work life and personal life, but we also should show an interest in the whole person.

WHAT CAN WE DO AS INDIVIDUALS TO PREVENT STRESS AND PROMOTE WELL-BEING?

There are things we can do to prevent stress and promote well-being. We can take responsibility as leaders and lead by example, showing that we can prevent and deal with our own stress.

Even though we're primarily responsible for keeping our stress at bay, that shouldn't lead to complacency and inaction on the part of the team or the organization. We may be responsible for our own health, but there are many other conditions beyond the individual factors that determine whether we'll fall prey to stress. As leaders, we have a wide range of options for promoting the well-being of individuals. This point will be discussed in more detail later.

Preventing stress in ourselves

First, we'll look at some of the things we can focus on while we're still able to take measures to prevent stress.

PREVENTING STRESS

1. Identify and eliminate stressors.
2. Increase resilience to stress.
3. Promote humor and a light-hearted atmosphere and activities that produce energy and joy.
4. Work on taking a constructive approach when situations look to be challenges rather than threats.
5. Organize and plan workday routines.

1. Identify and eliminate stressors

It's important that we identify the things that are stressful to us and the symptoms that occur when we experience stress. This awareness will enable us to respond to the warning signs/symptoms before the conditions develop into actual stress and to assess which of the stressful situations we may be able to avoid or even change in the future. The key is to know our limitations and to prioritize our energy. Because we can't and shouldn't be expected to do everything ourselves, we should carry out a constructive analysis to identify the things we find stressful when we're under pressure.

REFLECTION

Which factors in the workplace do you worry about excessively?

In which situations do you typically find that you are exposed to an uncomfortable level of pressure?

What is particularly stressful to you?

What patterns do you see in your stress history?

How important is the balance between work life and personal life to you?

Our answers will determine the necessary actions. If we make an effort to prepare ourselves during this preventive period, we'll be in a far better position to meet the challenges if they do grow large enough to trigger stress symptoms later on.

For example, we can identify the tasks that are most important for us to deal with when the strain exceeds our resources. Doing so will help us prioritize so that we don't have to worry about that when we're up to our neck in work. We also can consider our own ideas about what we should be able to deliver and achieve—and adjust our ambitions, expectations, and surroundings to be more realistic. Or we can prepare for an upcoming busy period by making sure we've established healthy habits concerning diet, exercise, and relaxation.

2. Increase resilience to stress

Being in shape is an important "buffer" against stress. When we're fit, it's easier to bring our body back to equilibrium after a physiological state of alertness that was brought on by a stressor. And we help our body release the unhealthy hormones that can build up during a long workday, when the stress hormones adrenalin and cortisol can "fire up" the body when they're not expended in physical activity. Thus, exercise helps us feel better and makes us physically strong and capable of resisting the influences we encounter.

Our social and professional network also serves as a "buffer" to reduce the level of stress that results from a particular strain. Therefore, it's important to identify the individuals we can rely on for support. To whom can we talk when necessary? There's a difference between receiving help with practical tasks and emotional issues. One person may be a good source for helping in practical terms (for example, by helping us move or lending a hand with a task at work), whereas someone else is better at helping with emotional challenges.

3. Promote humor and a light-hearted atmosphere and activities that produce energy and joy

By taking a light-hearted approach, we develop an ability to forgive ourselves, which is constructive during pressure-filled situations. A light-hearted atmosphere and a sense of humor are not the same as indifference and sarcasm, respectively. The former produces flexibility and a sense of security, whereas the latter produces the opposite—stubbornness and insecurity. Light-hearted means that we do our best and that we put things and ourselves in perspective. We appreciate our good health even if we discover a mistake in the document we just sent out—not because we don't care about the mistake, but because we can see the big picture and realize that this mistake isn't the end of the world.

Focusing on and seeking the things that produce energy and joy will boost our resilience and ability to be positive in our communication with others. It's energizing. Therefore, we should cultivate these aspects as part of a preventive effort and look for them during pressure-filled situations. A good laugh or a silly comment can take the sting out of even the most serious situations, which is no small thing. We need these moments where we indulge in a liberating laugh and regain our ability to see things in a larger perspective.

A sense of humor can be learned, and we should use it when we have some latitude. It's easier to laugh at ourselves and with others when we're not under a great deal of pressure. During these times, we can practice turning things on their head and learn to discover the quirky angles. When we've practiced for a while and noticed what people with a good sense of humor pick up on, we may find it easier to use humor at the right time in the right place.

Everybody has a sense of humor! But it comes in many forms. The humor discussed here has us poking fun at ourselves, not at others.

4. Work on taking a constructive approach when situations look to be challenges rather than threats

When we incorporate stress management skills into our repertoire, we're teaching ourselves to see the links between thoughts, emotions, body, and behavior. Based on the notion that these factors are interconnected and interdependent, we can affect our own situation, physically as well as mentally, by altering one or more of these components. If we learn to think about or interpret events in a new way, our bodily sensations will change, just as our thoughts and emotions will change if we act differently. In other words, we can interpret situations differently (as challenges rather than threats) as well as act differently.

Avoid unnecessary worries

In situations where you worry, answer the following questions:

- What is it I have to do?
- How am I going to do it?
- Have I done everything that I can to prepare?

If so, there is no reason to worry or fret.

If not, then I have to learn from this experience and manage and prioritize things better the next time. I can't improve matters by blaming or scolding myself for being useless. That will only make things worse! So I'll stop doing that and look forward.

5. Organize and plan workday routines

Butler and Hope (1995) outline the following tools and rules for time management:

Good advice for time management

- Get started right away on the task you are facing. Don't procrastinate.
- Use the "salami" approach—break up tasks into small, manageable pieces and deal with them one at a time.
- Deal with issues only once: Decide right away where they should "go."
- Stick to appointments. Arrange time for meetings to start and end.
- Plan and take breaks.
- On Monday mornings, form an overview of your calendar for the week ahead and look forward to it.
- Avoid making yourself available to others while you're busy with important scheduled tasks (for example, you can close the door or wear headphones).
- Organize your work and work area so that you don't waste time looking for things.

Another simple model is the urgent/not urgent approach to planning and prioritizing in a larger strategic perspective (Butler & Hope, 1995; Covey, 2007).

1. Urgent and important	2. Not urgent but important
3. Urgent but not important	4. Not urgent and not important

We can try plotting a few of our everyday tasks in this table. That might provide an indication of what we should assign as a high or low priority. According to Covey (2007), Box 3 should be empty, as should Box 4. If a task isn't important, why should we do it? Covey recommends spending 80 percent of our time in Box 2 and only 20 percent in Box 1. How is our time allocated on average? And whose "fault" is that? What are we going to do about it?

Managing stress

Below are some measures we can take when we're busy and thus have less room to maneuver.

> MANAGING STRESS
>
> 1. Use your head. Make a plan, avoid interruptions, and do one thing at a time.
> 2. Find someone to talk to about the situation.
> 3. Take a break even when the pressure is on.
> 4. Do relaxation exercises and use your body.

These measures won't eliminate the factors that cause stress, but they can help us feel better for a while. That enables us to make better use of our resources, which is essential at a time when the pressure is higher than normal. But we shouldn't allow this to become our default approach; our body won't sustain that in the long run. So while we draw inspiration from the stress management tools, we should try to achieve a balance between demands and resources in the workday. Here the preventive initiatives can be helpful.

1. Use our head. Make a plan, avoid interruptions, and do one thing at a time

When the pressure is on, we must focus on what is important—prioritize. Of course, this is important at times with less pressure too, but in the stress management phase, it is crucial simply because we can't do everything—however much we may want to. We'll probably have to delegate tasks, ask for help from colleagues, and move less essential tasks farther down the list.

The ability to focus and concentrate fully on the tasks that we decide are most important is essential if we want to be efficient. To do our tasks well, we must focus on one task at a time, insofar as this is possible. This is important because every time we're interrupted or must deal with other issues, we have to start over to regain our concentration. We tax our ability to concentrate every time we are interrupted. Thus, with every interruption, it takes us longer to get back to where we were. To avoid that, we can try the following:

Maintain your concentration

- Avoid interruptions as much as you can. Let the answering service take your phone calls, turn off the e-mail pop-up function, wear headphones, work at home.
- Bundle your tasks. Reply to e-mails at specific times of the day. Do the same with the answering service. Check it at certain times and return calls at certain times.
- Learn mindfulness, the ability to be present in the moment, and use this ability to help you focus on one thing at a time.
- Consider when the task has been done "well enough." Steer clear of the pitfall of perfectionism, where the time you spend achieving the last level of "perfection" rarely pays off.

Many leaders and employees are challenged by their level of ambition to the extent that it disrupts their ability to concentrate. Paradoxically, perfectionism can disrupt their efficiency unless it is managed well.

2. Find someone to talk to about the situation

We probably find it difficult to ask for help in dealing with our workload and stress. It can be helpful to have someone else's input and to receive specific help, for example, from fellow leaders within or outside the organization. Other people's input and ideas can open new possibilities that we may have missed because we were so busy. Having someone else ask us challenging questions can be highly effective and serve as an eye-opener for us. We may not like the advice or the conclusions we draw after being asked these questions, but we should challenge ourselves when confronted this way.

3. Take a break even when the pressure is on

It won't do us, our family, or our workplace any good if we overload. Just gritting our teeth and laboring on actually makes us less efficient. In fact, we often wear ourselves out and aren't as efficient or creative as we would have been if we had gone home and relaxed. The reason is that when we keep going without taking a break, we make mistakes. And those mistakes take time to correct, which is why we become less efficient in the long run.

For the sake of our body *and* our creativity, we need to relax once in a while (Boyatzis et al., 2013). One consequence of overworking may be "tunnel vision" where we fail to pick up inspiration and renew our energy outside work. We must take time off, turning off our computer for the weekend when we're busy, for example. Our family probably deserves it too. We'll likely find that this change of pace doesn't result in a disaster. In fact, the time off may help us be more efficient the following Monday. Stressed leaders often resent the idea of taking time off and make excuses, but once they try it (sometimes forced by consultants, their leaders, their spouse, their friends, or their children), they find that they don't have time *not* to take time off. There's a saying by Insoo Kim Berg:

If you wanna go fast, go slow.

And that saying points to the fact that when we go slow, we see more, experience more, and in the end do more. It's when we hurry that we stumble and fall.

4. Do relaxation exercises and use the body

Relaxation exercises can help us lose some of the tension we may have built up after having been under strain or having been stressed for a prolonged period of time.

For example, we can do relaxation exercises when we take a break from computer work. More workplaces have begun to incorporate these exercises as a natural part of the workday, where everyone takes part. If that's not the case in our workplace, we can try the exercises at home first and then gradually introduce them to our colleagues.

Exercise is good for us. But exercise isn't just a preventive measure. It's equally important as a way to manage stress. The stress hormones buzzing around our body when we're under excessive stress are more easily burnt off when we do what our body was made to do: move.

Now let's look at our options as leaders to engage in dialogue with individual employees, depending on their position on the "well-being staircase."

MANAGING THE INDIVIDUAL EMPLOYEE ON LEVELS FROM CALM TO BURNT OUT

Most leaders have had one or more employees who needed to talk to management about their well-being. This must be taken seriously and must be handled properly.

Stress doesn't develop from one day to the next day. It develops gradually. How we handle the individual employee depends on the number of symptoms we notice in the person and where he or she is on the "stress ladder." The following discussion will explain the different stages and what we can/must do at each stage to manage the stress.

Calm conditions

On this level, our management improves well-being and helps prevent stress in the employees. For instance, we may focus on identifying strengths and bringing them into play more often. That provides energy. We also may spend time on team building and strategic processes and other engaging activities that get the employees involved, making it clear to everyone *why* we're doing things this way and working this way and *how* we work together toward a common goal. In addition, we may ask the team to engage in a dialogue about how to prevent stress in the future.

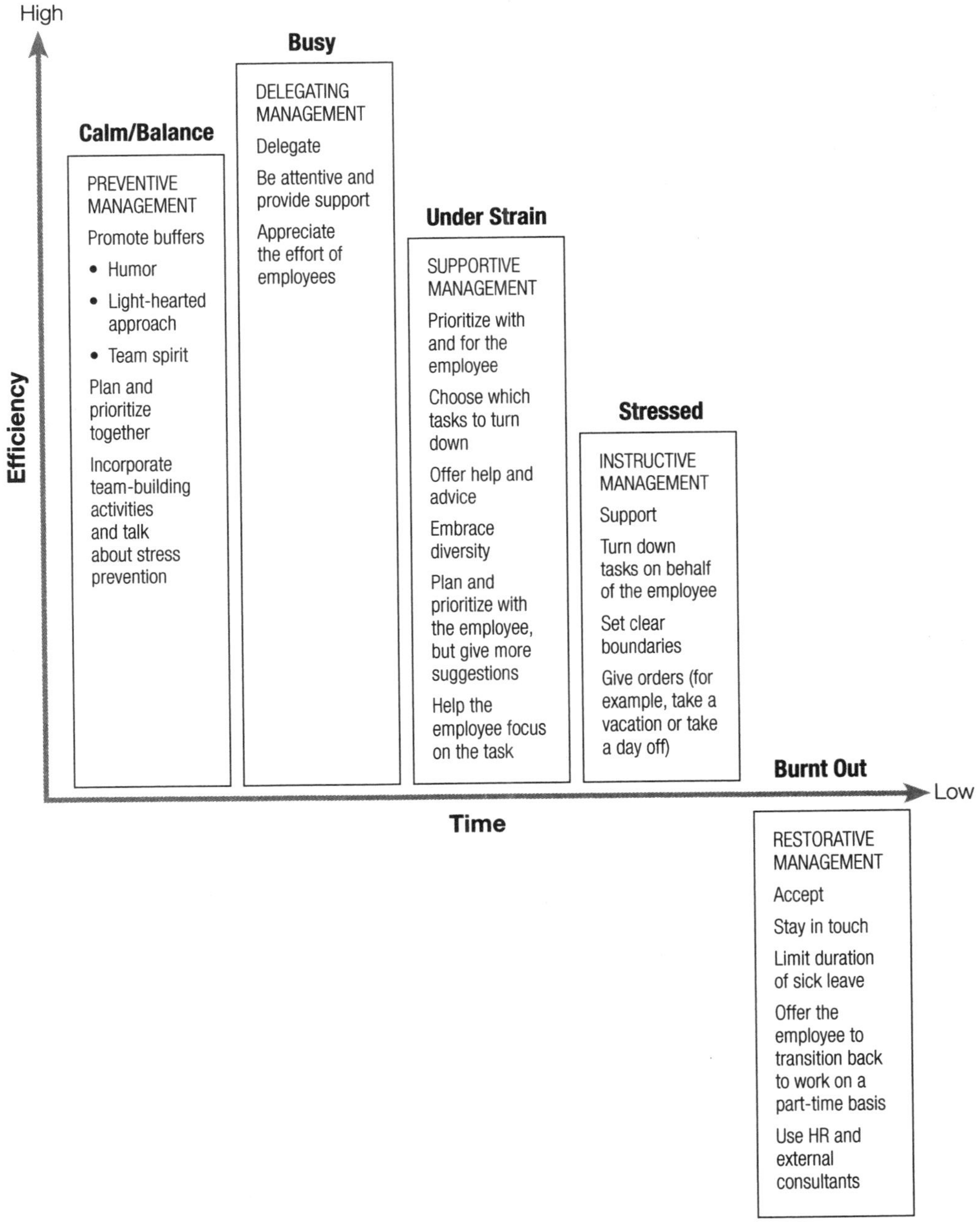
High
Efficiency
Low
Time
Calm/Balance
PREVENTIVE MANAGEMENT
Promote buffers
• Humor
• Light-hearted approach
• Team spirit
Plan and prioritize together
Incorporate team-building activities and talk about stress prevention
Busy
DELEGATING MANAGEMENT
Delegate
Be attentive and provide support
Appreciate the effort of employees
Under Strain
SUPPORTIVE MANAGEMENT
Prioritize with and for the employee
Choose which tasks to turn down
Offer help and advice
Embrace diversity
Plan and prioritize with the employee, but give more suggestions
Help the employee focus on the task
Stressed
INSTRUCTIVE MANAGEMENT
Support
Turn down tasks on behalf of the employee
Set clear boundaries
Give orders (for example, take a vacation or take a day off)
Burnt Out
RESTORATIVE MANAGEMENT
Accept
Stay in touch
Limit duration of sick leave
Offer the employee to transition back to work on a part-time basis
Use HR and external consultants

By creating good conditions for speaking openly about well-being, stress/feeling under pressure, *and* steps to prevent stress, we help to dismantle the taboo, making it a legitimate topic for discussion. A benefit of this is that employees become better at noticing signs and signals of stress so that they can respond in time. Often the workplace is where stress is a taboo (with employees collapsing from stress or experiencing burn-out) because all of their symptoms have been swept aside or trivialized. Unfortunately, it's no exaggeration that people are collapsing with stress in many modern workplaces. [See, for instance, Arianna Huffington's book *Thrive* (2013), where she tells her personal story.] So there are many advantages to building the foundation for communicating openly about well-being and stress.

At the same time, however, it matters how the topic is framed. The more forward-looking and strengths-based the dialogue, the more constructive the debate.

Following are questions that might be helpful for the team to address from time to time. They give the employees answers about specific initiatives for promoting well-being, they facilitate the sharing of knowledge within the team in relation to "best stress management practices," and they highlight the initiatives that are already in place. As a start, we can ask employees to interview each other based on the questions. Subsequently, we can summarize and share these insights in the larger group. The precise process depends on the number of people in the group.

Dialogue aimed at preventing stress and promoting well-being in the individual employee

- When do you feel happiest and most relaxed even when you're busy at work?
- What factors are present in these situations?
- What will it take for things to be like that more often?
- When do you experience real commitment—where the excitement/commitment doesn't lead to stress, but to added energy for the task at hand?
- Which strengths would you like to bring into play even more? Point out your main strengths in relation to the position you occupy.
- For what and where can your competencies and strengths be used (perhaps even more than they are today)?
- What are your best ideas for initiatives to promote well-being and job satisfaction in your team/organization?
- What have you done this week to promote well-being and job satisfaction in your team/organization?
- Tell me about a situation when you saw a colleague who was busy but who, from your perspective, was handling it well.
- What did the person do?
- What is your best stress management tool?

(continued on next page)

Dialogue aimed at preventing stress and promoting well-being in the individual employee (continued)

- How will you boost your energy the next time you have a period marked by low energy?
- If a colleague looks stressed or states that he or she is under too much pressure, what should each of us do?
- Some people prefer to be left alone; others like people to inquire about their well-being. What's your preference? Do you know the person to go to for help when life is "too much"?
- What's the best thing people can say to you when you're really busy?
- How do we make sure we can speak openly of these issues even when we're busier than usual?

In themselves, the type of questions listed above will probably have a positive effect on well-being. They also may prepare and strengthen the employees for future busy periods.

Busy

On this level, as mentioned earlier, the employees are busy, but they recognize that the condition is probably temporary. On this level, the employee can be highly efficient. We might catch ourselves thinking that it would be ideal if the employees always performed as they do when they're busy, where they still do a satisfactory job while getting more done than usual. But employees can't perform on this level for prolonged periods of time. At some point, the employees have to experience a calmer period to continue to perform and keep up their spirit. It may be challenging and fun to be busy for relatively short periods of time when there is a high level of productivity. But in the long run, the situation will slip to the "under strain" level unless people get a chance to recharge their batteries. And at that point, there is a big drop in efficiency. In the long term, the drop in productivity will outweigh the period of above-average production.

On this level, it is particularly helpful if we clearly express that we see, recognize, and appreciate the employee's work effort while also expressing that we don't expect or want this level to continue in the long run. To back up our words with action, we can intervene directly and help the employee by delegating tasks.

We may want to engage in a dialogue with the employee based on the following questions:

Dialogue with the busy employee

Suggestion for introduction:

I can see that you're busier than usual these days. You appear to be dealing well with your tasks, and I've noticed that you really deliver in terms of quantity and quality. Specifically, I've observed that you use your strength X and that it seems to be working well for you, the product's development/sales, and the other team members.

Questions:

- How do you experience your situation right now?
- In what ways do you bring your strengths into play in the tasks you handle?
- Do the tasks that drain you play a big role in your current situation?
- How long do you expect to remain busier than usual?
- Does it look as though your workload is beginning to lighten? If so, when?
- If not, what are your thoughts on how we can deal with that?
- Do you think you'll need help with any of your tasks in the long run?
- Is there anything we can do to ease your workload? If so, what?

Under strain

At this level, the employee has several stress symptoms. Specifically, the strain is showing when an employee is so much busier than usual that he or she must work evenings, nights, and weekends. It may not be worthwhile for the employee to work longer hours, though, because he or she tends to be running around in circles and easily loses focus. The employee may already have developed symptoms such as dizziness and headaches and no longer enjoys the work. Part of the dissatisfaction may stem from the fact that the employee can't meet his or her high quality standards—and probably not others' either. Of course, it may also stem from not being able to bring his or her strengths into play.

Our task as leaders on this level is to establish clear conditions, help the employee prioritize, plan and turn down tasks, offer help and support, and minimize the employee's frustration. We won't help the employee by pointing out that "things really aren't that bad"; reality for the employee is that they are that bad. He or she may be looking for another job. On this level, the employee still has the energy to do that, so if we fail to show understanding and direct leadership, we risk losing the employee.

We shouldn't ask the employee to take on additional tasks. Also, we shouldn't expect the employee to turn tasks down without guidance and support. The energy to do that isn't there as it requires an overview of whether the employee can get things done on time. That overview is missing. Therefore, the employee will likely accept the task if it's placed on his or her desk—perhaps at the cost of more frustration. The task probably won't be completed any time soon. So it's preferable to give the task to someone who has more room in his or her schedule or to change priorities to remove other tasks from the employee's to-do list.

We should have a specific talk with the employee about his or her experience of the situation. In this talk, we should listen with an open mind even if we disagree with the employee's perception of the situation.

Dialogue with an employee under strain

Start: Tell the employee that you have requested this dialogue because he or she seems to be extraordinarily busy right now. Show the employee the well-being staircase and explain that in your opinion, he or she seems to be under strain. Describe the observations that have led to this. Next, ask the employee where he or she would place himself or herself on the staircase—from calm to burnt out. Also use the scaling exercise to gauge the severity of the situation from your perspective as well as the employee's. You and the employee should be more or less in agreement that he or she is under strain; otherwise, you won't achieve resonance in the conversation.

When you and the employee basically agree on the reality of the situation, proceed with open-ended questions. Let the employee do most of the talking. (That's a sign that he or she feels heard.) Feeling heard and understood usually helps diminish the employee's frustration, and it becomes easier to put things into perspective. Tell the employee that you are sympathetic to his or her situation, that your purpose is to assist the employee, and that the goal of this dialogue is to discuss the tasks that you think he or she ought to give up in the current situation.

During the conversation: Once the conversation is off to a good start, proceed with the following questions:

- What have you done in the past to handle this type of situation well?
- In your experience, what worked well for you?
- How do you think you would view the situation if you saw it from a less strained position?
- Have you noticed whether others here are handling their situations differently? Now that you're thinking about it, does that give you any ideas about what you can do to change the situation in which you clearly feel stressed?

Also ask the following:

- How can I assist you? What do you need from me?
- How can your colleagues help you?
- Is there anything we can do right now?

End the dialogue by summarizing what you've talked about and what proposals for solutions you have agreed on. Don't draw conclusions in your own words unless the employee approves. Always ask: Did I get this right? Is that your perception as well? So is that what we'll agree to do?

Stressed

This level involves many of the same signs that are described in the section "Under strain." What distinguishes this level from the preceding one is the number of symptoms and the fact that the employee may seem less frustrated but more passive and defeatist about his or her situation. That is also evident in the quality of work the employee is capable of, which, briefly put, is deteriorating. The employee may make obvious mistakes or forget important details. Sick days also may increase.

In this case, our management style must be more direct. That is, we have to intervene and take tasks away from the employee, even if the person doesn't think that's necessary. On this level, the employee has lost his or her sense of reality in terms of what he or she can handle. Consequently, the employee needs specific instructions—for example, leave work on time, leave work early, take a vacation, or work less on this project (we'll get coworkers to help you). Of course, this has to be conveyed in a respectful but direct way.

It's difficult being the leader of an employee who's dealing with stress. We probably need the employee, so it may run counter to ask the employee to go home early and work less. Nevertheless, in the long term, this is the best decision for us, the team, the workplace, and the employee. The alternative is that the employee goes over the edge and has to take sick leave due to burn-out, in which case we'll really miss the person's contribution!

Dialogue with an employee with stress

This is less a dialogue than the talks on the previous levels, as the employee requires specific directions and actions from you. However, you still need to listen and let the person speak.

Start: Tell the employee that you perceive his or her situation as being severe. Describe the symptoms you've noticed and explain that you interpret this as stress. The more specific your examples of observations, the better. This may involve disagreements the person has had with colleagues (perhaps atypically); it may be a performance that was not up to the usual high standards; it may be things the employee forgot to do or check.

Ask the employee whether he or she recognizes the examples you mention. Let the employee describe his or her situation and his or her perception of it. As in the other dialogues, listen and be understanding. Here too you may include the scaling exercise; also use the well-being staircase to check whether your views and those of the employee are consistent with regard to level of stress. However, you should know if the employee doesn't have a realistic grasp of his or her situation. Stress affects people's sense of reality and their ability to see themselves differently.

(continued on next page)

Dialogue with an employee with stress (continued)

During the conversation: Explain that you want to reassign some of the employee's current tasks to others and that you've prepared a list of those tasks. Present the list and explain that you aren't doing this because the employee isn't doing a good job (provided that's the case); rather, you're taking this step because the employee has too much on his or her plate right now. This is affecting delivery times, for example, which is why you have to take this step. You've already decided who can take over or whatever else is going to happen to the tasks in question. The fact that you have assumed responsibility for the tasks may lift some of the stress from the employee's shoulders. Don't ask an employee who is on this level to get into a discussion with you about what should happen to the tasks you're looking to reassign. Part of your responsibility as a leader is to deal with the issue and show the employee that he or she needn't worry about it. Ask about the employee's perception of what you've said. In general, be direct and tell the employee that he or she must respect work hours (in other words, work less), vacation plans, etc. Tell the employee that you appreciate his or her effort but that the current state of affairs regarding his or her workload isn't tenable in the long run—for the employee or the workplace.

End: Summarize what you have agreed on or what you're asking the employee to do. Ask the employee what it was like to have this conversation and whether there is anything else he or she would like to discuss. Schedule a follow-up conversation at a time that's convenient for both of you.

Burnt out

On this level, the employee is on sick leave. The employee is sick, and the condition may be characterized by depression, ennui, anxiety attacks, and apathy. The expected length of the sick leave is often proportional to the duration of the person's experience of stress. If the condition has been developing for years, the employee will probably be away from the workplace for a long time. Employees who have been under intense stress for "merely" six months may need only a few weeks of sick leave.

This issue depends on the individual involved, which is why it's hard to make generalized predictions. Experience shows, however, that the sick leave shouldn't be too short or too long. The plan for a return to the workplace must be found in a dialogue between us and the employee. For example, a good idea is for the employee to return on a part-time basis at first. That can only happen, however, if in the interim period we've made a genuine effort to eliminate as many of the work-related stressors as possible—for example, restructuring tasks and discussing with the employee which workplace factors are particularly stressful for him or her.

Our first task is to make a plan for handling the employee's job tasks while he or she is on sick leave. This probably involves shuffling tasks and changing priorities. It is important to deal with the tasks and not have them "waiting" until the person returns.

Relatively soon after the sick leave is announced, depending on when the employee is ready for it, we should have a conversation with the employee.

Dialogue with the employee who is on sick leave

Start: Ask how the employee is doing.

During the conversation: Tell the employee the following:

- The employee shouldn't worry about urgent tasks (or any tasks). They will be handled in the person's absence. The tasks have been dealt with, and you've made sure they're not "waiting" until the person returns to work.
- Offer the employee some sessions with a psychologist.
- Determine what you should say to colleagues. Make a suggestion and listen to what the employee wants.
- Ask how much contact the employee wants to have during his or her sick leave and ask whether the person's boss or a colleague should oversee the contact.

In closing: Agree when you will contact the person again. Give the other colleagues the information that you agreed on with the employee during your dialogue. If this information isn't provided, unfortunate rumors may emerge.

After the initial conversation with the person who is on sick leave, we need to have ongoing conversations with the employee about how he or she is doing and whether there are things that need to change in the person's work assignments. We should ask whether the employee thinks there are too many or not enough tasks, which tasks he or she enjoys, and whether he or she finds any tasks too stressful or too draining.

If we have a close relationship with the employee, we can ask how big a role the workplace played in the stress and what role private factors played. Many employees don't mind discussing this. In fact, they're often well aware of the factors that triggered the stress and whether those factors are related to work or to their personal life. We also should discuss general work conditions with the employee, including relationships and cooperation issues.

Toward the end of the sick leave, we can have a dialogue with the employee about how to work together to make sure the person brings his or her strengths into play when he or she returns to work. We should schedule a series of meetings once the employee returns (for example, initially twice a week). It's our responsibility to call these meetings.

We now know how we must act as a leader in relation to employees on various levels of the well-being staircase. The following section reviews recommendations for how to promote well-being and thus prevent stress in the team or department.

PROMOTE WELL-BEING WITHIN THE TEAM

Certain areas or themes may be particularly important to address in promoting well-being in the team or department. These themes are linked to the general stressors that were discussed at the beginning of the chapter. We can take the following steps to enhance the well-being in our department, team, or organization.

1. Establish clear goals—a clear purpose of the work.
2. Provide a working environment that doesn't have too many conflicts.
3. Provide predictability and clarity by means of communication and ongoing alignment of expectations.
4. Provide a "suitable degree" of influence.
5. Provide "suitable amounts" of work.
6. Ensure a good match between demands and control.
7. Promote a culture of useful feedback.

Let's take a closer look at each of them.

1. Establish clear goals—a clear purpose of the work

It appears that we experience the greatest sense of well-being when we know the goal and can see the higher purpose of our work. Therefore, from time to time, we should bring up the following questions in our team/department:

Talk with your team about the goals and purpose of the work

- What is it that we're passionate about?
- What difference would we like to make in the world?
- What difference do we want to make for our customers/users?
- What was the reason you applied for this job?
- What is the unique position of our team in relation to the rest of the organization?
- Where can we make a difference in relation to the overall vision of the organization?
- What are our unique individual contributions?
- What would the organization lack if we weren't here?
- What would the world lack if the organization wasn't here?

Ideally, the purpose of an employee's work should be clear. That makes the work meaningful to him or her, which is important in today's workplace. Besides putting the overall purpose of the organization on the agenda, we also should discuss the partial goals or actions. This is when the partial goals become clear to the employee (for example, something as specific as meeting a deadline), which will bring us closer to the overall goal of the organization. Then things make sense, and that sustains the employee's will and energy to make an effort.

2. Provide a working environment that doesn't have too many conflicts

We can promote a good working environment by making sure the employees get along. We manage the negative conflicts as described in Chapter 10. We enhance the social relationships by means of social events and team-building activities. For example, we can encourage the employees to have lunch together and establish a buddy system where pairs of employees follow up on each other, ensuring their well-being. In short, the key is to ensure that the individual employee believes that he or she has social supports at work.

3. Provide predictability and clarity by means of communication and ongoing alignment of expectations

Predictability is about giving employees the right information at the right time (for example, information about a new strategy or an upcoming restructuring). That places demands on our ability to provide adequate and timely information, which can be a balancing act. With our fellow managers, we probably should practice our ability to convey a message clearly and timely before speaking to our employees about certain organizational matters. That will help us deliver more coherent messages, and it will ensure that everybody in the management team delivers the same message at the same time. That can help prevent misunderstandings and ensure predictability.

Predictability also is about matching employees' expectations on an ongoing basis.

REFLECTION

Is it clear to the individual employee and to the team what is expected of them?

What is your main strength in communicating and matching expectations?

On a scale from 0 to 10, how good are you at communicating the right information at the right time? (How would your employees rate you?)

What can you do to climb one step up the scale with regard to communicating clearly and appropriately about information that your employees need on an ongoing basis?

4. Provide a "suitable degree" of influence

As mentioned earlier, we like being able to affect our environment and to have influence; it's human nature. That gives us a sense of control and ownership, which are emotions that help prevent stress. Therefore, it makes sense to let our employees influence, for example, how to plan their workday, in what order to carry out their tasks, when the workday begins and ends, what tools they use to carry out their tasks, and what the interior design/layout of the office should be. Different workplaces have different degrees of influence.

The key is to give the employees a *suitable* degree of influence so that it doesn't seem like an added burden to be involved in planning and prioritizing.

In this respect, employees are different. Some like having a high degree of influence, whereas others prefer leaving decisions up to others. And the issue can be further complicated by the fact that different people in the team/department have different preferences about where they want these boundaries drawn and in what way. In this regard, there are no simple solutions. As leaders, we have to uncover the preferences of each employee as well as the team. That dialogue is never-ending and must be repeated regularly.

As leaders, we often fail to involve our employees enough. This isn't done out of malice, but often stems from the faulty assumption that the employees want to avoid or lack the ability to consider, for example, strategically appropriate steps in a given project. In a strengths-based approach, we assume that the more the employees are involved in the decision-making processes, the greater their sense of responsibility and ownership in relation to the given task and its execution. We'll return to this point in Chapter 12. Therefore, a suitable degree of influence not only has the potential to prevent stress, but also makes good strategic sense.

5. Provide "suitable amounts" of work

Who gets the most recognition in an organization—those who take on extra tasks and put in more than 50 hours a week or those who draw the line and stick to 40 hours? Which behavior is rewarded? The culture in many organizations encourages people to take on too much work. As leaders, we need to notice when some of our employees tend to do this. In some cases, we must challenge those employees or instruct them to work less.

We should encourage our employees to try to complete their work in a "normal" workweek. Otherwise, a workplace culture develops where putting in the normal number of hours is considered inadequate—where we're expected to stay up late if we don't finish our tasks during the day but don't find time to relax and rebuild our strength. It's not healthy to set this precedent.

It is more constructive to create a culture where working late is the exception, where working weekends is not the norm, and where management also sends the signal that this sort of behavior is expected only in peak periods and isn't the norm. Management should clearly convey that it wants well-rested employees who maintain a work-life balance (or work-family balance because work is also life).

REFLECTION

What sort of workplace culture does your organization encourage?

What sort of workplace culture do you encourage?

What sort of behavior do you recognize/praise in your staff?

Have you ever asked an employee to work less? Why or why not?

What would it take for you to do so?

How much overtime would you let an employee work before you asked him or her to go home?

Is that inconceivable to you? Why or why not?

How does that benefit you?

The way we work is changing, and the modern workplace calls for flexibility. That means it might be okay to put in ten-hour days for a while, but then it should be possible to work four-hour days or to take days off. Some workplaces offer flexible schedules. In others, the hours are fixed. A flexible schedule requires an ongoing dialogue about the way the workday is managed and about mutual expectations.

6. Ensure a good match between demands and control

As leaders, we have a number of options that we can use to ensure that employees experience a match between demands and control. The most important thing is to keep an open dialogue about this. We may ask them "How do you perceive the level of demands these days?" and talk with them about their perceived level of resources (personal, professional, and economical) compared with the level of demands they face. Remember that an employee also may feel that he or she isn't challenged enough, in which case we need to consider changes based on this information.

7. Promote a culture of useful feedback

In a culture of useful feedback, people on our team talk about and receive feedback related to their tasks, performance, and achievements on an ongoing basis. This may be in the form of business results, text documents, information the employees have communicated, their way of cooperating with colleagues, or their ability to accomplish a process. In this culture, feedback is not only something we give the employees, but also something the employees incorporate as part of their interactions. A high-functioning culture of useful feedback is a bottom-up process: There is enough openness and a sufficiently safe environment that the employees are comfortable giving us feedback. Chapter 7 discussed more about how to build a culture that encourages useful feedback.

CLOSING REMARKS

This chapter discussed the different styles we apply in the various dialogues on well-being and stress. Our goal should be to gain inspiration so that we can promote well-being on our team/organization, helping us to blossom and flourish even more in the future.

12

STRENGTHS-BASED CHANGE PROCESSES

CONTENTS

This chapter takes a closer look at what we can do as strengths-based leaders to help move our team and the organization in a desired direction—toward a burning desire to create or be something for and in the world that will make a positive difference, something that will help make the world a better, more sustainable, flourishing, and wonderful place. That may sound lofty, but visions should be lofty.

A vision should be within sight but out of reach.

This means that the vision is what we want to pursue because we can imagine the positive impact it will have if it is realized. The vision should be ambitious, desirable, and meaningful—and achievable if we strive to bring it about. It's not something we can achieve without an effort, though. We have to make it happen. Therefore, there should be a burning desire to make it happen. That's the driving force.

We often hear that the burning *platform* is what makes people see the need to take action, change the organization, or generally pull themselves together. The burning platform is the factor that motivates and drives change processes. This is based on the idea that people are motivated by escaping from something undesirable. Some research suggests that people can be motivated by "the stick": with punishment and the knowledge of the severe consequences of inaction. That definitely has the capacity to make us act to prevent or escape "the bad stuff" (Daft, 2008). That is the underlying premise of the campaigns about lung cancer, high cholesterol levels, obesity, and companies that need to do something *now*—or else. These are scare campaigns that show us the terrible burning platform we're standing on and that seek to motivate us to act now. And they appear to be effective. At least they have driven many people to lose weight, quit smoking, and change their corporate strategy because they envisioned (or were forced to envision) what would happen if they did nothing (Mabeck, 2005).

Thus, conventional strategy processes rely on the notion of avoiding something undesirable. The terminology and the thinking in traditional strategy and change processes are strongly influenced by the fact that historically the military was the first to employ strategic thinking. Plans were made for outmaneuvering the enemy, conquering new markets (countries, regions, etc.), and killing efficiently. The impact of the military mind-set is evident in the language that is still used in conventional strategic thinking. Here the goal is to outgun, conquer, command and control, kill, and destroy (Mohr et al., 2008).

This thinking and this mind-set are so embedded in our ideas about change and strategy that we rarely question whether it's the "right" or the only way to change organizations. That's a shame, as the aggressive, competitive mind-set has a number of unfortunate side effects. It instills in us the sense of being at war and experiencing fear, dominance, and submission; us versus them; and the goal of exploiting the resources (grab what we can while we can).

With the strengths-based mind-set, there is a different perception of what it takes to motivate people to change and of the overall strategy. There's no doubt that people can be motivated by fear and horror. But as human beings, we're also highly motivated by cooperating, by building on the best there is, and by imagining ourselves as the best version of ourselves (*without* killing a lot of people to get there). The focus is on the positive aspects of making sure that as we move toward a desired goal, we keep hold of ourselves as whole persons who also think beyond ourselves to the benefit of society and the larger world. We think with our heart as well as our brain (Scharmer, 2009; Watkins et al., 2001; Weisbord & Janoff, 1995; Lazlo et al., 2014).

It's far wiser to motivate through a burning desire—visualized at the right time and in the right spirit—than through a burning platform, where we have no time to think things through properly and thus incorporate a holistic perspective, where our only thought is to *get away*. The burning platform only catches fire if we act too late. As leaders, we should motivate our employees to change *before* the platform catches fire. We need to *work toward something* rather than *move away from something*. Naturally, we should be honest about the state of the platform (it's our foundation), but as strengths-based leaders, our focus is on the burning desire.

We must create a timely burning desire to motivate change before the burning platform forces our hand.

We must be proactive and innovative rather than reactive and aggressive.

The idea is that we should involve the employees in determining the burning desire. We need to look at the "end of the rainbow" for the intended outcome of our shared work and efforts. We must consider why it is so important for us to do the work we do and what we then need to change to accomplish that work.

This chapter touches on how we can create a clear, burning desire and a clear strategy that will move us, our team, and our organization toward the desired goal.

SUCCESSFUL CHANGE PROCESSES

In 2008, a study on change processes carried out by McKinsey found that what characterized *really* successful transformation processes in organizations was that the employees had been involved and engaged in the process as early as possible (McKinsey, 2008). In these processes, management led by example; they painted the big picture and clearly showed what the organization "would look like" once the vision was realized. Management clearly articulated "the burning desire" and advocated the "noble cause."

Disastrously, however, the same study also found that only 6 percent of the 3,199 top executives who had been interviewed replied that their transformation processes had been successful in terms of accomplishing the goals they had set and in terms of managing to include the entire organization in the process of reaching the goals. In other words, only 6 percent of the organizations had managed to change systems and structures as well as the more informal levels represented by the culture, values, and "mood" in the organization.

However, the processes that *were* successful had managed to bring everybody on board. The box below summarizes the findings from the study (McKinsey, 2008).

Recipe for successful transformation processes

- Engage and energize the entire organization by means of continuous communication and involvement (for example, by celebrating small victories along the way).
- Establish clear ownership in top management by setting clear goals for managers and holding them accountable for achieving those goals.
- Allocate resources to develop desired competences in the organization.
- Mobilize role models, individuals, and teams to head up the process and "lead the way" (desired behavior and changes in ways of working and cooperating).
- Break up the transformation process into small manageable parts.
- Focus on business-related and human achievements (for example, the economic bottom line as well as human learning).
- Create and communicate emotionally attractive stories about the transformation.
- Enhance the transformation that contributes to anchoring the process by means of clear goals and incentives.
- Make sure all managers understand and are able to communicate what is desirable about the transformation.

In other recent literature on successful change processes and literature about innovation and strengths-based leadership (Steensen, 2008; Anderson, 2008; Whitney, 2010; Hamel, 2012; Kotter, 2014; Lazlo, 2014), a uniform picture emerges. The key to lasting change and transformation is to involve individual employees and trigger their commitment, creativity, and passion in the change process—and not only the employees, but also relevant stakeholders, customers, and citizens impacted by and interacting with the organizations on a day-to-day basis.

Hamel (2007) describes how the organization and its leaders must earn the employee's initiative, creativity, and passion—these factors only thrive under a certain kind of leadership, where employees are set free to think for themselves and bring out the best of themselves. Hamel sets up the goals in a hierarchy, together with three other employee contributions that also help the organization reach its goal—a total of six employee contributions that enable the organization to achieve its goals.

The top three employee contributions cannot be expected to occur automatically, as mentioned. Leaders have to do something in organizational and management terms to bring them out. The bottom three contributions, however, are capabilities that leaders can *buy* and can *expect* of employees. Once the employees have been hired, they're expected to show up at work and do what they are told (obedience and diligence) using whatever intellect or expertise that secured them the position in the first place. But simply having employees do these basic things will not in itself make the organization flourish or help accomplish a burning desire and vision. To achieve that, the employees need to show initiative, creativity, and passion in relation to the task they are performing (Hamel, 2007, 2012).

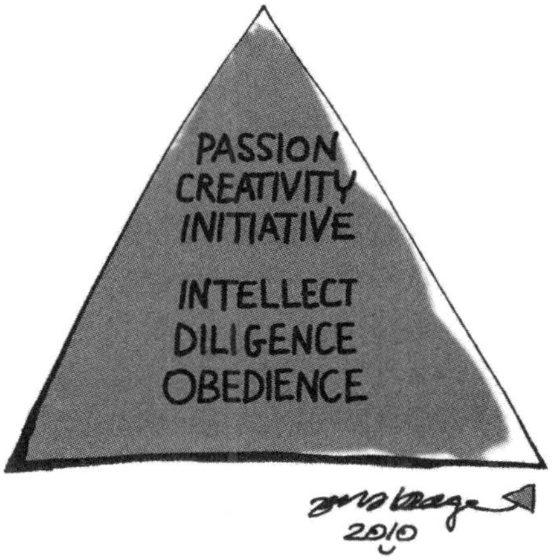

So what can we do as an organization and as leaders to strengthen and promote the "top" three contributions from the employees? We need to ask, involve, and engage them—that is talk with them about the burning desire, visualize it, and find new ways of working together.

Hamel calls it *management innovation* when leaders come up with new ways of involving employees, new ways of triggering their passion and commitment, and new ways of generating initiative and creativity (Hamel, 2007, 2012)—briefly put, new ways of bringing their strengths into play. In his books, Hamel offers many specific examples of innovation by managers that inspire initiative, creativity, and passion. Some of the principles behind management innovation were mentioned in Chapter 9. Here are some more.

Examples of management innovation that brings out initiative, creativity, and passion in employees

- The managers bring the employees together around a common purpose/a noble cause that deserves everyone's best effort.
- The teams/employees are allowed to decide who is hired for a four-week trial period, after which time they are again allowed to determine whether the new colleague will be offered a permanent position. This also counts for the hiring of new leaders.

(continued on next page)

Examples of management innovation that brings out initiative, creativity, and passion in employees (continued)

- There is full transparency about pay and ownership. Everybody knows what everyone is paid, what leads to a pay increase or decrease, and what it takes to become a partner or co-owner.
- There is room for slack—room for thinking, tossing around ideas, and developing possibilities that don't necessarily have to turn into something concrete.
- Power is distributed downward. The employees choose projects and their managers.
- There is support for what may seem to be opposites and paradoxes—for example, democracy and discipline, freedom and accountability, and community and internal competition.
- Everyone is allowed to be creative. It's not left to any one group, but to everyone, to offer ideas for ongoing improvements and to carry them out.
- Internal games are organized to find the best ideas for development; the best project wins and receives funding. The money for the project comes from previous years' earnings.

Thus, if we want to move our team or organization, our path as leaders is paved with involvement, positive stories, committed leaders, and employees who are allowed to use their strengths every day. This includes taking small steps, setting up role models, and bringing everyone's ideas into play. It includes top-down management to provide the general direction and communication, but bottom-up management with regard to ideas for action as well as the actions themselves (Cameron & Lavine, 2006; Whitney, 2010). Whitney et al. (2010) refers to it as getting results with "positive power" when leaders apply these five I's (Inquiry, Illumination, Inclusion, Inspiration, and Integrity) in their leadership approach and processes of transformational organizational change.

The next sections discuss specific ways in which we can apply a strength perspective in our organizational change processes.

STRENGTHS-BASED CHANGE

The following discussion explains a strengths-based process model. It can be used in any strengths-based process (that is, in small or large development processes with teams or the whole organization).

The strengths-based process helps us devote time on the strength axis, leveraging existing strengths and bringing new strengths into play in the future. The model is inspired by the Appreciative Inquiry model developed by David Cooperrider of the Weatherhead School of Management (Cooperrider, 2005).

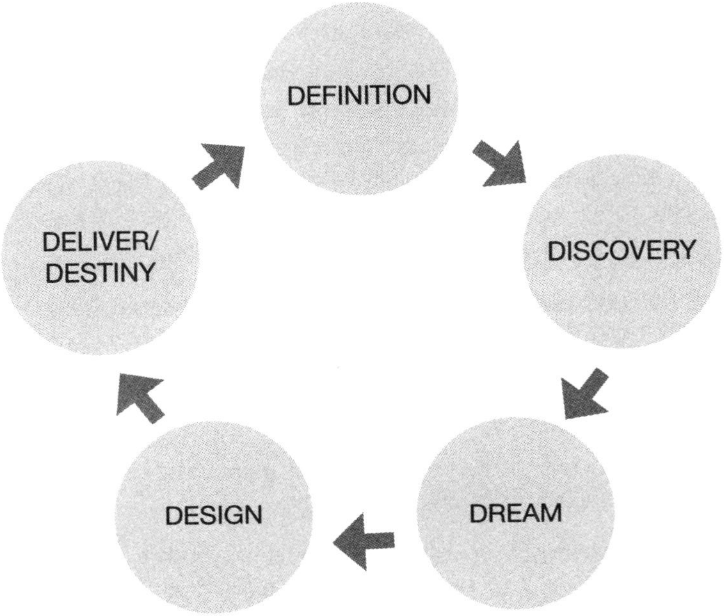

The strengths-based process model. Cooperrider's 5D model.

In the **definition stage**, we define an existing problem or challenge that we want to do something about. We talk about the problem, but also talk about what we want to see instead, thereby defining the real topic—the topic we'd like to dig into further. Instead of talking more about the problem, we shed light on what it is we want to see more of—the desired future. For example, if pollution is a by-product of our company's production process, we need to deal with it. But instead of talking about pollution, who or what created it, etc., for a longer period, we talk about whatever it is we want instead—for instance, 100 percent clean production. By talking about this, we find solutions to the original problem and thereby solve it, but indirectly. This is called the principle of obliquity (Kay, 2012).

In the **discovery phase**, we engage as many employees as possible in articulating which strengths and best practices exist in the organization, in the surrounding community, and within the team and/or in individuals that we can build on and learn from to solve the problem. We talk about the best of what has been and what is, building self-esteem and hope and showing everybody that we don't start from scratch when trying to solve the problem at hand.

In the **dream phase**, we dream of "what might be" if/when the problem is solved and a "future perfect" has emerged. We think outside the box and use creative methods such as drawing, singing, and/or poetic articulation to show what we want to happen—as if it's happening right now. This phase is often challenging for many down-to-earth and to-the-point people, but if introduced properly and explained well, even the most straightforward person ends up seeing the benefit of this phase and getting something out of engaging in it.

The **design phase** is characterized by a more concrete and action-oriented approach, yet we're still in the future. We imagine and design those structures and work methods and ways of collaborating that will best fit the "future perfect" envisioned in the dream phase. We're still allowed—and in fact expected—to think outside the box, so more realistic thinking such as "this will never work" or "that's not possible" isn't part of the dialogue yet.

In the last phase, the **delivery phase**, we experiment and try out the new ways of working and structuring ourselves and inviting new stakeholders to collaborate. "There is nothing to it but to do it." We try out wild ideas and see what happens, not judging whether something will work before we try it (unless, of course, it will do harm). In this phase, we also start evaluating: Was this a good idea? Does it work? But we still try to keep an open mind and not judge too soon; maybe an idea needs time before it will work. Patience, open-mindedness, courage, and perseverance are key words for the strengths-based leader and everyone else engaged in this phase.

Below we'll look at the application of the models in strengths-based change processes. For an in-depth understanding of its application though, we need to read more literature and perhaps take a course in Appreciative Inquiry to become capable of leading this process. The Literature section at the end of the book provides suggestions. In addition, the website for the Weatherhead School of Management (www.weatherhead.case.edu) offers courses/foundations in the Appreciative Inquiry model.

When we apply the strengths-based model in a change process in our organization, we bring together many minds that together can envision and design a future that is beyond our imagination. Before we can embark on this exciting journey of solving problems and finding solutions based on this mind-set, we need to understand some fundamentals about the process. Some basic conditions must be present for the change process to be successful (Cooperrider & Whitney, 2005, p. 55). These "fundamentals" consist of the following, in which people must:

- Be Known in Relationship.
- Be Heard.
- Dream in Community.
- Choose to Contribute.
- Act with Support.
- Be Positive.

So we must remember to design the process in such a way that these basic conditions can be brought to life. It's important to instill a certain level of trust, for instance, not only by encouraging others to listen well, but also by listening to ourselves, by being positive, and by meeting (making eye contact with) the human beings around us with a certain level of intimacy.

Two other aspects of the process need to be emphasized before we, as strengths-based leaders, try the methods in the Appreciative Inquiry change process. These deal with our ability as leaders to let the process "do its work" and to "give life to the fundamentals" mentioned above.

First, note that the strengths-based process is a bottom-up process. This means that as leaders, we have to let go of the idea that we know best and that we have to control everything. Instead, we need to trust that the employees, stakeholders, customers, and maybe people from society have valuable ideas that can help us move in the direction of a burning desire that we might not have considered or been able to come up with ourselves. Imagine how many ideas and initiatives can surface if we involve X number of employees/customers with X number of years of experience in dreaming and providing input for action—and in adding new perspectives to the situation.

Second, prepare to let go of control for a moment. The process is managed and controlled by us and possibly other leaders of the organization and experts. But even when the process is controlled, it still must be able to flow freely and allow people to offer ideas they've come up with or want to bring into play. This is how their enthusiasm is realized. If the involved parties sense that we're reluctant or that whatever they say, we'll go ahead and do what we want regardless, this pseudo-process never should have been launched. Of course, we have to frame the dialogue and strive to keep it on track, preferably with help from others (maybe even external consultants). But we need to try to let go for a while and see what direction the process takes. Most people are well aware that suggestions, ideas, and initiatives must fit into a context. But if they begin to think that we'll shoot down ideas or be "realistic" too soon, we'll kill the creativity and out-of-the-box thinking.

Many leaders are challenged by strengths-based change processes because they sometimes feel out of control when engaging in them. People come up with wild ideas and use creative sides of themselves that we might not have imagined. At times, we may be thinking that engaging in this kind of process is a waste of time that is taking us nowhere. But that's not true. Because the strengths-based change process takes time in the short run, it might seem like a waste of time. We do spend a great deal of time bringing everybody together and brainstorming and listening carefully to people's ideas. But Watkins et al. called one of their first books *Change at the Speed of Imagination* (2001). All the time we spend involving people in important dialogues related to the organization, its product, its processes, and its collaboration styles is saved when we put ideas into action. As was already mentioned, people are sometimes skeptical when they see how fast and easy things seem to change after a process such as this. But that's because the process is well framed, it involves everybody, and everybody knows what to do and why to do it afterward. So during the process, we need to let go of our fear and know that the process has proved its worth (Cooperrider & Whitney, 2005; Cooperrider et al., 2008; Whitney et al., 2011; Lazlo et al., 2014) and that all the wild ideas and dreams will be framed as concrete action points by the end of the process.

Now let's look at the strengths-based change process step-by-step.

Definition. Describe the foundation: what the challenge/problem is, what your basic strengths are, and what you would like to see happen in the future.

A strengths-based change process begins with our burning desire to change something and involves our employees and others to make that change happen. But instead of using the traditional mind-set of looking deeper into the root causes of the problems and analyzing everything that has led to the current problem, we want to apply the strengths-based mind-set (the ideal pit), bring everybody on board, and make the strengths of the many compensate for whatever weaknesses there might be in the system.

Once we've identified a problem that we think is important for the organization to solve, we can involve people to help find solutions used to solve the problem from a strengths-based mind-set. That is basically the goal of the strengths-based change process. We want to solve a problem but are tired of using the old methods. As Cooperrider and Whitney framed it the book *Appreciative Inquiry: A Positive Revolution in Change* (2005, p. 6):

> *Are you ready for a positive approach to change? Are you tired of the same old discussions of what's not working, how hard it is to overcome, and who's to blame? Do you have hopes and dreams for your organization? Would you like to see engagement, commitment, and enthusiasm rise along with revenues and profits? Are you searching for a process to open communication, unleash human potential, and create a truly learning organization? If your answer to any of these questions is yes, you are ready to accept the invitation to the positive revolution, to embrace Appreciative Inquiry, and to benefit from a positive approach to change management.*

In the definition phase of the process, which might take up to a year to complete, the following happens:

STEPS IN THE DEFINITION PHASE

- Choose a representative group to help you find the right topic and headline for the future process.
- Analyze the platform on which you're standing.
- Educate AI agents.
- Choose an inspiring, engaging, and motivating headline.
- Establish measurable success criteria.
- Find a suitable venue.
- Send out an exciting invitation.

Let's take a look at these steps one by one.

Choose a representative group to help you find the right topic and headline for the future process

Before involving everybody—the whole organization/department/team, important stakeholders, customers, and people from the community—in the strengths-based change process, we ask a representative group of people from these different groups for help in finding the right topic for the process.

Interestingly, once we've identified a problem to solve, we have a tendency to think that the solution is the opposite of our problem. For example, if the problem is "too much sick leave" in the company, the solution might be "less sick leave." But how aspiring is that for people to aim for? Not that aspiring. People do not necessarily want "less sick leave." Imagine asking a leader what the company's vision is and what the desired state for the working environment is and he or she answers: "Less sick leave." Would anyone be convinced that this leader had ambitions and could motivate the people around him or her? Probably not. Instead, this leader might aspire for "full-spectrum engagement and flourishing" in the team/organization. But once we've identified a problem, we might find it hard to determine what we want. This is where the representative group comes into the picture. When solving organizational problems, we need to think about what we want to accomplish in the world, not just what we want to avoid.

Analyze the platform on which you're standing

Another important thing happens during the definition phase. As part of finding the right topic and headlines for our process, we should analyze what sort of platform we're standing on. Everyone must be able to envision what the point of departure for the process is and what made us decide that this was the most important topic for initiating a change process in which everyone is involved. This analysis should contain a thorough investigation of the market in which we're operating, our stakeholders, and the demand for our services and products now and in the future. Where do our earnings come from? Where might they come from in the future? What are our strengths and weaknesses, our potentials and aspirations? Where do we make our most important contributions? What does the world need and thus want us to do now and in the future?

This chapter won't discuss all the analytical tools we might use to carry out this strategic analysis. There are countless possibilities, and a thorough discussion goes beyond the scope of this book. The Literature section at the end of the book provides inspiration for strengths-based ways of carrying out strategic analyses. One recommendation is the article on Appreciative Strategy (Stavros et al., 2003) that discusses the SOAR model (analysis of Strengths, Opportunities, Aspirations, and Results), among others. SOAR is a strengths-based alternative to the better-known SWOT model (Strengths, Weaknesses, Opportunities, and Threats).

Educate AI agents

As part of getting to know the platform, we might want to educate/train a select group of people from the organization in Appreciative Inquiry and the strengths-based paradigm, asking them to conduct interviews with people in and around the organization about what the organization should focus on in the future. Having local change agents with a deeper understanding of the strengths-based mind-set also kick-starts the change that we ultimately want to see happen in and around the organization (Cooperrider & Whitney, 2005).

Below are examples of questions the change agents might ask relevant stakeholder, employees, leaders, and customers when delving into a strategic topic.

QUESTIONS ABOUT TRENDS

- When you look at society (media, politicians, trends, legislation, etc.), what developments do you see that should be addressed in the coming years?
- When you look at current developments and trends in your industry or profession, what developments should be addressed in the coming years?
- What do you think the customers/citizens/users will be focused on in the coming years?
- What is your opinion about what the world/society calls us to do?
- What do these developments mean to the company and to the strategies and goals it will be pursuing in the future?
- If the company was to engage everybody around a strategic and vitalizing topic that was relevant not only for the company, but also for the world, from your perspective, what might that be? What might everybody's perspective and ideas for implementing be? What do you think the company needs to shed light on and see grow in the future?

Questions such as these let us engage in good dialogues about what the future calls our organization to do. That may be a very important dialogue to have before we decide what the headline for the process should be, and as already discussed, the questions we ask may determine the future we get.

Choose an inspiring, engaging, and motivating headline

When we know our platform (challenges and possibilities) and what people in and around the organization think is important to focus on in the future, it will be easier for us to find the right focus for a process.

When selecting a headline for the process, we must consider the following:

The headline for the strengths-based change process should be:

- Simple and clear.
- Bold.
- "Stretching."
- Worth striving for.
- Energizing.
- Inviting.
- Anchored in history—and reaching out to the future.

The headline is important. We're touching on some essentials about how language shapes our world and turns our focus, energy, and efforts in a particular direction.

Below are some examples of exciting headlines and thus topics of strengths-based change processes that consultants have been involved in over the years.

CASE

How do we become the "most wanted"?

The starting point for this process was a concrete problem in a factory under the pharmaceutical company Novo Nordisk. The company had high employee turnover of great employees and the possibility of the factory closing due to its inability to attract a new product and a high incidence of sick leave. Instead of focusing on these problems, the head of the factory asked external consultants and a representative group from the factory to come up with an inspiring headline for an AI change process. The process should help the members of the group solve the concrete problems they face, but also be engaging for the employees. When asked what the company wanted to become, the leader of the factory initially had no answer. He then said, "We might be closed a year from now." But he was encouraged to imagine that the company still existed and that by becoming a success, it could attract the right employees, keep the best employees on the team, and deliver a great product. What would accomplish that and help that happen? After reflecting on these questions, one of the stakeholders answered, "We would become 'most wanted.'"

We ended up choosing the headline "Most Wanted" because it was appealing, but also because it was two-sided. It summarized ideas for attracting new products as well as ideas for the employees making themselves attractive elsewhere in the organization in case they failed to attract a new product.

(continued on next page)

CASE (CONTINUED)

Ultimately, this process lead to some amazing results. By engaging the whole organization in this topic—how to become most wanted—the factory was able to attract a new product, cut down the production time per unit by 80 percent, decrease the price per unit by 17 percent, lower the incidence of sick leave (from 12 percent to 6 percent), and attain a higher engagement score in the annual Gallup engagement survey (from 3.48 to 4.08). And the factory didn't shut down!

CASE

How do we generate "growth through values"?

This example comes from the Danish bank Sydbank, the Copenhagen Region, which a few years ago made a dedicated effort to generate more growth economically for the individual as well as the team.

The process was initiated because the regional CEO wanted to bring the region together around a common goal. The time leading up to the start of the process had been characterized by considerable turnover in staff. With so many new faces, the leader felt a need to highlight the core values of the bank and create a common basis for generating growth. As regional director, he had a natural interest in economic growth as well and knew that happy employees create better results. Besides, based on strong values, he wanted to strengthen and promote the already exciting spirit of "What can I do for you"" toward the customers and believed that the "Growth through values" process could help the bank do exactly that.

To achieve this, the bank decided to build on its common strengths and best ideas for future actions. The process that was initiated came to include the following:

- Preliminary meetings with a representational steering committee to ensure that the bank had the right focus throughout the process.
- An AI Summit, where the entire part of the organization was involved in identifying strengths and potentials in the organization; here it brainstormed on, prioritized, and planned feasible local activities that would create added value.
- Four "passion days" where local enthusiasts were trained in the strengths-based method to ensure that the project would be grounded and implemented with the initiation of and follow-up on specific strengths-based projects and initiatives in all branch offices.

(continued on next page)

CASE (CONTINUED)

- A management day that included additional training in the method and time to follow up on achieved results and put them in a larger perspective. This event also identified ways for the leaders to support and sustain achieved and desired results.
- A final conference on a two-day cruise from Copenhagen to Oslo that again involved everybody in the region. At this event, the individual departments presented their projects/results to the rest of the region.

The fact that the headline involving the word *growth* was linked to the word *values* reflected Sydbank's long-standing tradition of being a value-based organization. The bank considered its historic foundations in selecting its focus. Instead of focusing on "securing themselves," the bank focused on its core strengths and on abundance, which gave the bank a head start with regard to the 2008 financial crisis. The bank not only survived this crisis, but also endured it without the need to lay off employees, with higher earnings in the years to come and with employees thriving and flourishing in their daily lives. In fact, employees who had left the company now wanted their old jobs back because they missed the spirit in the bank and had heard about the results and new initiatives implemented as a result of the strengths-based process. In addition, the employees were number one on the bank's sales list, achieving approximately 20 percent growth in new customers in 2009.

Establish measurable success criteria

Before initiating the change process, it is important to establish success criteria for the process. Success criteria can be based on objective as well as subjective parameters:

- Objective parameters (productivity, quality, sick leave, etc.)
- Subjective parameters (mood, sense of flow, employee feedback, etc.)

Below, Henning Juhl Jessen, the director of the bank mentioned previously, talks more about how the bank set up concrete success criteria in the definition part of the process:

> *The main thing for me, the first time we sat down in my management team and asked ourselves what we should do, was that we should set a goal that was very measurable. So the goals we set up were:*
>
> - *Personal growth in the form of challenges and possibilities.*
> - *Common growth because we help each other even more.*
> - *Less staff turnover.*
> - *Heightened number of new customers.*
> - *Regional growth based on achieving the ambitious earnings goal of at least 150 million kroner by 2010.*

Especially the last parameter is extremely objective and easy to deal with. It provided a landmark that we were constantly able to refer back to. It was an ambitious goal we set, and it was wonderful to achieve it. To us it was important to set a goal that was as straightforward as possible. That felt right for us. Perhaps other companies would have had to set a completely different type of goal. We set a goal that was demanding but also very broad. We were aiming for growth through values—personal values as well as common values—and we set this earning goal. But the personal and common values were the means we used to accomplish the goal. So by tying it all together, we were able to make everything pull in the same desired direction.

Once we find a compelling headline and topic for our process and set up success criteria, it time to find a nice venue and send out invitations.

Find a suitable venue

Nothing drains and inhibits good dialogue more than a dull room with theater-style rows of chairs. This is inappropriate for a strengths-based change process. We must find a place where we can sit in groups and draw up a seating plan that mixes different stakeholders. That produces more synergy in the dialogues around the tables. In this process, no one is too important or too insignificant to sit around a table with anyone else. We need to ensure that everyone feels welcome (for example, by making the room inviting) and pay attention to details [for example, distributing a small folder that contains all the information the employees will need during the process (schedule, handouts, interview guides, etc.)].

Send out an exciting invitation

The invitation should contain information about the following:

- The process in which the participants can look forward to being involved: purpose, aspirations, and a high degree of involvement and dialogue
- The background (the focus of the process) and the names of those who have been involved in defining this topic as the strategic focus
- Time and place

Get the process started in a good way

Once we've completed the preparations that allowed us to select the focus for the process, found a venue, and invited and brought together relevant people, it's time to give an initial introduction where we explain how we chose the topic on the agenda and provide some details about the day's schedule. To set the mood, we might show an amusing or thought-provoking video clip and then conduct a sing-along. Perhaps the venue is so unique that we can open with a knowledgeable person talking about its history. Only our imagination sets the limit for a good start to the strengths-based change process. But we need to remember how resonance and positivity are important factors and how they set the stage for the rest of the day. If the participant don't see the purpose of doing the interview (the next phase of the process) or don't understand why they're there, they won't want to "play along." In addition, if they're full of negativity, their creativity, their ability to think outside the box, and their willingness to collaborate with others and bring their best selves into play will be limited. So from the beginning, we must set the stage that ensures a positive and meaningful atmosphere.

Discovery. Find "the best of what is" and what brings life.

Once the headline, background, and topic of the process have been introduced, the first part of the process, where everybody is gathered, begins. Here we ask the employees, customers, and other relevant stakeholders to talk about the strong foundation on which everyone is standing. We don't ask the staff to identify the weaknesses. (We can decide how to deal with those later.) The point now is for the attendees to realize that they're not starting from scratch in relation to the topic—they're already standing on a working foundation and a positive core. Even in cases when the foundation is somewhat shaky, everybody should be involved in discussing what is working well with regard to the issue at hand. The purpose is to build organizational and individual self-esteem—something we'll need when it's time to act.

During this part of the process, we ask the participants to interview each other in pairs. We have to develop an interview guide to frame the process. Below is an example of an interview guide used in the strategy seminar in Sydbank (the case mentioned previously) on the topic "Growth through values."

INTERVIEW GUIDE: GROWTH THROUGH VALUES

The purpose of this interview is for all of us to learn more about how we can generate **growth through values** for the individual, the branch offices, the entire region, and ultimately our customers.

Based on your thoughts, values, and ideas, we want to use this morning session to discuss the values that form and may come to form the foundation of a workplace where everybody pulls together, where everybody flourishes, and where job satisfaction, development, and earnings go hand in hand.

Tips for a good interview:

- Remember, this is an interview, not a conversation.
- Allow time for reflection. Silence is often a sign of thoughtfulness. You may use follow-up questions to ask your interview partner to elaborate on something and to add more depth and nuance to your learning.
- Pursue the points you find most exciting and interesting, but cover the questions that are included in the question guide.
- Make notes during the interview so that you can recall and relate the most important learning points and insights.

(continued on next page)

INTERVIEW GUIDE: GROWTH THROUGH VALUES (CONTINUED)

This interview is also a good opportunity to get to know a colleague, so enjoy!

First part: Sharing a little bit about yourself

How long have you been working in our part of the bank? What is your job, and what do you like about it?

Please tell me a little bit about your family, friends, and hobbies; something you find important in life; or anything else you might want to share.

Second part: Digging into the basic values

Our attitudes and convictions are based on our values. Therefore, our attitudes and convictions can tell us a great deal about our values and the things we appreciate.

- What was it that originally attracted you to work in Sydbank and in the Copenhagen Region?
- What do you appreciate most about being with Sydbank today?
- What do you appreciate most in your colleagues, your department, and/or your team?
- Without being modest, what do you appreciate most about yourself as a colleague?
- What values and attitudes do you share with your colleagues that help make it meaningful for you to go to work? Which of those contribute to making this a "good job," a job that you (you personally or your team) are proud of and that you enjoy?

Events that made a positive difference

When you think back on your time as an employee in Sydbank/Copenhagen Region, there have probably been ups and downs—times when you took a more reserved and cautious position; times when you were passionate and excited about your work; and times when you believed that what you were doing was important and beneficial to you, to other employees in the bank, and to the customers.

Tell me about an experience when you were really excited about your job—where the teamwork with your colleagues clicked and where you created something unique together to your own benefit as well as the benefit of your colleagues, the customers, and the bank.

- Who was involved?
- What did they do?
- What did you do?
- What do you think made this situation possible?
- What basic values played a role in your common approach to this situation?

(continued on next page)

INTERVIEW GUIDE: GROWTH THROUGH VALUES (CONTINUED)

Third part: Sharing wishes and ideas

- What ideas do you have about what we might do in the region that would strengthen us as a workplace to the benefit of everybody employed here as well as the customers and would promote our basic values?
- What steps could we take internally that would enhance our job satisfaction, our commitment, and our level of flourishing?
- What steps could we take externally that would enhance our customers' satisfaction with being customers of this bank?

"Predictions are hard to make, particularly about the future"
as the Danish writer Storm P. said. But that doesn't mean we shouldn't try!

Imagine that while you are asleep tonight, a miracle happens. When you wake up tomorrow, everything about Sydbank/Copenhagen Region has become exactly as you hoped it would be based on the common values we share in the region. What is the first thing you notice when you show up for work? Describe your workday:

- What is going on?
- How do we work together? (with teams, with branches, between branches, between the branch and regional headquarters, with customers, etc.)
- How do we address and treat our customers? What are they saying about us?
- What are our goals, and how can we achieve them?
- What is the smallest step we could take as a region/bank to move in that direction?
- What is the smallest step you could take to move the region/bank in that direction?

We should give the participants two 45-minute sessions to complete this interview. That may sound like a long time, but it isn't. There is a great deal to talk about. Before sending people off to conduct the interviews, we should review the guidelines for a good interview that were outlined in the preceding interview guide. This is important so that the participants don't think that they're going to have a loosely structured dialogue. We also should tell the whole group to take notes and that they're expected to share the main points from the interview upon their return.

When the participants return from this interview, we ask them to sit down with two or three other interview pairs. These groups do the following:

EXERCISE (45 MIN.)

Summary of the interviews

1. Take turns sharing the main points of the interview partner's input to the positive core, shared values, and good ideas for achieving X.
2. Summarize these points in the small group and find the common positive core, values, and ideas of the stories you have shared. What are our strengths? What positive core are we standing on that we can build from? What should we continue doing, and what could we start doing in the future?
3. Prepare to present your findings to the group.

Whether we ask all the groups present what they talked about and what they found to be the "positive core in the company" depends on the size of the group. Remember that too many presentations in a large assembly or presentations that are too long drain the energy. If a group is small (up to 30 people), everyone should present, or if there are only a few groups, all of them should present. With larger groups, we may want to hear a few representative presentations.

Dream. About what might be.

This is the part of the strengths-based change process that some leaders (and employees, stakeholders, and customers) find challenging because it's creative, meaning that it may seem "out of control" and unrealistic. The preceding stages have prepared the way for this phase, though. But to make sure people are ready for this, we can ask them to stand up and do a scaling exercise.

EXERCISE

Scaling exercise in preparation for drawing the dream

Ask the participants to imagine where they would place themselves on a scale from 0 to 10 in relation to achieving X (the topic of the day). This should be simple because they worked on this point in the preceding stages of the process.

Then ask the participants to go to 10 (they've arrived, their dream has come true, and they're living in a reality where X is fully alive and present and happening all around them). Ask them to close their eyes for this part and to visualize what it is like to be living the dream—where they manage to be or generate X.

(continued on next page)

EXERCISE (CONTINUED)

- What is happening in and around our organization, what do I do, what do others do? Why?
- What has changed in the surroundings in the way we work together and in the way we relate to customers, society, stakeholders, and each other in the organization now that the dream has come true?
- What do you notice when you look around the office and when you look outside the office? Is there an office at all? Who is present? Why?
- Whom do you greet?
- What is the first thing you do when you arrive at work?
- What is your workday like?
- With whom do you cooperate internally and externally?
- How do you communicate?
- How do you conduct your meetings?
- What organizational strengths have we put into play?
- How have we dealt with our weaknesses?
- What individual strengths have you in put into play, and how have you dealt with your weaknesses?
- What are we accomplishing with our product?
- How does what we do help make a better world?

Now all of the participants should be ready to talk about their vision of a future, where everybody has put his or her strengths to work and has accomplished X/generated Y (the topic of the process).

What we want now is to ask the smaller groups (the same groups that did the exercise at the end of the last phase) to produce a concrete, creative product that shows what happens when we manage to create or be whatever (for example, being the most wanted or generating growth through values or ensuring well-being in a hectic workday). We may sing the dream; draw the dream; or build the dream using toy characters, paper-mâché, or pipe cleaners. Singing, drawing, and constructing activate the right side of the brain, which provides access to more creative parts of ourselves. That is just what is needed at this stage, as the goal is to show a future dream that is within sight but out of reach. We show the dream as if it's happening right now, but we know that what we envision doesn't have to be realistic right now. It's about the future, and it's about thinking outside the box.

An outsider may have a difficult time figuring out what the dreams symbolize. But years later, the participants who made the dream pictures, will be able to recall what every element of the dream symbolizes. It's much easier to remember images than words and sentences (Ashcraft, 1994). We never forget our dreams. But for the sake of others, before we finish this part of the process, we must ask the participants who co-created the dreams in the smaller groups to make a few written headlines about their dream. The headlines should be framed as "provocative propositions," as Watkins et al. (2001) call them, which are statements providing clear directions for all of the organization's activities. The propositions must be phrased in the active form, such as "we aim to, will do, aspire to, strive for." The following provocative proposition was developed by a group that worked through the process.

When you walk into our department, you will experience:

- *An open dialogue between leaders and employees, between employees and customers, and between customers, us, and the wider community.*
- *How customers and the wider community help us deliver our service.*
- *Ideas that thrive. Even on stony ground, they don't die, but find water or are protected in times of drought by special idea agents taking care of them.*
- *Open work procedures throughout the organization and into the wider community.*
- *Times of high energy and times of silence and stillness depending on the time of the day, year, and product phase.*
- *That everybody's strengths are put into play by continuous feedback, dialogue, and openness.*
- *A nurturance of the personal as well as the common purpose.*

Once the dreams and provocative propositions have been produced, the groups present them to each other unless, of course, the process involved only one group. The point of this presentation is to find similarities between the dreams so that the larger group can find a shared focus in one common dream. At this point, we may ask ourselves: "Will the dreams necessarily have similarities? Is there not a risk that the dreams might point in different directions?" That seldom happens, but if it does, it's usually a good indication that something is fundamentally wrong in the makeup of the group or the organization. And then we'll have to "take it from there."

Design. Co-construct the wanted future—new structures, work flows, collaborations, and ways of measuring.

At this stage of the process, the participants engage in designing and creating the ideal organization working as if it is fully alive and is "living the dream." In other words, the participants craft a set of organizing principles for a future dream organization.

Edgar Schein, Professor Emeritus in Organizational Development and Leadership, claims that an organization needs to be changed in three dimensions if the change is to last (2010):

1. Underlying assumptions, convictions, and expectations
2. Values and norms
3. Behavior and artifacts (artifacts being the physical components in an organization, such as furniture, clothes, logos, technology, and art)

According to Schein, it is easiest to change behavior and artifacts and most difficult to change underlying assumptions, convictions, and expectations. These underlying thought patterns influence the values—what cultures see as appropriate and wanted—and the values influence what people do (that is, their behavior). It works the other way around as well—people's behavior might change their values and underlying assumptions.

If we want to change an organizational culture and create new structures, according to Schein, we should start by setting up new structures that enable (and maybe even force) individuals to change their behavior. Then they'll gradually change within other parameters as well. Weick and Sutcliffe (2007, p. 114) claim the same thing and state that:

Organizations act their way into what they become.

And as Winston Churchill once said:

First we shape our buildings, then they shape us.

What he meant is that if we change the way a building is shaped in a set of rules or in procedures/ guidelines for how to act and behave, it will influence our values and assumptions in the long run.

But it is not enough to change only the structures. We also need to change the other parts of an organization, as Pradhan shows using the following model (2005).

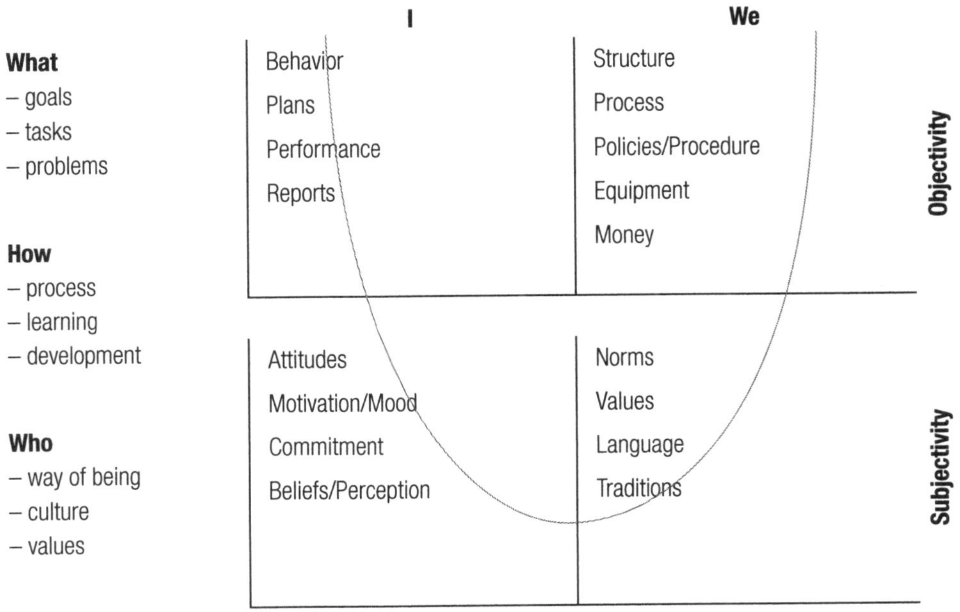

About the model, Pradhan says:

> *The traditional approach in change management focuses mostly on the structure, goals, and performance. While such an approach may generate results in the short run, it often cannot be sustained because the underlying patterns within the organization have not kept pace with the new strategies and goals. In many cases, unless the subjective aspects of the organization are changed, a new strategy or reorganization will not be executed successfully. (p. 6)*

So in the following part of the process, we want the participants to engage in dialogues about changing the artifacts and concrete structures in the organizations (for example, workflow and spreadsheet procedures) as well as dialogues about what structures help ensure that the wanted values, traditions, beliefs, and commitments are implemented.

We may first ask the participants to discuss what has already been done that might help the dream come true. For instance, we can ask the following questions:

"FIND AND AMPLIFY" QUESTIONS

- What are we really good at already that can help us achieve the dream? How can we bring these strengths into play even more?
- What forms of cooperation, internally and externally, facilitate the dream? How can we improve this cooperation?
- What ways of working facilitate the dream?
- What strengths represented in each of us can be used to make the dream come true?

During this phase, the group must uncover the good ideas that everybody has, individually and together, for making the dream come true—in addition to the steps that already exist. This activity is based on the dream and on the positive core on which the participants are already standing in relation to the topic. (These were identified in the discovery phase.)

During the design phase, the participants should be encouraged to think outside the box to produce new (and maybe unusual and novel) ideas and solutions for making the burning desire/the dream come true.

There are certain things we can do to facilitate unconventional ways of inventing innovative organizing principles for the future. For example, we can ask for 15 minutes of silence with the group where participants silently reflect on what might move them closer to the dream—what specific steps they can take, what others can do, and what we can do. They have 15 minutes of silence to reflect on what it will take to bring the dream to fruition. We can ask a couple of questions for people to reflect on during this silence. Of course, it's important to follow up on what people envisioned.

Instead of silence, we can use a brainstorming process. In that case, we should review the rules for brainstorming described in Chapter 8. In a true brainstorming process, the participants are not restricted by assumptions about what they can/should/must/cannot do. The main obstacle for being innovative and for inventing the future is statements such as "we can't," "we've already tried that," and "that's too far out." Indeed, some ideas may be too far out, but during this phase, it's important to let ideas flourish.

We can do a number of things to make the brainstorming more specific. For example, we can divide the department/organization into four smaller groups. Those groups then take turns brainstorming on what they can do more of, do less of, stop doing entirely, or begin doing to realize the dream. This concrete activity requires subsequent follow-up to make sure it happens—we should arrange who does what and when in the final phase, the delivery phase.

As described earlier, we may be inspired by the concept of *proflection* as an indication of what it takes to invent the future during this phase. While reflection means looking back and learning from the past and one's experiences, proflection means looking into the future and learning from it. Scharmer's Theory U may be an important source of inspiration here. In Theory U, he discusses how we can engage in dialogues that create something novel and innovative—something that isn't inhibited by what we think we know based on past experiences. Scharmer tries to teach us to combine seeing a desirable image of the future with being present in the moment, where we use our intuition more deliberately. We have to learn from the future, so to speak, while it's unfolding. Scharmer (2009) calls it "presencing." Presencing combines the shared silence described previously with a brainstorming session where presence in the moment is a powerful tool. Silence lets us listen inside ourselves, and brainstorming combined with presence in the moment links with the ideas that emerge. In many respects, this is an interesting and innovative theory and method. Leaders should take a more in-depth look at Scharmers U-process, which challenges them to take an innovative approach to innovation and change management.

Before ending this phase of the process, we should ask the groups to write down recommended steps that the teams, the departments, the whole organization, and possibly the stakeholders can take to bring the organization in the desired direction. Another option is to have the groups write down these steps as the provocative propositions described at the end of the dream process. These propositions can be viewed as guiding design principles that must be worked with in another process where people who are interested in a specific topic sign up. For instance, there may be propositions about workflow or implementation of a new IT system, a new organizational structure, or a collaboration model with customers. All those ideas will be further debated and implemented in the next and final phase of the process.

Delivery

Before we break up the event and conclude the part of the process where everyone is together, we should discuss what small steps can be taken, together and individually, to move closer to the burning desire/the dream. This is when it all comes together and takes on a concrete form. Many leaders are concerned about waiting until this late stage in the process to become that specific, concrete, and action-oriented. But in the preceding parts of the process, we should allow the participants to think outside the box. And once we get to this stage, things will become specific and action-oriented.

We can, for example, ask the group to produce a map or chart describing how to fulfill the burning desire. The map/chart should contain the following:

- The headline/the burning desire, which now includes the dream for which everyone is aiming
- Specific activities and strategies that will bring everyone in the desired direction
- Partial goals and the persons/teams/units responsible for each
- Potential barriers and ideas for how to overcome them

In the early stages of this final phase, the description may involve other people beside the individual. For example, the employees can be expected to have many good ideas for things management can do and vice versa. But as the process proceeds, everyone must consider what specific steps he or she will take to move the organization or the department closer to the burning desire. The point is that progress will begin to happen once everybody assumes personal ownership and is able to tell how he or she can help make a difference.

For us as leaders, this is a crucial moment. And it is paramount that we inspire the participants to take responsibility by (1) doing so ourselves and (2) providing motivation without coercion. This is the point where every participant commits and becomes involved. How would I like to contribute? What idea would I like to promote? What will I do tomorrow? Where can I bring my unique strengths into play? What is it that I'm particularly good at that will move us closer to the burning desire?

When everyone is personally committed to taking small steps, the long-term progress can be substantial. Every single person must commit to one or two specific steps he or she will take before the event is over. For example, we can ask the participants to take part in a commitment exercise where they speak to one or two of their colleagues and tell them specifically what they intend to do. This obliges the participants and increases the chance of action. We also can establish a system where two colleagues commit to following up on whether the other person does what he or she intended to do.

It also is important that local teams and units get a chance to meet and discuss what to do next as a consequence of this process. We should allow at least a couple of hours for this at the end of any process. This ensures that teams commit to and talk and coordinate with other teams and/or stakeholders, customers, and possible leaders higher up in the organization with whom they might want to collaborate in the future.

Before we end the process, we also need to address the following questions:

Summarizing questions before the end of the strategy seminar

- How will we know if we are moving closer to the dream?
- What partial goals can we check up on regularly?
- When is the next follow-up for everybody in smaller groups?
- What are the remaining steps in the process?

One final point to be made regarding the delivery phase: We might consider not calling it the "delivery phase" because that signals a "neatly packaged or engineered product" (Cooperrider & Whitney, 2005, p. 34). Instead, we could call it the "destiny phase," which implies allowing the transformation to happen by itself, emerging, and coming to life as a result of all the dialogues and actions from the previous part of the process. If we look at the process as a movement that is now shaping new ways of collaborating, communicating, and empowering each other in and around the organization, after a strengths-based process, organizations should be able to fulfill their dream and take action. Therefore, we should make concrete plans and then move on to final step where we anchor the process.

Anchoring the process

Once the formal part of the process is over, it is time for everyone to take action. As in our meetings, we must follow up on the process. We may do that with e-mails, phone calls, meetings, and the Internet, sharing good stories about what is happening in and around the organization now and helping to implement the initiatives to bring the organization in a desired direction. Perhaps working groups have been established that must be launched and that require follow-up. Together with the groups, we should follow up with regard to our success criteria, shed light on what works well, and correct any steps in new directions that aren't working. This is an experimentation process as well, which means that we might have to come up with many great ideas, but now when we try to implement them, they may not work.

We shouldn't evaluate too soon, though. The idea may not work because there hasn't been enough time for the idea to show its worth or because other parts of the structure of the organization, communication channels, or ways of collaborating haven't yet been corrected. This chapter ends with a quote from Scharmer and Kaufer (2013), showing how transformative change takes time and needs time:

> *From biology we know what happens, when the new is not supported by kind surroundings. The immune system is activated and do, what it is meant to do: Kill the new. Why? Because it is different. Because it threatens status-quo. Because it doesn't belong here. That's why all new (wanted) initiatives need a safe place and kind surroundings, which support the new life in growing. On a farm you do not walk around and dig out plants once a day to see how it is going with the growth. You water it and give it time.*

We should do the same.

13

STRENGTHS-BASED EVALUATIONS, SURVEYS, AND ASSESSMENTS

CONTENTS

Employee surveys, 360-degree reviews, workplace environment assessments and evaluations, engagement surveys—there is no shortage of evaluations, surveys, and assessments in the workplace today. Some surveys aim to identify problems and shortcomings, areas where performance is unsatisfactory. A growing number of surveys aim to show the areas in which we are doing well and the areas in which we can continue what we've been doing well because it's clearly working. It's crucial that we design the right surveys so that we can ask the right questions. Remember:

What we ask for grows.

In workplace surveys that involve us, we should try to influence the types of questions that will be asked. We should try to shape the questions to ensure that they provide answers about the issues we want to know more about—that is, the information we need to move the organization in the right direction and to become the best version of ourselves as leaders.

With any survey, the phrasing of the questions, which determines the insights that are generated, is a task in and of itself. There is no such thing as a "neutral question." In the moment it's asked, a question exercises an influence in a particular direction. When we measure the temperature in a glass of water, the thermometer affects the temperature of the water slightly. The same applies when we check the temperature of our organization. The organization changes depending on how we ask (Cooperrider & Srivastva, 1987)—sometimes a little bit sometimes a lot. It's an illusion to think that a survey can be carried out without the objective of the survey being affected. This means that the right questions must be asked.

We can influence the entire organization if we begin to address *how* surveys, evaluations, and assessments are phrased. The more negatively phrased the questions, the greater the likelihood of nourishing seeds of negativism in the organization.

For example, if the question "How often do you experience conflicts in your workplace?" is asked, people will begin to think carefully about conflicts and look for examples. This will make conflicts loom larger in people's minds. If, instead, the question is "When do you experience a good team spirit in your workplace?" people will begin to look for examples of good team spirit. The things we notice are usually the things we look for, and they grow not only in our minds, but also in the real world as a consequence of this awareness.

However, this chapter is not about designing questionnaires; it's about our options as leaders, when we follow up on evaluations, assessments, and surveys. The outcome of any survey must be understood in light of the wording of the questions. And if we're in a position to affect the direction or the slant of the survey questions, we should consider the points outlined previously and use our position to shape the survey. But now we'll take a closer look at how, from a strengths-based perspective, we can follow up on surveys and assessments once they've been conducted.

THE NUANCED SCALE

A survey checks the "temperature" on a number of issues. On the one hand, it's straightforward: we have the answers in numbers. On the other hand, we lack nuances: All of the questions may not be relevant to us, just as the survey probably left out other relevant questions. It's also important to remember that the questions (and thus the answers) can be interpreted differently by different people. The answers to the questions will always provide some ambiguity.

Traditionally, people are asked to provide an unambiguous answer on a scale (for example, a scale from 1 to 5, where 1 is the lowest rating and 5 is the highest rating). For instance, we could be asked to rate this book on a scale from 1 to 5.

Based on my impression of the book so far, in my assessment, this book is . . .

1 Really bad	2 Bad	3 Okay	4 Good	5 Really good

We might think the book is good, but we may have missed a few things. So maybe our assessment is a 3. That raises a whole host of questions. Why was the rating not a 4 or 5? What would it take to achieve that? Why wasn't our rating a 2? What's good about the book? What's bad? To learn anything from feedback on the book, in terms of a number, the authors would need to know more about the nuances implied in the answers to the questions. The situation is the same for us and our organization regardless of whether we're looking at the outcome of a management evaluation or a well-being survey.

Therefore, we must try to include nuances in the feedback we receive on survey outcomes in general and help others take this perspective when they look at the evaluations, the feedback, and outcome of surveys.

One way of doing that is to ask people to add nuance to their numbers: If you had 100 percent, how would you distribute it on a scale from 1 to 5? Consider the following example.

Compared with the previous assessment of this book, the rating could be made even more nuanced: "What percent of the book is really bad?" "How much of the book is really good?" "What percent is okay?" Now the feedback may look like this:

1 Really bad	2 Bad	3 Okay	4 Good	5 Really good
5%	10%	10%	50%	25%

This paints a more nuanced picture. The authors are happy to see that the person thinks that 25 percent of the book is really good, but they're curious about the 5 percent and the 10 percent at the low end of the scale. What is it about the book that is really bad? And which sections are okay?

Asking about nuances provides a more subtle picture of what lies behind a score of 3. The authors can begin to ask questions about what the different ratings imply. This is a different use of scaling questions, a technique that was described in Chapter 5.

It's very helpful to ask about nuances when following up on surveys, so we should include percentage ratings whenever possible. Alternatively, we can discuss what is behind the figures in the survey.

Here's an example that illustrates how this approach worked for a leader who was encouraged to try it.

CASE

A leader received an okay score (3) in the category Credible on a 360 survey. The leader was frustrated because he perceived himself as being very credible. By using a nuanced scale with his respondents, however, he realized that the score of 3 reflected a perception among most of the employees that his credibility was generally somewhere between 4 and 5. But a couple of incidents in which he had been forced to withhold information and to change decisions at the last moment had reduced his overall score. In these situations, his credibility had been perceived as being somewhere between 1 and 2, fairly low. Thus, when the employees were asked to rate him in the management evaluation, many of them opted for a 3 to express their dissatisfaction with these specific incidents. The leader was thankful to get this perspective and to be given an opportunity to explain his motives for acting the way he did in the situations that had reduced his average. It also was a relief for the employees to have an opportunity to explain their scores.

Looking at results from an evaluation, an assessment, or a survey

Now we'll take a closer look at what else we can do to follow up on the findings of a survey. The survey probably contains findings about which we're pleased as well as findings that surprise (or concern) us. As discussed previously, it may be difficult to know exactly what the individual results reflect and who is experiencing what. Therefore, we may find it difficult to act on the basis of the survey.

One way of dealing with the survey may be to ask ourselves a number of questions in preparation for a dialogue with the respondents of the survey (knowing very well that because of anonymity, we often don't know who answered what). We should first consider our immediate response to the survey and then look at it more closely.

REFLECTION ON SURVEYS

First impressions

- What is my immediate reaction to the outcome of the evaluation?
- Which results make me happiest and proudest?
- Why those results in particular?
- What was my result for the same questions last year?
- Are there any results that worry me?
- What is the main source of my concern?
- Which questions are most important for me as a leader (regardless of the distribution of answers to the question)?
- Why are these questions/themes particularly important to me?
- In my immediate assessment, what are the three most important things my team should focus on right now?
- Why?
- What would I like to achieve?
- What would my employees, the other managers in the organization, and my superior like to achieve?
- What are their reactions to the survey findings likely to be?

(continued on next page)

REFLECTION ON SURVEYS (CONTINUED)

Reflections on positive scores

- In which areas do I receive a high score?
- Why is the score so high in this particular area?
- What are the possible reasons for the high score?
- What do I do, specifically, that brings about that high score?
- What else contributes to the high score?
- As a leader, how can I maintain the positive score?
- What could the employees, the other leaders in the organization, and/or my superior do that would maintain or elevate the score?

Reflections on negative scores

- Which questions/themes have the lowest score?
- What are the possible causes of the low score?
- What do I do, specifically, that might cause the low score?
- What else contributes to the low score?
- Why, after all, is the score as high as it is and not lower?
- Is it sometimes higher?
- What happens in those situations?
- What might raise the score a little bit?
- What could the employees, the other managers in the organization, and/or my superior help me do that would have a positive effect on the score?

Reflections on the overall score for the team

- What is the score for my team compared with the total for the organization?
- In what areas are the team's scores higher than the scores of the organization as a whole?
- In what areas are they lower?
- Are there big differences?
- What is the likely cause of this?

(continued on next page)

REFLECTION ON SURVEYS (CONTINUED)

Summing up

- Am I satisfied when I compare myself and my team with the rest of the organization?
- Why or why not?
- What could I do myself and we do as a team to heighten the score in the future?

FOLLOW-UP MEETING

Far too many surveys are carried out without proper follow-up, which is a waste of time. In fact, it is only in the subsequent process that the survey shows its true worth.

> *We all visit branch offices after a survey. Here we follow up on the factors that helped create the good results and any suggestions as to what we can do about the things that are not quite up to par. That gives us a sense of what is happening in the branch offices. The bosses out there handle most of it in the dialogue they have with the staff. But I can tell that it makes a difference when we show up, as top management, and show an interest. And it really serves to qualify the results of the surveys when we know the local challenges and successes, and it gives us a chance to engage in a dialogue about what we can to do to get even better ratings next time.*
>
> *—Henning Juhl Jessen*

We should consider setting up dialogue meetings if the organization doesn't already do this to follow up on surveys. We also need to allocate sufficient time for the meetings; one hour is rarely enough time to deal with the main themes and issues indicated in the survey as key topics. At a minimum, we'll probably need two to three hours—maybe even a whole day. At the meeting, we can address any issues and potential solutions. Everyone should feel free to point out something that already works well and should be preserved, as well as to raise his or her voice on issues of concern. We may want to use the survey findings to examine which strategic areas to focus on in the future.

To prepare for the follow-up meeting, we should reflect carefully on the survey findings and plan a process to ensure a constructive and forward-looking meeting. In terms of question techniques and process formats, Chapters 5 and 8 provide information for planning the meeting. In addition, we can ask ourselves the questions below in preparation for what we want to say and bring up at the follow-up meeting.

REFLECTION

... before the follow-up meeting

- *What should characterize the meeting where the survey is discussed—what kind of atmosphere, level of honesty, seriousness, etc., would I like?*
- *How am I going to ensure that?*
- *What questions is it important for me to ask the employees?*
- *How should I ask and frame those questions?*
- *What questions are they likely to ask me? What answers will I give them?*
- *What is the most important issue for me to discuss at the follow-up meeting (the three most important themes)?*
- *What is the most important aspect for us to act on together?*
- *What am I going to do?*
- *What do I want others to do?*
- *What specific ideas do I have for things we should do together?*

Imagine that the dialogue meeting has gone really well.

- *What happened at the meeting?*
- *What did you do that led to a good dialogue?*
- *What did the employees do?*
- *How and what did you decide or conclude together?*
- *What was the best thing that happened at the meeting?*

Follow-up meetings can be a potential conflict zone. Therefore, we have to pay particular attention to our roles as leaders to ensure that the meetings go well. In closing, the box below provides a few important points.

Accept personal boundaries	It is not essential to have each participant's assessment or opinion. Contributing to the dialogue should be voluntary, so don't force anybody to speak, especially in front of others. *(continued on next page)*

Look for possibilities rather than truths	There are as many truths about a situation as there are people in the room. Discussions about who is right and who is wrong usually don't lead to anything good. What is helpful is the dialogue about the different perceptions of the situation.
Be curious	When others do or say something we don't understand, we tend to reach a negative conclusion. An open and curious search for other possibilities can open doors that would otherwise remain closed.
Ask questions	Answers close! Questions open! There is no end to the positive effects of asking questions. Particularly important effects are that questions force others to think and that we usually learn something when we ask them.
Listen	By listening actively and sincerely, we create openings in the dialogue and make others want to listen as well.
Be appreciative and challenging	We should accept and acknowledge other people's points of view. But by challenging them in a respectful way, we also give them something to think about.
Be frank	The point is not to give in to others and allow them to walk all over us. We should be frank in telling people how their actions and words affect us. Without that feedback, they don't know if they're overstepping our boundaries.
"Break the curve"	One side of the coin may be a problem or a frustration. Look for what's on the other side of the coin. Remember, behind every problem lies a wish for something else. So what's the underlying wish behind the frustration? Talk about it. That's where the solutions can be found—together.
Be specific	We should make specific suggestions about what we want more of (what should I/we do) and what we want less of (what should I/we stop doing). *(continued on next page)*

"Toward" rather than "away from"	By focusing on and asking questions about wishes and possibilities in the future rather than barriers and fear/worries, we can create a "toward-motivation" rather than an "away-from-motivation."

CLOSING REMARKS

With these closing points, this book has come to an end. However, there is never an end with regard to leading from a strengths-based perspective. Human beings and organizations are living, ever-changing systems and therefore are never finished. We may get a new employee, superior, or customer, which means starting all over again by strengths-training our team, having one-on-one conversations, and the like. What a joy! Sometimes we may find ourselves in a situation we've been in before and may need to draw on experiences from the past. In other situations, we may have no idea what to do and will have to try something new. Whatever situation we're in, though, we should stay open and curious. The ideal pit will then, for sure, show itself. Good luck on your further strengths-based journey.

POSTSCRIPT

REFLECTION

What have you been successful at as a leader today? What was the best thing you did as a leader yesterday?

What great things have your employees done this week? How did you as a leader facilitate that?

What has your superior done recently that you perceived as helpful?

What does the future call for you to do more of?

Where do you see yourself and your company going—how will you help make the world an even better place in the future?

Questions generate reflection. Perhaps the preceding questions stirred reflection and thoughts about what you, your employees, and your superior are doing well now and should be doing more of in the future. These reflections and thoughts may be a source of inspiration and positive learning for you based on your achievements—in other words, your positive experiences.

A goal of this book is to inspire you to collect positive experiences, to ignite profound organizational and individual change, and to catch yourself and others doing the right things. We hope it has gotten you started on the journey to build on your strengths and to deal with your weaknesses and to help your staff, colleagues, and the organization do the same. If you read the book, could relate to the contents, and tried some of the methods and exercises, we believe you are off to a good start as well as an adventure. We hope it is an exciting adventure that brings you joys and thrills and challenges—everything that makes you feel alive.

Now it's up to you to keep up the good work. You should keep challenging yourself and others around you to think and act in a strengths-based way. You should continue to try the methods in the book, reflecting on their effectiveness and modifying them as needed. Then you'll be able to take a strengths-based approach based on your specific strengths as a leader.

To keep up your spirit, you can share the experiences you had in applying the strengths-based approach. As described in the book, research shows that it is much easier to instill new habits if you're highly motivated and you consider a strengths-based approach meaningful. You should be able to envision the positive results of incorporating the strengths-based approach. Therefore, it's important to have people around you who know and support you in incorporating the new habits or maintaining and developing the strengths-based paradigm. Find people to reflect with and cultivate the good relations you already have. Ask these individuals to be your "sparring partners" and to remind you if you're about to slip back into an old "fault-finding" paradigm.

On the Internet (on Facebook, for example), you can find groups of people who share experiences and exchange methods within the strengths-based paradigm. Use these resources to discuss the approach used in your organization. Turn to your social circle to draw inspiration for thinking and working in a strengths-based perspective (in relation not only to work, but also to parenting or friendships or recreational activities). Notice your children's and your friends' strengths. Perhaps you'll notice new qualities in them or discover fascinating nuances in what you see as their weaknesses. And notice your partner's strengths. Chapter 7 discussed how that's the path to a successful relationship. No matter what you do, maintain a positive attitude, share, and give and receive feedback—and stay in touch. That's the only way you can move yourself and others.

We wish you luck on your future leadership journey.

LITERATURE

Anderson, H., Cooperrider, D. L, Gergen, K., Gergen, M., McNamee, S., Watkins, J. M., & Whitney, D. (2008). *The Appreciative Organization.* Chagrin Falls, OH: Taos Institute Publishers.

Ashcraft, M. H. (1994). *Human Memory and Cognition*. New York: HarperCollins College Publishers.

Ashford, S., & Tsui, A. S. (1991). Self-regulation for managerial effectiveness: The role of active feedback seeking. *Academy of Management Journal*, 34.

Axelrod, D., & Axelrod, E. (2014). *Let's Stop Meetings Like This: Tools to Save Time and Get More Done.* San Francisco: Berrett-Koehler Publishers.

Barge, J. K., & Oliver, C. (2003). Working with appreciation in managerial practice. *Academy of Management Review*, 28(1).

Barret, F. (2012). *Yes to the Mess: Surprising Leadership Lessons from Jazz.* Boston: Harvard Business School Publishing.

Barrett, F., Cooperrider, D., & Fry, R. (2005). Bringing every mind into the game to realize the positive revolution in strategy. *Practicing Organization Change & Development*. San Francisco: Pfeiffer.

Bateson, G. (2000). *Steps to an Ecology of Mind*. University of Chicago Press.

Beer, M., & Eisenstat, R. A. (2004). How to have an honest conversation about your business strategy. *Harvard Business Review*.

Berg, I. K., & Szabo, P. (2005). *Brief Coaching for Lasting Solutions*. New York: W. W. Norton.

Bernstein, S. (2003). Positive organizational scholarship: Meet the movement. *Journal of Management Inquiry*, 12.

Boyatzis, R., & McKee, A. (2005). *Resonant Leadership*. Boston: Harvard Business School Publishing.

Bregman, P. (2012). If you're too busy to meditate, read this. *Harvard Business Review*.

Brinkerhoff, R. O., & Apking, A. M. (2001). *High-Impact Learning: Strategies for Leveraging Business Results from Training*. Cambridge, MA: Perseus.

Bryan, L. L (2007). *Mobilizing Minds: Creating Wealth from Talent in the 21st Century Organization.* New York: McGraw-Hill Professional.

Buckingham, M. (2005). *The One Thing You Need to Know … About Great Managing, Great Leading and Sustained Individual Success.* New York: Free Press.

Buckingham, M. (2007). *Go Put Your Strengths to Work.* New York: Free Press.

Buckingham, M. (2008). *The Truth About You: Your Secret to Success.* Nashville, TN: Thomas Nelson.

Buckingham, M. (2011). *StandOut: The Groundbreaking New Strengths Assessment from the Leader of the Strengths Revolution.* Nashville, TN: One Thing Productions.

Buckingham, M., & Clifton, D. O. (2002). *Now, Discover Your Strengths.* New York: Free Press.

Bushe, G. (1998). Appreciative Inquiry with teams. *The Organization Development Journal*, 16(3).

Bushe, G. R. (2000). *Generativity and the Transformational Potential of Appreciative Inquiry.* Atlanta, GA: Elsevier.

Bushe, G. R. (2010). *Clear Leadership: Sustaining Real Collaboration and Partnership at Work.* Boston: Davies-Black Publishing.

Butler, G., & Hope, T. (1995). *Manage Your Mind: The Mental Fitness Guide.* New York: Oxford University Press.

Cameron, K. (2008). *Positive Leadership. Strategies for Extraordinary Performance*. San Francisco: Berrett-Koehler Publishers.

Cameron, K., Dutton, J. E., & Quinn, R. E. (2003). *Positive Organizational Scholarship: Foundations of a New Discipline*. San Francisco: Berrett-Koehler Publishers.

Cameron, K., & Lavine, M. (2006). *Making the Impossible Possible.* San Francisco: Berrett-Koehler Publishers.

Carroll, M. (2007). *The Mindful Leader: Ten Principles for Bringing Out the Best in Ourselves and Others.* Boston: Trumpeter.

Clifton, D. O., & Harter, J. K. (2003). *Investing in Strengths.* San Francisco: Berrett-Koehler Publishers.

Collins, J. (2001). *Good to Great: Why Some Companies Make the Leap . . . and Others Don't.* New York: HarperCollins.

Collins, J., & Hansen, M. T. (2011). *Great by Choice: Uncertainty, Chaos, and Luck—Why Some Thrive Despite Them All.* New York: HarperCollins.

Cooperrider, D. (2008). Going green maximum velocity through AI's sustainable design factory. *Global HR News*.

Cooperrider, D., & Srivastva, S. (1987). Appreciative Inquiry in organizational life. *Research in Organizational Change and Development*, Vol. 1, 129–169.

Cooperrider, D., & Srivastva, S. (1999). Positive image, positive action. *Appreciative Management and Leadership*, 91–125.

Cooperrider, D. L., & Whitney, D. (2005). *Appreciative Inquiry. A Positive Revolution in Change.* San Francisco: Berrett-Koehler Publishers.

Cooperrider, D. L., Whitney, D., Stavros, J. M., & Fry, R. (2008). *The Appreciative Inquiry Handbook: For Leaders of Change.* Brunswick, OH: Crown Custom Publishing.

Covey, S. (2007). *The Speed of Trust.* New York: Simon & Schuster.

Covey, S. (2013). *The 7 Habits of Highly Effective People: Powerful Lessons in Personal Change.* New York: Simon & Schuster.

Csikszentmihalyi, M. (1990). *Flow: The Psychology of Optimal Experience.* New York: HarperCollins.

Daft, R. L. (2008). *The Leadership Experience*. Stamford, CT: Cengage Learning.

Dahrendorf, R. (1969). *The Modern Social Conflict*. New York: Weidenfeld & Nicolson.

Dickman, M. H., & Stanford-Blair, N. (2009). *Mindful Leadership: A Brain-Based Framework.* Thousand Oaks, CA: Corwin Press.

Dolman, E., & Bond, D. (2011). Mindful leadership. Exploring the value of a meditation practice, 360°. *The Ashridge Journal*, Spring, 36–43.

Drucker, P. (1966). *The Effective Executive.* New York: HarperCollins.

Einarsen, S., Hoel, H., Zapf, D., & Cooper, C. (Eds.) (2010). *Bullying and Harassment in the Workplace.* Boca Raton, FL: CRC Press.

Eisenhardt, K. M., Kahwajy, J. L., & Bourgeois, L. J. (2007). How management teams can have a good fight. *Harvard Business Review*.

Elstein, K., & Driver, K. (2007). Fostering a continuous-learning mind-set in a federal research organization. *Organizational Development Journal*, 25.

Everly, J., & George, E. (1990). *A Clinical Guide to the Treatment of the Human Stress Response*. New York: Plenum Press.

Fredrickson, B. (2009). *Positivity.* Brunswick, OH: Crown Custom Publishing.

Fredrickson, B., Cohn, M., Coffey K., & Finkel, S. (2008). Open hearts build lives: Positive emotions, induced through loving-kindness meditation, build consequential personal resources. *Journal of Personality and Social Psychology*, 95(5), 1045–1062.

Fredrickson, B., & Losada, M. (2005). Positive affect and the complex dynamics of human flourishing. *American Psychologist*, October.

Fredrickson, B. L. (2000). Why positive emotions matter in organizations: Lessons from the broaden-and-build model. *Psychologist-Manager Journal*, 4.

French, W. L., & Bell, C. H. (1995). *Organization Development: Behavioral Science Interventions for Organization Improvement*. Upper Saddle River, NJ: Prentice Hall.

Gallup. (2006). Feedback for real. Retrieved from www.gallup.com/businessjournal/811/feedback-real.aspx.

Gallup. (2013). State of the global workplace. Retrieved from www.gallup.com/services/178517/state-global-workplace.aspx.

Gardner, H. (2006). *Five Minds for the Future.* Boston: Harvard Business School Publishing.

Gelles, D. (2015). *Mindful Work: How Mediation Is Changing Business from the Inside Out.* New York: Houghton Mifflin Harcourt Publishing Company.

George, B. (2010). Mindful leadership: Compassion, contemplation and meditation develop effective leaders. *The European Financial Review*.

George, B., Sims, P., & McLean, A. (2007). Discovering your authentic leadership. *Harvard Business Review*.

George, J. M., & Bettenhausen, K. (1990). Understanding prosocial behavior, sales performance, and turnover. *Journal of Applied Psychology*, 75.

Gergen, K. (2009). *An Invitation to Social Construction*. London: Sage Publications.

Gladwell, M. (2005). *Blink: The Power of Thinking Without Thinking.* New York: Little, Brown.

Gladwell, M. (2008). *Outliers: The Story of Success.* New York: Little, Brown.

Glasl, F. (1980). *Konfliktmanagement: Diagnose und Behandlung von Konflikten in Organisationen*. Bern: Verlag Paul Hapt.

Glock, J. W. (1955). *The Relative Value of Three Methods of Improving Reading—Tachistoscope, Films, and Determined Effort.* University of Nebraska–Lincoln.

Goffee, R., & Jones, G. (2006). *Why Should Anyone Be Led by You? What It Takes to Be an Authentic Leader*. Boston: Harvard Business School Publishing.

Goleman, D. (2013). *Focus: The Hidden Driver of Excellence.* New York: HarperCollins.

Goleman, D., Boyatzis, R., & McKee, A. (2013). *Primal Leadership. Unleashing the Power of Emotional Intelligence.* Boston: Harvard Business Review Press.

Gordon Training. Learning a new skill is easier said than done.
Retrieved from www.gordontraining.com/?s=learning+a+new+skill.

Gottman, J. (1995). *Why Marriages Succeed or Fail: And How You Can Make Yours Last.* New York: Simon & Schuster.

Grimes, C. F. (2005). The self-fulfilling prophecy: Better performance by perception. Retrieved from www.accel-team.com/_pdf/atpdf_11_pygmalion_np.pdf.

Hamel, G. (2002). *Leading the Revolution.* New York: Plume/Penguin Group.

Hamel, G. (2006). The why, what, and how of management innovation. *Harvard Business Review*.

Hamel, G. (2007). *The Future of Management.* Boston: Harvard Business School Publishing.

Hamel, G. (2012). *What Matters Now.* San Francisco: Jossey-Bass.

Hamel, G., & Prahalad, C. K. (2010). *Strategic Intent*. Boston: Harvard Business Press.

Hammond, S. A., & Royal, C. (Eds.) (1998). *Lessons From the Field: Applying Appreciative Inquiry.* Minneapolis, MN: Practical Press.

Harter, J. K., Schmidt, F. L., & Hayes, T. L. (2002). Business-unit-level relationship between employee satisfaction, employee engagement and business outcomes: A meta-analysis. *Journal of Applied Psychology*, 87(2.)

Harter, J. K., Schmidt, F. L., Killham, E. A., & Agrawal, S. (2012). Q12® meta-analysis: The relationship between engagement at work and organizational outcomes. Retrieved from www.gallup.com/services/177047/q12-meta-analysis.aspx.

Hornstrup, C., & Johansen, T. (2009). From Appreciative Inquiry to inquiring appreciatively. Retrieved from www.taosinstitute.net/Websites/taos/Images/ResourcesManuscripts/Hornstrup-AIP-HornstrupJohansen.pdf.

Hotvedt, T. (1999). *Konflikt og konflikthåndtering i arbeidslivet*. Copenhagen: Gyldendal.

Huffington, A. (2013). *Thrive: The Third Metric to Redefining Success and Creating a Life of Well-Being, Wisdom, and Wonder.* New York: Harmony Books.

Jackson, P. Z. (2003). *58 ½ Ways to Improvise in Training.* Williston, VT: Crown House Publishing.

Jackson, P. Z., & McKergow, M. (2002). *The Solutions Focus: Making Coaching & Change Simple.* Boston: Nicholas Brealey Publishing.

Jaffe, D. T., & Scott, C. (1994). *Rekindling Commitment.* San Francisco, Jossey-Bass.

Kabat-Zinn, J. (1991). *Full Catastrophe Living: Using the Wisdom of Your Body and Mind to Face Stress, Pain, and Illness.* New York: Random House.

Kabat-Zinn, J. (2005). *Wherever You Go, There You Are: Mindfulness Mediation in Everyday Life.* New York: Hyperion.

Karasek, R. A., & Theorell, T. (1990). *Healthy Work: Stress, Productivity, and the Reconstruction of Working Life.* New York: Basic Books.

Katzenbach, J. R., & Smith, D. K. (1993). *The Wisdom of Teams: Creating the High-Performance Organization*. Boston: Harvard Business School Press.

Katzenbach, J. R., & Smith, D. K. (2005). The discipline of teams. *Harvard Business Review*, July–August.

Kay, J. (2012). *Obliquity: Why Our Goals Are Best Achieved Indirectly.* New York: Penguin Group.

Kelley, T. (2001). *The Art of Innovation: Lessons in Creativity from IDEO, America's Leading Design Firm: Success Through Innovation.* London: Profile Books.

Keltner, D. (2009). *Born to Be Good: The Science of a Meaningful Life.* New York: W. W. Norton.

Keyes, C. L. M., & Haidt, J. (2002). Flourishing: Positive psychology and the life well lived. *American Psychological Association.*

Kierkegaard, S. (1849, 1980 trans.). *The Sickness unto Death.* Princeton University Press.

Kim, W. C., & Mauborgne, R. (2004). *Blue Ocean Strategy*. Harvard Business School Publishing.

Kirschenbaum, D., Ordman, A. M., Tomarken, A. J., & Holtzbauer, R. (1982). Effects of differential self-monitoring and level of mastery on sports performance: Brain power bowling. *Cognitive Therapy and Research*, 6(3), 335–342.

Kofman, F. (2006). *Conscious Business: How to Build Value through Values.* Boulder, CO: Sound True.

Kotter, J. P. (2014). *Accelerate: Building Strategic Agility for a Faster-Moving World.* Boston: Harvard Business School Publishing.

Langer, E. (1990). *Mindfulness.* Boston: Da Capo Press.

Laszlo, C., & Brown, J. S. (with Ehrenfeld, J., Gorham, M., Pose, I., Robson, L., Saillant, R., Sherman, D., & Werder, P.). (2014). *Flourishing Enterprise: The New Spirit of Business.* Stanford University Press.

Linley, A. (2008). *Average to A+: Realising Strengths in Yourself and Others.* Coventry, England: Capp Press.

Linley, P. A., & Joseph, S. (Eds.) (2004). *Positive Psychology in Practice.* Hoboken, NJ: Wiley.

Losada, M., & Heapy, E. D. (2004). The role of positivity and connectivity in the performance of business teams: A nonlinear dynamics model. *American Behavioral Scientist*, 47(6).

Ludema, J. (2001). *From Deficit Discourse to Vocabularies of Hope: The Power of Appreciation.* Champaign, IL: Stipes Publishing.

Ludema, J. D., Whitney, D., Mohr, B., & Griffin, T. (2003). *The Appreciative Inquiry Summit: A Practitioner's Guide for Leading Large-Group Change.* San Francisco: Berrett-Koehler Publishers.

Mabeck, C. E. (2005). *The Motivating Dialogue.* Copenhagen, Denmark: Munksgaard.

Majchrzak, A., Malhotra, A., Stamps, J., & Lipnack, J. (2004). Can absence make a team grow stronger? *Harvard Business Review*.

Maturana, H., & Varela, F. (1987). *The Tree of Knowledge: The Biological Roots of Human Understanding.* Boston: Shambhala Publications.

McAdam, E., & Lang, P. (2009). *Appreciative Work in Schools. Generating Future Communities.* West Sussex, England: Kingsham Press.

Maslow, A. (1954). *Motivation and Personality*. New York: Harper.

McKinsey Quarterly (2008). McKinsey Global Survey results: Creating organizational transformations. Retrieved from http://gsme.sharif.edu/~change/McKinsey%20Global%20Survey%20Results.pdf.

Miller, D., Eisenstat, R., & Foote, N. (2002). Strategy from the inside out: Building capability-creating organizations. *California Management Review*, 44(3).

Miller, W. R., & Rollnick, S. R. (2012). *Motivational Interviewing: Helping People Change.* New York: Guildford Press.

Mohr, B., McKenna, C., & Daykin, J. (2008). Strength-based organizations: The challenge for Appreciative Inquiry 2.0? *AI Practitioner*.

Murray, S., Holmes, J., Dolderman, D., & Griffin, D. (2000). What the motivated mind sees. *Journal of Experimental Social Psychology*, 36.

Ofman, D. (2004). *Core Qualities: A Gateway to Human Resources.* London: Scriptum.

Patterson, K., Grenny, J., Maxfield, D., McMillan, R., & Switzler, A. (2013). *Crucial Accountability. Tools for Resolving Violated Expectations, Broken Commitments, and Bad Behavior.* New York: McGraw-Hill.

Patterson, K., Grenny, J., McMillan, R., & Switzler, A. (2011). *Crucial Conversations. Tools for Talking When Stakes Are High.* New York: McGraw-Hill.

Pescosolido, A. T. (2000). *Emotional Intensity in Groups* (Unpublished doctorate dissertation). Case Western Reserve University, Cleveland, OH.

Pink, D. (2011). *Drive. The Surprising Truth About What Motivates Us.* New York: Penguin Publishing Group.

Pradhan, R. (2005). Why is soft so hard? Retrieved from http://ourkirtipur.com.np/index.php/education/career/624-why-is-soft-so-hard-part-1 and http://ourkirtipur.com.np/index.php/education/career/624-why-is-soft-so-hard-part-2.

Rath, T. (2007). *StrengthsFinder 2.0*. New York: Gallup Press.

Rath, T., & Conchie, B. (2008). *Strengths Based Leadership: Great Leaders, Teams, and Why People Follow*. New York: Gallup Press.

Reis, E. (2011). *The Lean Startup: How Today's Entrepreneurs Use Continuous Innovation to Create Radically Successful Businesses.* New York: Crown Business.

Rohrig, P., & Clarke, J. (Eds.) (2008). *57 SF Activities for Facilitators and Consultants: Putting Solutions Focus into Action.* Cheltenham, England: SolutionsBooks.

Rosenthal, R., & Jacobson, L. (1968). *Pygmalion in the Classroom: Teacher Expectation and Pupils' Intellectual Development.* Norwalk, CT: Crown House Publishing.

Rothwell, W. J., Stavros, J. M., Sullivan, R. L., & Sullivan, A. (Eds.) (2005). *Practicing Organization Development: A Guide for Leading Change.* Hoboken, NJ: Wiley.

Sabini, J. (1992). *Social Psychology*. New York: W. W. Norton.

Scharmer, O. C. (2009). *Theory U: Leading From the Future as It Emerges.* San Francisco: Berrett-Koehler Publishers.

Scharmer, O., & Kaufer, K. (2013). *Leading from the Emerging Future: From Ego-System to Eco-System Economics.* San Francisco: Berrett-Koehler Publishers.

Schein, E. H. (2010). *Organizational Culture and Leadership.* San Francisco: Jossey-Bass.

Scott, V. (2011). *Conflict Resolution at Work for Dummies.* Hoboken, NJ: Wiley.

Seligman, M. (1998). *Learned Optimism: How to Change Your Mind and Your Life.* New York: Pocket.

Seligman, M. (2003). *Authentic Happiness.* New York: Simon & Schuster.

Seligman, M. (2012). *Flourish: A Visionary New Understanding of Happiness and Well-being.* New York: Free Press.

Senge, P. (1990). *The Fifth Discipline*. New York: Doubleday.

Senge, P., Scharmer, C. O., Jaworski, J., & Flowers, B. S. (2005). *Presence: An Exploration of Profound Change in People, Organizations, and Society.* New York: Doubleday.

Senge, P., Smith, B., Kruschwitz, N., Laur, J., & Schley, S. (2010). *The Necessary Revolution: How Individuals and Organizations Are Working Together to Create a Sustainable World.* New York: Crown Publishing Group.

Sibbett, D. (2010). *Visual Meetings: How Graphics, Sticky Notes and Idea Mapping Can Transform Group Productivity.* Hoboken, NJ: Wiley.

Stavros, J., & Hinrichs, G. (2009). *The Thin Book of SOAR: Building Strengths-Based Strategy.* Bend, OR: Thin Books Publishing.

Stavros, J., Sutherland, J., & Schiller, M. (2003). On appreciative strategy.
Retrieved from www.aipractitioner.com/ai-practitioner-november-2003.

Swanson, R. A., & Holton, E. F. (1999). *Results: How to Assess Performance, Learning, and Perceptions in Organizations.* San Francisco: Berrett-Koehler Publishers.

Tan, C.-M. (2012). *Search Inside Yourself: The Unexpected Path to Achieving Success, Happiness (and World Peace).* New York: HarperCollins.

Thomas, W. P., & Collier, V. P. (1997). Two languages are better than one. *Educational Leadership*, 55(4), 23–26.

Thomas, W. P., & Collier, V. P. (2003). The multiple benefits of dual language. *Educational Leadership*, 61:2, 61–64.

Tuckman, B. W. (1965). Developmental sequence in small groups. *Psychological Bulletin*, 63(6), 384–399.

Tuckman, B. W., & Jensen, M. A. C. (1977). Stages of small-group development revisited. *Group & Organization Management*, 2(4), 419–427.

Wagner, R., & Muller, G. (2009). *Why Partners Need Complementary Strengths*. Retrieved from www.gallup.com/businessjournal/122237/why-partners-need-complementary-strengths.aspx.

Watkins, J. M., Mohr, B., & Kelly, R. (2001). *Appreciative Inquiry: Change at the Speed of Imagination.* San Francisco: Pfeiffer.

Weeks, H. (2001). Taking the stress out of stressful conversations. *Harvard Business Review*.

Weick, K. E., & Sutcliffe, K. M. (2007). *Managing the Unexpected: Resilient Performance in an Age of Uncertainty*. Hoboken, NJ: Wiley.

Weisbord, M. R., & Janoff, S. (1995). *Future Search. An Action Guide to Finding Common Ground in Organizations & Communities*. San Francisco: Berrett-Koehler Publishers.

West, M. (2004). *Effective Teamwork: Practical Lessons from Organizational Research*. Hoboken, NJ: Blackwell Publishing.

Wheatley, M. J. (2005). *Finding Our Way: Leadership for an Uncertain Time.* San Francisco: Berrett-Koehler Publishers.

Whitmore, J. (2005). *Coaching for Performance: Growing People, Performance and Purpose.* Boston: Nicholas Brealey Publishing.

Whitney, D., Trosten-Bloom, A., Cherney, J., & Fry, R. (2004). *Appreciative Team Building: Positive Questions to Bring Out the Best of Your Team.* Lincoln, NE: iUniverse, Inc.

Whitney, D., Trosten-Bloom, A., & Rader, K. (2008). *Appreciative Leadership: Focus on What Works to Drive Winning Performance and Build a Thriving Organization*. New York: McGraw-Hill.

Woods, E. (1998). *Training a Tiger: A Father's Guide to Raising a Winner in Both Golf and Life.* New York: HarperCollins.

ABOUT THE AUTHORS

Pernille Hippe Brun
Business Consultant, Change Agent, and Author

Pernille earned a master's degree in psychology from the University of Copenhagen, Denmark, and the University of Irvine, California, in 1997. She has a foundation in Appreciative Inquiry from the Weatherhead School of Management (2006) and a foundation in Theory U from MIT (2008). From 2006–2010, Pernille owned and led a small- to medium-sized company based in Copenhagen, Denmark. She is now self-employed and works with strategic advising, consultancy, and large-scale change processes in organizations both large and small and in the private and public sector. Pernille also is co-creator of and facilitator/lecturer at an executive MBA program in Denmark and Kenya and works in many different countries. She has lived in Denmark and in San Francisco, California. During her stay in San Francisco, Pernille became part of the start-up culture in Silicon Valley, which gave her a nose for "what's next" in business opportunities and development.

David L. Cooperrider

David is Professor of Appreciative Inquiry at the Weatherhead School of Management, Case Western Reserve University, where he is faculty chair of the Fowler Center for Business as an Agent of World Benefit and Co-director of the Strategy Innovation Lab.

David is best known for his pioneering theory on Appreciative Inquiry and has served as adviser to senior executives in business and societal leadership roles, including projects with five Presidents and Nobel Laureates such as William Jefferson Clinton, His Holiness the Dalai Lama, and Kofi Annan. David has brought appreciative inquiry to a wide variety of organizations including Apple, Verizon, Johnson & Johnson, National Grid, Fairmount Minerals, Keurig Green Mountain Coffee, and Walmart as well as United Way, Cleveland Clinic, and World Vision.

David has published over 20 books and authored over 100 articles and book chapters. He has served as editor of the *Journal of Corporate Citizenship* with Ron Fry and the current research series for *Advances in Appreciative Inquiry* with Michel Avital. David's books include *Appreciative Inquiry: A Positive Revolution in Change* (with Diana Whitney), *The Organization Dimensions of Global Change* (with Jane Dutton), *Organizational Courage and Executive Wisdom* (with Suresh Srivastva), and the four-volume research series *Advances in Appreciative Inquiry*. David was named Visionary of the Year by *Training* magazine and was awarded the Peter F. Drucker Distinguished Fellow by the Drucker School of Management, a designation recognizing his contribution to management thought.

(continued)

Most recently, Champlain College's Stiller School of Business honored David with an academic center in his name. It is called the David L. Cooperrider for Appreciative Inquiry. For the center's dedication ceremony, Marty Seligman wrote: "David Cooperrider is a giant: a giant of discovery, a giant of dissemination, and a giant of generosity" and Harvard's Jane Nelson at the Kennedy School of Leadership said: "David Cooperrider is one of the outstanding scholar-practitioners of our generation."

Mikkel Ejsing
Business Consultant

Mikkel earned a master's degree in psychology from the University of Copenhagen in 2000. He is a partner in the management consultancy company Resonans in Copenhagen. Resonans works with change processes and implementation of strategies in international organizations. Often the change processes are directly linked to the development of leaders and talents. Resonans is engaged in challenging organizations and people to release their potential for a future of new customer demands and habits, an accelerating speed of change, exponential technologies, and new management systems. When working with organizational change and the development of leaders and talents, Resonans has a strong foundation in the strengths-based approach in connection with the core business of clients.